THE MONSTERS

THE MONSTERS

Adrian Rigelsford

and

Andrew Skilleter

First published in Great Britain in 1992 by
Doctor Who Books
an imprint of Virgin Publishing Ltd
338 Ladbroke Grove
London W10 5AH

Copyright © Adrian Rigelsford and Andrew Skilleter 1992
'Doctor Who' copyright © British Broadcasting Corporation 1963, 1992

Photographic illustrations
© BBC Photographic Library

Cover illustration by Andrew Skilleter

This book is published by arrangement with BBC Books, a division of BBC Enterprises Ltd.

Typeset by D&S Design
1 Edith Grove
London SW10 0JY

Printed and bound by
Singapore National Printers

ISBN 1 85227 283 X

CONTENTS

Introduction

The enduring appeal of *Doctor Who* can be ascribed to various factors: the concept of limitless travel, by police box, in time and space; the Doctor's regenerative physiology, which has ensured continuity through three decades and seven different Doctors; the high standards of scripting and performance.

But what everyone remembers is being scared stiff as a child.

And what was so terrifying?

The monsters.

This book is a celebration of the creatures that sent us scurrying behind the sofa at tea-time.

Each of Adrian Rigelsford's cunningly crafted stories provides a new and unusual insight into the history, mythology or misdeeds of one of the races of monsters against which the Doctor has fought. Each story is much more than a mere sequence of words, however. Andrew Skilleter's remarkable illustrations illuminate almost every page, combining with the narrative to make the story of each monster a uniquely compelling experience.

Among the dramas enacted here in words and pictures are: the Sontarans' records of their clashes with the Doctor, replayed as a training programme for an officer cadet; the Menopteran history of their conflict with the giant ant-like Zarbi, and of the crucial intervention of the traveller known as the Doctor; the ancient legends of the monster-cursed planet Peladon; the UNIT files on the case of the terrifying Autons; the computer records of the discovery of the Ice Warriors under the glaciers covering a future England; and extracts from the casebook of Miss Olive Hawthorne, demonologist, which tell of the visits of other-worldly beings to our planet.

The final section of the book, *The Monster Makers*, takes us behind the scenes to meet the people who invented and gave shape to the alien creatures that menaced us from the television screen.

Anyone who has held their breath and averted their eyes as the latest scaly horror loomed behind one of the Doctor's unsuspecting companions will find their nightmares realised in *The Monsters*.

Biographies

Andrew Skilleter

Andrew Skilleter has worked as a professional illustrator since the '70s ans is most widely known for his *Doctor Who* work which has appeared on numerous covers, in books, calendars and on various merchandise. More recent *Doctor Who* work includes *The Cyberemen* book and covers for the first four *New Adventures, The Gallifrey Chronicles* and BBC Video.

His illustrative experience is extensive and varied including many book covers – he has painted over forty covers for the famous Ruth Rendell crime series – an illustrated edition of *The Decameron* which received critical attention and appearing this year, a calendar devoted to his art of nostalgic Britain. Original paintings from *Doctor Who* and other work are in private collections in the UK and USA. He is married to another illustrator and lives on the South Coast of England.

Adrian Rigelsford

Adrian Rigelsford was born in Cambridgeshire, where he still lives, and works as a writer and actor. He worked with Brian Blessed on the film *Galahad of Everest,* and the subsequent book of the film, *The Turquoise Mountain – Brian Blessed On Everest.* Tow of his scripts, *Inebriate's Rhapsody* and *The Sons of the Desert,* are to be filmed in 1992. A follow-on to *Galahad of Everest* is in the planning stages, provisionally entitled *The Abominable Snowman.*

Adrian has worked on various projects with Andrew Skilleter since they met in 1985, including the book *Doctor Who – Cybermen,* with David Banks. He's written for various magazines such as *Fantasy Zone, Fear, Skeleton Crew,* etc., regularly contributes to *Film Review* and *Doctor Who Magazine,* and has broadcast on the radio on classic fanatasy television.

Acknowledgements

Andrew Skilleter

First and foremost I have Adrian Rigelsford to thank for bringing about my involvement in this book. I responded enthusiastically to the possibilities he outlined and found we had a shared vision of what could be achieved.

Peter Darvill-Evans, our editor, must take full credit for encouraging my entré into the project, to supporting us in every respect and in helping shape the final form of the book - it is his book as well as ours.

To Mark Stammers, the designer, my appreciation for coping calmly with the complexities presented to him, some at the eleventh hour! My personal thanks go to a small number of individuals who have helped me with visual reference, a commodity that cannot be over-estimated. First and foremost to Richard Landen who so generously provided me with a selection from his own Whovian archive for a longer period than was ever envisaged. Finally to Kevin Judd and Stephen James Walker for their added assistance.

Adrian Rigelsford

There's several people I'd like to thank for their time and energy in making this book possible : Andrew Skilleter, an artist of consumate skill, and Pat, his wife for their sympathy, advice and admonition; Clive Banks, for his tireless and comprehensive research work; Ian McClachlan, for helping in all matters visual; Peter Darvill-Evans, for having the faith to give me a chance, and enduring the trials and tribulations that followed; Riona MacNamara, for her encouragement and help.

John Freeman, who was always happy to advise alternate routes for my wild ideas, and Gary Russell, the successor to John's Marvel throne; Brian Blessed, for letting me use his comprehensive Everest material for research; The late Innes Lloyd, who dug deep in his memory time and time again; and Graeme Harper, for helping to bring strange ideas under budget.

Bobbie Mitchell, and eveyone at the BBC Photo Library for helping me unearth some hidden treasure; David Shepperd, for my other 'photo finds'; Vicky Thomas and Vicki Haig, for all their help at 'BBC Enterprises' and most importantly of all, the writers, without whose ideas and imaginations thre would have been no stories . . . and no book!

And finally : Ricky Waller, Nick Jagels, Markus Van Natten, Nic Crawly, Mr C., Mum, Nicola and Midge . . . !

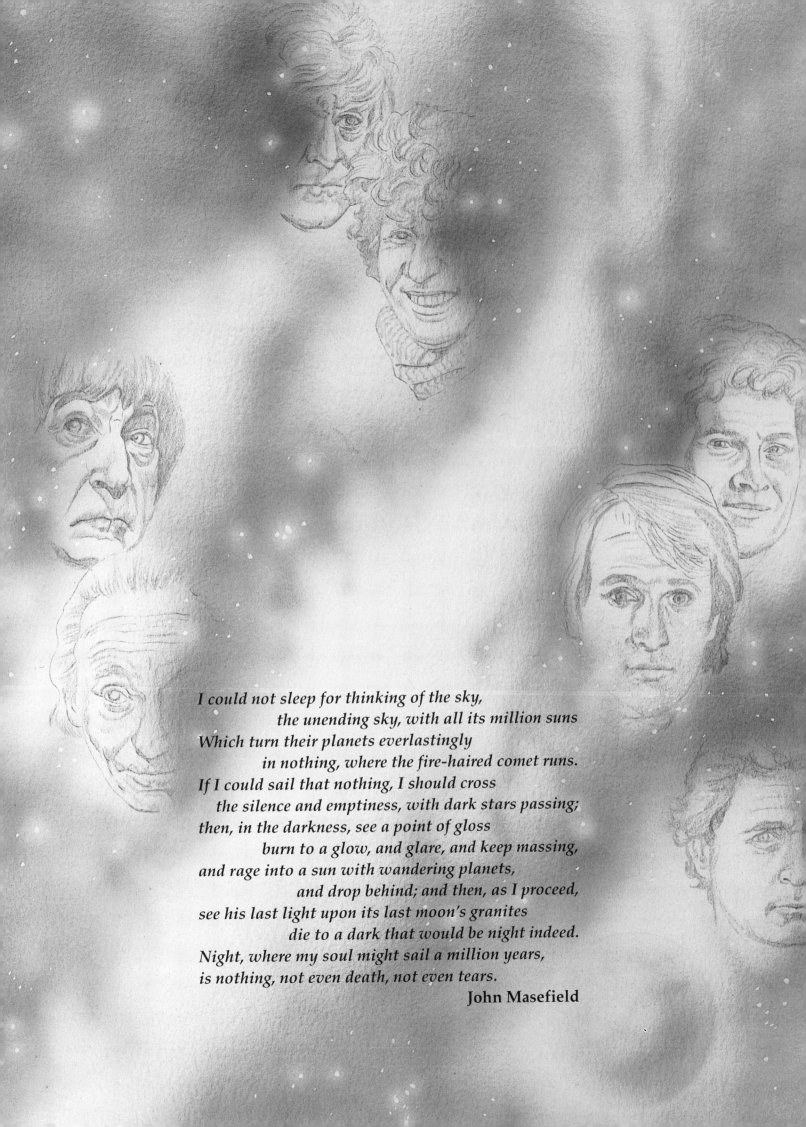

I could not sleep for thinking of the sky,
      the unending sky, with all its million suns
Which turn their planets everlastingly
      in nothing, where the fire-haired comet runs.
If I could sail that nothing, I should cross
      the silence and emptiness, with dark stars passing;
then, in the darkness, see a point of gloss
      burn to a glow, and glare, and keep massing,
and rage into a sun with wandering planets,
      and drop behind; and then, as I proceed,
see his last light upon its last moon's granites
      die to a dark that would be night indeed.
Night, where my soul might sail a million years,
is nothing, not even death, not even tears.

                    John Masefield

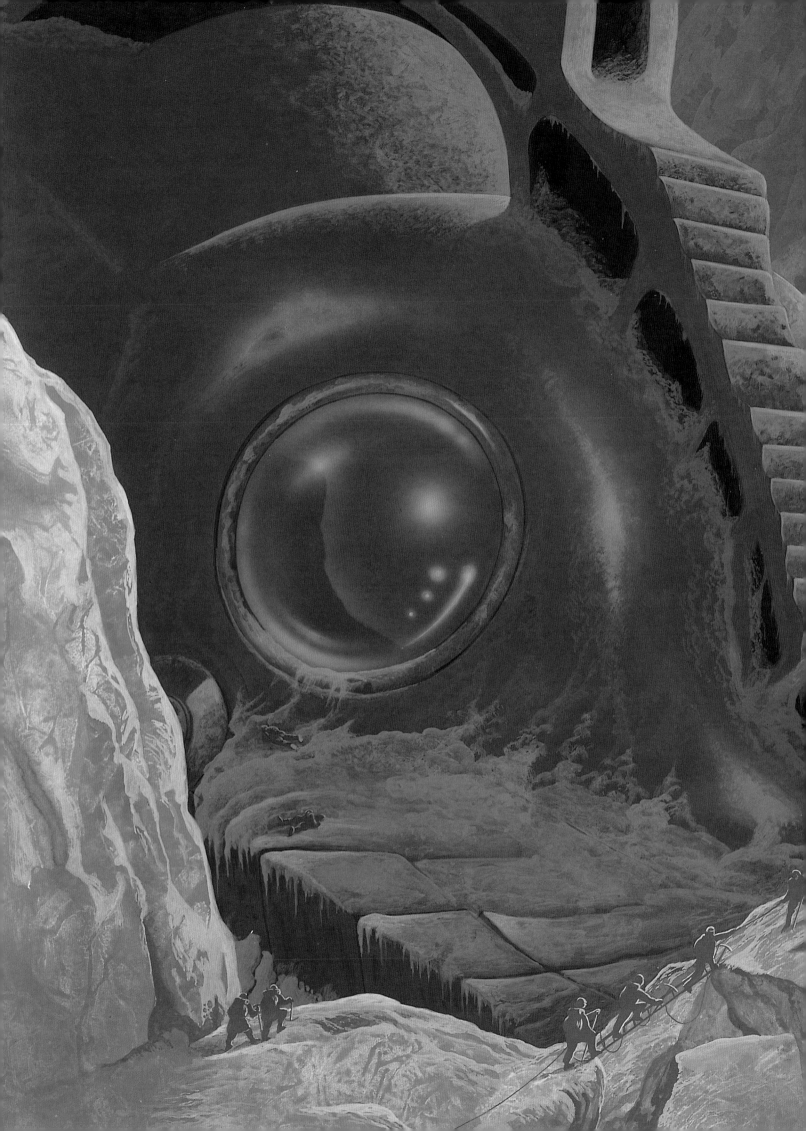

THE ICE WARRIORS

Terrestrial man fancied there might be other men upon Mars . . . Yet, across the gulf of space, minds that are immeasurably superior to ours . . . Intellects vast and cool and unsympathetic, regarded this Earth with envious eyes . . . And slowly and surely, they drew their plans against us . . .

Herbert George Wells

Can all warriors be such,
    that their souls are of ice?
Could the colour of conquest,
    be as pure as white snow?

JD Turner

Monstrous blizzards have forced us reluctantly to abandon our quest for the North Pole; if we were to continue, we would surely perish. The bad weather and the events of the past day have drained our confidence, and I fear for the sanity of my men. Captain Trasker and Corporal Wilde have returned from their trek to Mount Erebus, several miles from our base on the Taylor Glacier, with tales that only minds tormented by the cold could tell.

Through a storm of unrelenting sleet, Trasker and Wilde saw a gigantic metal craft entombed in the ice. Charred and jagged cracks revealed the full horror of the catastrophe that had befallen the ship, yet it was the sight of the crew that most haunts my men's memories. Towering figures encased in body armour exuded a green haze through the ice; their eyes stared blankly through the red visors of domed helmets.

Trasker's efforts to excavate the apparatus from the grasp of one body before darkness and the storm closed in have provided an unfathomable mystery. The corroded metal sphere he retrieved has failed to yield its secrets to a team of the most knowledgeable of scientists. Perhaps on my return to England, my cousin's inventiveness and imagination will be able to solve the mystery.

Extract from the diaries of Commander Frederick William Wells, dated 12 August 1896, during the first main reconnaissance expedition to the North Pole

20th December 1896

My dear Frederick,

Your most perplexing gift from the furthest reaches of this planet has, in a most cryptic and enigmatic way, revealed its innermost secrets to, as you reportedly describe, 'that genius cousin chap of mine'.

As far as exterior qualities suggest, your deductions were most accurate: the object appears to be no more than a rusty metal sphere. These signs of outer normality, however, conceal a more complex purpose.

By accident or chance, I concluded my preliminary examination with a stethoscope to determine whether anything moved within. A mild, presumably electric, current passed through me as I touched the sphere, causing me to jerk my head back and pulling the instrument's earpieces forward so they rested on my temples. Some form of circuit must have been completed, for there was surely no other explanation for the images that proceeded to course through my mind.

I saw another world, one totally unlike ours. Its sky was a molten, burning red; jagged amber mountains towered over the desolate landscape; and there were deep craters and canyons in which water may once have flowed freely, yet which were now filled with dry dust. In my mind's eye I could see the world covered in ice; perhaps centuries ago its environment had been changed by some great heat. Could the planet have been moved closer to the sun in some way?

My mind was then transported to the underworld, where I saw tunnels and caverns carved in unending reaches of ice. There were vast caves, some as big as the interior of St Paul's. It was then that I saw the inhabitants of this world . . .

Their nobility and dignity struck me instantly: they were far from the beasts of nightmares. Encased in coarse-looking green armour, every movement of the warriors of this martial race exuded power. Surely the strength of such creatures would exceed that of any man? I was mortified by fear, and only my curiosity compelled me to witness more.

Death is regarded as a logical sacrifice for honour; a slain warrior is burned in a great ceremonial pyre, ejected into the atmosphere within a glass dome while his companions respectfully salute his passing.

Could these inhabitants of Mars be the true gods of war? It seems that from an early age their reptilian grace is honed to an extraordinary fighting prowess. These warriors strive for success right from the first stages of induction. A young warrior achieves his ultimate goal when the Elders present him with the ornate holy sword of their god, which blazes with heat to test the warrior's strength.

Additions are made to a warrior's armour as he progresses. Communication and recording devices are fitted to his helmet; vice-like clamps are eventually grafted to the end of his arms.

The strongest warriors protect the slender aristocrats of the race. Free from the cumbersome armour, these nobles look resplendent in their simple uniforms. Taking their commands from the Elders, the nobles instigate the tactics and strategy that are so relevant to their lives.

The mystery of your discovery became clear, my dear cousin, as the images began to fade. As the icy expanse of the creatures' domain began to melt, a new home world became a matter of necessity. The craft of which you spoke was one of many that left Mars in search of a new home. All but one returned.

A search expedition for the missing ship headed towards what I presume to be Earth, landing on a terrain of mist and ice.

It is here I must regretfully report that the sphere began to smoke; by the time I had extinguished the resulting flames, only the smouldering metal husk remained. Therefore I can only conclude that the search mission failed; perhaps the first craft arrived on Earth years, possibly centuries earlier. We will never know what became of that first ship.

I thank you for the intrigue of the sphere; it has provided material enough for another book. I shall set my imagination to work over the imminent winter.

Yours, as ever,

HG

P.S. Perhaps the day will come when another expedition, not unlike your own, will find evidence of the other craft they sought.

COMPUTER INPUT «

TRANSMISSION DATA: INCOMING «

LOCATION: COTSWOLD HILLS «

MESSAGE BEING RECORDED ■

'Is anybody there, over? This is Arden. I want to speak to a communications officer, not a damn machine! This is Science Officer Arden reporting to Brittanicus Base. I'm with Walters; Davis has been killed in an avalanche, over. The ice gave way before we could insert the seismic probe. We found something in the ice – I don't know what it is. It's gigantic . . . humanoid . . . could be prehistoric, any period up to three thousand years old. We've cut it free, we'll bring it in on the airsled. Over and out.'

TRANSMISSION DATA: MESSAGE TERMINATED «

POWER OFF ■

AUDIO DATA STORAGE «

LEADER CLENT'S JOURNAL ■

I dreamt last night that spring had returned. The world was without ice, and the colours of the land were more than just white. I strive to maintain my image of authority, yet sometimes the memory succumbs, and I require a systematic reminder of the danger we face. Only the most respected scientists dared to postulate what was happening to the Earth's atmosphere in the final years of the last century. Massive over-population and the world famine were solved in tandem, the former with a continual programme of city construction, the latter with the mass production of synthetic food substitutes and the recycling of proteins.

Carbon dioxide in the air was slowly destroyed by recycling waste gases and through the decline in the world's plant life. But the air temperature dropped too quickly: the polar ice caps started to advance, and before long, vast icebergs started to appear in the Atlantic.

A cold white infection spread across every ocean. England was reunited with France after years of geographical separation, linked by an umbilical cord of ice.

It is my duty to maintain the equilibrium of the situation, with the saviour of mankind, the Ionizer. Through the world-wide ECCO computer system, the Ionizer can be used to project concentrated beams of heat at any point on the Earth, effectively controlling the onslaught of the ice. Seismic monitors monitor the movements of the great floes of ice.

One of our top geologists – Arden, I believe – is investigating a stray ice floe reported to have come from the North Pole. While he battles the ferocious weather, I can only sit and wait incapacitated and reliant on a stick for support, in this grandiose Georgian mansion, protected by its radiation-proof dome.

There are simply not enough technicians here trained in the delicate techniques of ionization; the merest fraction of a fault could reduce a country to smouldering lava, yet I manage to maintain a sense of order.

I find the Ionizer is my constant companion during every waking hour and thought. My life revolves around it; nothing must be allowed to interfere with its work. I cannot bear to contemplate shutting it down: the ice would destroy everything within hours. The machine must not stop, that is unthinkable.

ECCO COMPUTER TERMINAL ACCESS «

VOICE ACTIVATION «

STATE NAME AND RANK ■

Clent, Leader.

STATE COMPUTER FUNCTION REQUIRED, LEADER CLENT ■

Access clearance date on new member of Brittanicus staff, acting as replacement for Penley.

DATA RECALL: PENLEY, PROFESSOR RJ. HEAD OF RESEARCH AND «

DEVELOPMENT ON IONIZER IMPROVEMENT AND INSTIGATION. REPORTED«
MISSING FOR 46 DAYS, PRESUMED DEAD OUTSIDE THE PERIMETER OF THE «
PROTECTIVE DOME. REASON FOR DEPARTURE: WEAKNESS DISPLAYED UNDER«
PRESSURE AND ANTAGONISM BETWEEN LEADER CL— ■

Yes, yes, yes. Now open the files.

CHANNEL OPEN. STATE DETAILS OF NEW STAFF MEMBER ■

Very well. A fault in the computer system for the Ionizer had reached Phase Three Evacuation. All the systems operatives found the problem insoluble. A man, accompanied by a male and female companion, all of whom were presumed to be scavengers, arrived and deduced the solution that would avert disaster. His intuition and knowledge could help to maintain 100% capacity operation for the Ionizer. He could prove invaluable – I need him on my team.

CANDIDATE VALIDITY ACCEPTED. STATE NAME ■

The Doctor.

ACCEPTED. OPEN FILE ON THE DOCTOR ■

STATE NAME AND REQUIREMENT ■

This is Arden. Access medical analysis system, complete physical prognosis equipped for sub-zero temperatures.

ACCESS GRANTED. STATE VISUAL CONDITION OF THE SUBJECT ■

Humanoid. Seven feet tall at least, could be taller. Main physical features are blurred, the figure is held frozen within a block of ice. Heated power packs have been attached to the lower section. Monitor the body and alert me when room temperature has been reached. Alert me to any sudden movements as well, if the ice becomes loose it mustn't be allowed to fall.

COMMANDS ACCEPTED. STATE POINT OF CONTACT ■

Leader Clent's general meeting in the library, something to do with a new member of staff, Doctor something or other.

RESPIRATORY MONITORING SYSTEM: 0.00% «

CARDIOVASCULAR SYSTEM: 0.00% «

SUBJECT ANALYSIS: DECEASED «

25% OF ICE BLOCK EVAPORATION COMPLETE ■

!!CORRECTION!! «

CARDIOVASCULAR SYSTEM: 35.00% «

LIFE SIGNS ARE REACTIVATING «

BODY TEMPERATURE INCREASED: 40.00% «

CONSCIOUSNESS REGAINED «

RESPIRATORY MONITORING SYSTEM: DIFFICULTY EXPERIENCED, «

50% EFFICIENCY «

CARDIOVASCULAR SYSTEM : 100% «

ICE EVAPORATION: 100% «

SUBJECT APPROACHING COMPUTER TERMI——■

ECCO COMPUTER SYSTEM «

TRANSCRIPTION OF LEADER CLENT'S REPORT ■

The Doctor's sense of logic is undeniable. He has accurately demonstrated the possible chain of events leading to the potential disaster that now faces Brittanicus Base. The implications of the discovery of the creature in the ice are truly devastating.

Arden is convinced that the depth at which the creature was found indicates that it has been there since the last Ice Age. Yet the Doctor's examination suggests that its helmet contains electronic wiring. Logically, this fact would suggest the creature is an alien that arrived on Earth in some sort of space craft.

Assuming the ship is trapped within the ice and that it is powered by a reactor propulsion engine, the use of the Ionizer at 20% power could trigger an explosion that would render the entire area radioactive and uninhabitable for several centuries.

But if the Ionizer is not operational on full power for at least 85% of the time, there is no way to check the progress of the ice.

RECORDING TERMINATED. LEADER CLENT NOW ABSENT «

REASON FOR ABSENCE: MALE COMPANION OF THE DOCTOR REPORTS «

FEMALE COMPANION HELD CAPTIVE. THE BEING FROM ICE BLOCK IS NOW«

MOBILE ■

CEREBRAL THOUGHT RECORDER ACTIVATED ■

I live. I, Varga, commander of the . . . My ship, what has happened to my ship? I can see the ice... the ship crashed, I led the survey patrol into the light. The incline of ice overhead gave way, I remember the ice, the white snow . . . closing in yet I still live.

The female earthling I have captured displays natural vulnerability through her lack of armour – a hereditary weakness of planets that are evolving in solar cycles.

Her description of how my body came to live again intrigues me. A form of high resistance heat generator, stimulating life through the ice. I must retrieve the apparatus, my men will live again. My sonic destructor remains functional – it should disintegrate the brains of the bipeds that inhabit such a low-gravity planet.

AUDIO DATA STORAGE «

LEADER CLENT'S JOURNAL ■

No one informed me of the regained mobility of the creature, so its assault as I entered the Medical Centre came as a shock. Damn thing knocked me unconscious and stole some power packs.

Displaying admirable military foresight, the creature appears to be intent on excavating the rest of its crew, or so the Doctor has deduced. A search will be mounted to track the creature at first light; with luck the creature will lead us to its ship. Hastier action might endanger Victoria's life. I thought I heard the Doctor say something about Penley trying to save my life . . . preposterous! I doubt whether we'll be graced by his presence again!

Our mutual attention must return to the Ionizer; continual maintenance and operation is paramount. The fate of the Doctor's companion is trivial compared with the work of the Ionizer, though I must admit a certain degree of concern over her fate.

CEREBRAL THOUGHT RECORDER ACTIVATED ■

The sonic waves of my gun have released my crew from their torment. The girl has activated the power. Soon the heat will make them live again. Isbur, Turoc, Rintan and Zondal will rise from the dead. The ice is truly our friend.

Together we will locate the ship. Our combined sonic power will make it worthy of flight again. A cave formation will be formed in the process. A useful trap. The humans will follow. I have the bait I require.

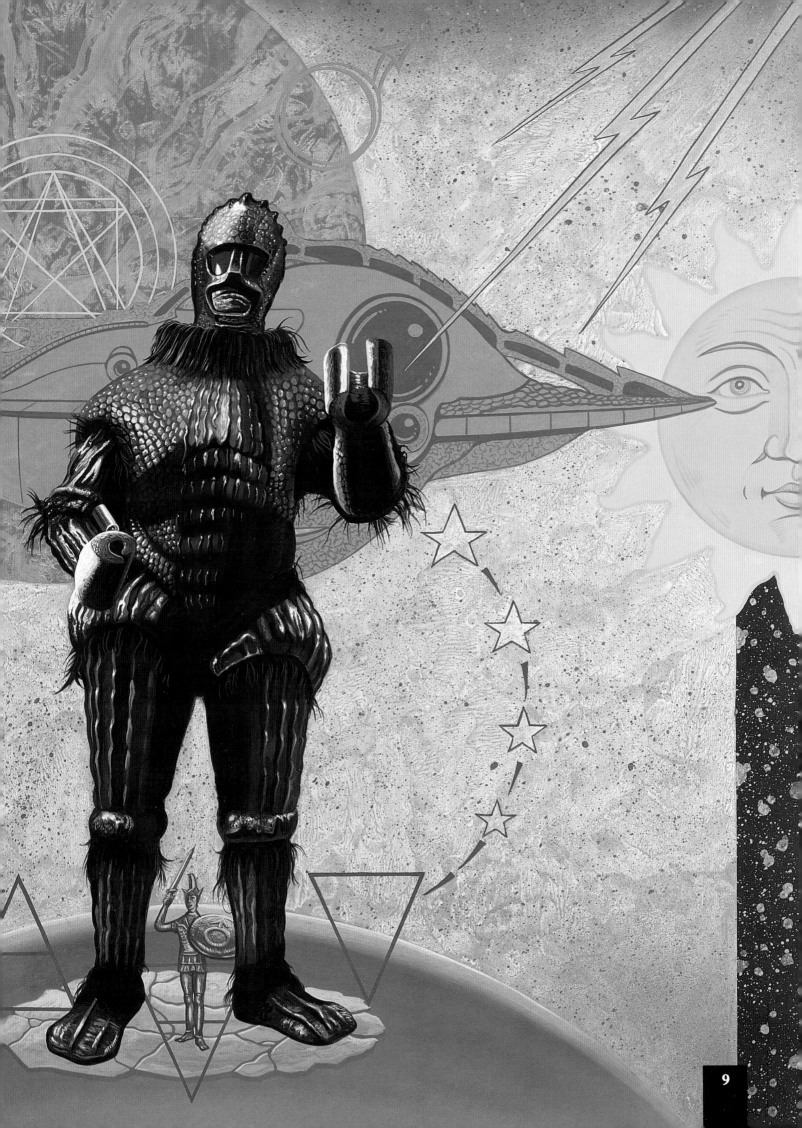

VOICE-ACTIVATED RECORDER ■

Perhaps an introduction is in order. This is Elric Penley and you, my friend, are a tape machine taken from Brittanicus for, shall we say, more important matters than normal. I have witnessed events that need documentation, and this is the most convenient way.

I am what Leader Clent tersely refers to as a scaveger, and for the sake of this record, I shall remain as such. My beliefs on the restrictions on the mind in a computer dominated society should not be aired at this moment.

I paid no attention to Arden's excavation site, but the avalanche resulting from the digging injured my companion of the wasteland, Storr. Out of necessity I returned to Brittanicus to acquire medical provisions. To say that the sight of the creature being active was a shock would be a considerable understatement: it held a girl hostage and Clent lay injured in its wake. Much as I despise the man, I administered medical treatment purely because I would not wish such an injury on anyone – even him.

I have seen the creature revive four more of its kind from the ice. They appear to be hollowing out a tunnel within the ice, the exact purpose of which remains a mystery.

The arrival of Miss Garrett, a young woman working under Clent's tyranny, with a plea for me to return to the base shows that Clent's mighty empire is about to crumble. Her willingness to pacify me with drugs proves the point, with only Storr's timely intervention stopping her.

Reluctantly, I have advised her to look at the Omega Factor files. I knew problems were inevitable with the Ionizer, so perhaps this is an admission from Clent that he should have listened to me.

I fear that the signs of activity outside the ice cave warrant investigation. I shall report news of my finds later, my friend.

COMPUTER REPORT «

ACCESS DATA: INSTIGATION OF THE OMEGA FACTOR PROGRAMME «

IONIZER STABILISATION: 75% AND RISING. INCREASE 25% «

IONIZER STABILISATION: 100% «

OPERATION ANALYSIS: COMPLETE SUCCESS ■

CEREBRAL THOUGHT RECORDER ACTIVATED ■

The first of the humans have arrived. My men terminated both creatures. One was familiar to me, the biped who freed me from the ice; the younger one was unknown.

Zondal has displayed impulsive urges; he desired to kill the humanoid girl. His compulsion was not without reason. She was communicating with the other bipeds, detailing data of my ship's propulsion units through a transmitter. Turoc is hunting her through the ice tunnels. Her escape bid is a futile gesture.

Our fuel supplies are drained, all power sources are extinct. That would surely require the passage of thousands of Earth years. There is truth in the words of the humans; my time in the ice was indeed longer than calculated.

The humans must have the means to replenish the ship's power. The female would have assisted in this matter by bargaining for our needs.

Turoc has not returned. Time can no longer be wasted. The sonic cannon will make them part with materials.

AUDIO DATA STORAGE «

LEADER CLENT'S JOURNAL ■

Against my advice, the Doctor is preparing to travel to the excavation site. Refusing to take any form of weapon, he will accept only a video communicator, purely to maintain contact with Brittanicus.

A phial of ammonium sulphide hardly seems enough to stop these creatures in their tracks, but the Doctor insists such a substance would be toxic to them, as they are used to a nitrogen-rich atmosphere. For his sake, I hope his theories are correct.

He is prepared to use it only if trapped, but as I pointed out, the only feasible way to conduct any communication face to face would be if the creatures held him prisoner in the first place.

I fear that time will shortly start to run out. We must know more about the creature's craft, before it's too late.

VOICE-ACTIVATED RECORDER ■

Well, my friend, I had my differences with Arden over the years – anyone would against a temperament like that – but he did not deserve the fate the creatures inflicted upon him. Fortunately, the young lad accompanying him seems to have taken the lesser brunt of the blast from their weapons.

Storr has assisted in tending to his wounds, but I fear the boy may be paralysed. With the last of the tranquillizers gone, Storr foolishly set out to get help from the creatures. I followed him to try to stop such a fatal gesture, but succeeded only in finding the Doctor, a man who on first impressions would appear to be a scavenger who I came across on my recent infiltration of Brittanicus. The boy is apparently a fellow traveller of his, so he was, to say the least, concerned about the state he found him in.

With great reluctance, I have agreed to transport the boy to the Medicare Centre at Brittanicus. Rather than accompany us, the Doctor has taken it on himself to enter the ice caves in search of the girl they hold captive. It's a brave move, but a task I do not envy him.

CEREBRAL THOUGHT RECORDER ACTIVATED ■

Servo mechanisms are worn, the sonic cannon has been aligned manually. The girl has returned without Turoc, a male humanoid, her companion. I detected a willingness to regard us as benevolent on the part of the male specimen. Foolish. He had no knowledge of use to us and his eradication was inevitable. The girl referred to him as Storr.

One of my warriors has fallen. The girl saw him slain by an ice fall.

I had not considered the humanoids to be capable of guile and cunning. The man they call the Doctor displays both. His bluff to gain access to my ship did not fool me. His plea of the danger of the Ionizer is a mere strategy to deceive us, a ploy to asses the power of my craft. Concealing his communicator failed – I now hold the device.

Threatening to terminate the girl's life has produced the desired effect. Information was forthcoming to save her. We will soon have all the power we need. My craft will live again.

Bombardier Zondal remains to operate the sonic cannon, Isbur and Rintan will follow me. Our mission to Brittanicus Base will not fail, total success is assured. The captive humanoids will remain here.

AUDIO DATA STORAGE «

LEADER CLENT'S JOURNAL ■

The ice is nearly upon us and I fear that things are turning against us. Disaster looms over Brittanicus like the shadow of death. Since contact with the Doctor was disconnected, we have no idea of his fate or that of Victoria.

In six hours, a mass Ionization will be instigated by all of the world's bases in a concerted effort to hold back the ice. Fate is a double-edged sword: one edge betokens the certain destruction of the ice; the other holds the possibility of the Martian's ship detonating when the Ionizer is operated. There seems to be no escape.

The return of Penley with the boy Jamie, whose wounds are being tended to by the computers in Medicare, has only worsened the situation. His theories of the power source on the spacecraft being decayed, and therefore no threat to the Ionizer, are hardly credible. Predictably, Penley turned hostile, and now lies sedated next to the boy in Medicare, thanks to the timely intervention of Security Chief Walters. My every hope is with the Doctor. I must return to my duties.

EMERGENCY – EMERGENCY – EMERGENCY «
ATTACK ON BRITTANICUS BASE «
DAMAGE REPORT «
WEAPON: HEAVY CONCENTRATION OF SONIC WAVES «
DAMAGE: DOCUMENTATION WING OF BRITTANICUS COMPLETELY «
DESTROYED. WOUNDED AND CASUALTIES BEING CONVEYED TO «
MEDICARE CENTRE. FURTHER DATA TO FOLLOW ■

CEREBRAL THOUGHT RECORDER ACTIVATED ■

The humans have now seen the forces we have at our control. Leader Clent offered a meeting in peace to negotiate. His betrayal was instant. A man within his chambers held a weapon. He was terminated.

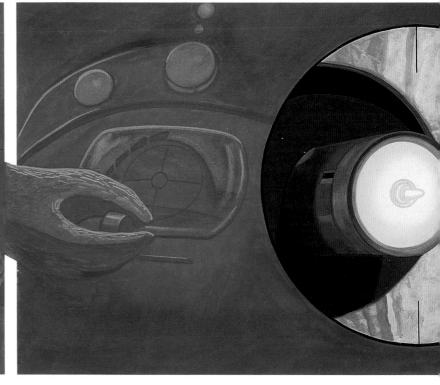

I have underestimated the Ionizer. A device capable of volatilizing rock is a most commendable weapon.

The human female, Garrett, is bringing the power level of the machine down. The risk of detonating an explosion in my ship will be minimized.

The Ionizer now operates safely. Shutdown will be instigated. Soon, we will be able to extract fuel. The mercury isotopes will be taken from their reactor – all the power we need for the ship.

VOICE-ACTIVATED RECORDER ■

I must admit, my friend, that I begin to appreciate the pressure Clent is under. In a way I can understand his lack of hesitation when he ordered Walters to sedate me. I am now recovered, and from my vantage point, I see that Brittanicus has one or two unwanted visitors, my tales of confronting bears on the snowy desert will have to wait for another time.

The main control room is under siege. Clent and Miss Garrett appear to be shutting the Ionizer down, and Walters is on the floor, quite dead. My own efforts to make life uncomfortable for the invaders have been outdone by the Doctor's, although I can only deduce exactly what has happened.

The creatures did indeed, as I calculated, suffer under the heat of increased humidity in the control room, thanks to the temperature controls next to me. A slight manipulation has made them decidedly hot under the collar.

I remember the sonic weapons they used to hollow out the ice cave, to excavate their ship. The Doctor must have gained access, perhaps he is held prisoner, but now seems to have control of a much larger version of the same kind of device. The creatures must have a high water content in their cell structure, so by changing the frequency of the device and aiming it at the control room, the Doctor has brought about their retreat.

The Martians have just staggered past my hiding place towards the exit. The pain of the sound waves echoing in their helmets must have been excruciating. I only hope that the Doctor manages to get out of the ship before they get back. I still feel weak from the drug...

AUDIO DATA STORAGE «

LEADER CLENT'S JOURNAL ■

I face a decision I never allowed myself to contemplate: the use of the Ionizer as a weapon. A machine that maintains peace turned to a tool of destruction. Penley is right, I have to admit it. The creatures must be stopped; if their ship were to break free of the ice they would be invincible. I understood their power was drained, but the Doctor estimates there would be enough left to cause considerable damage.

The computer has overloaded, unable to answer a question where there is no apparent solution. What is to be stopped? What is the priority? The Martians or the ice?

The Doctor revived Penley, who now sits at the controls of the machine. Penley will align the Ionizer with the Martian ship. Perhaps he was right all along; decisions can be made without computers.

CEREBRAL THOUGHT RECORDER ACTIVATED ■

The ice is moving. As I predicted, the humans are using the Ionizer. Soon my ship will be free of the ice. The water is rising . . . Zondal must raise the last vestiges of our power.

The one called Doctor has escaped; the sonic cannon is destroyed!

Power! The power is returning! Soon we will rise from the ice. So much power restored. My men, weakness... they are collapsing around me. No, it is not power, it is the heat. The humans have turned the Ionizer against us, destroying us...

The heat – the flames surround me. I die with honour . . . I die with pride . . . and no surrender!

VOICE-ACTIVATED RECORDER ■

I suppose this is an epilogue, my friend, Now let me see, insert disk? Right. The ice is under control; we have the first signs of a thaw for twenty years. Clent has reinstated me, he is once again the man of reason I knew for so many years. The computers no longer control his train of thought, the power to make our own decisions and progress has returned.

I can but wonder where the Doctor and his companions have gone, the man saved all our lives. Type in name and rank on keyboard? Right, something about those creatures stirred a distant memory – it's so long since I studied the Earth history files.

PRESS "SEARCH" FOR FILE LOCATION ■

Clent mentioned that if the creatures had been in the ice for so long, there could be other groups of them roaming the galaxy. He asked what if they'd already encountered mankind previously.

Of course! The old transmat teleportation system. I haven't thought about T-Mat for years. I knew one of these old disks would have a record of something to do with them.

PRESS "ACCESS" ■

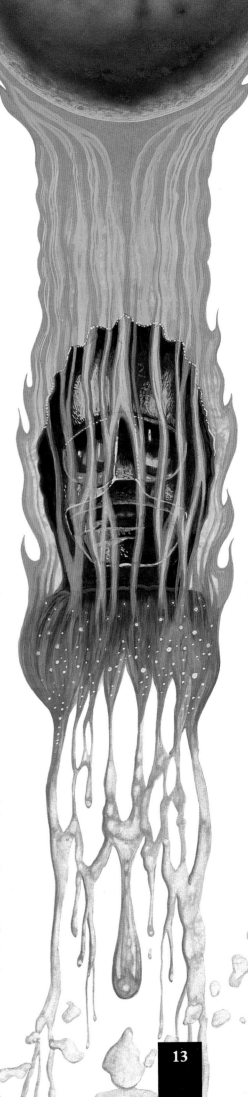

T-Mat – Shareholder Application Audio Presentation

Welcome, friends, to the eleventh wonder of the world; the miracle of the 21st century; a planet-wide matter transportation system, the Travel-Mat – T-Mat for short. All other transportation fades into nothing by comparison, Travel-Mat is undoubtedly the ultimate in designer transport. In almost the same instant of departure, you will arrive at your desired destination, eradicating jet lag and delays.

Safety precautions are paramount. We have ensured that all possibilities of mid-matter transportation collision have been eradicated. T-Mat is safe.

But what of the more important benefits from the system? From the T-Mat control base on the moon, major cargo transportation is controlled with all raw materials and food supplies being directed to every corner of the planet. With simple dematerialization and rematerialization at a different location, it is now possible to solve all problems of famine and disasters with instant help.

Reports of technical problems are unfounded. Although T-Mat is a relatively recent invention, you have our guarantee that the entire system is fully automated, and one hundred per cent foolproof against power failure. Nothing could possibly go wrong.

DECODED COMPUTER OBSERVATION DATA «

T-MAT MOONBASE ■

T-MAT TRANSPORTATION SHIPMENTS RUNNING TO DELAYS. ALL SHIPMENTS « ARE FIVE MINUTES BEHIND ■

COMPUTER ANALYSIS: TECHNICIAN FEWSHAM ON DUTY 36 HOURS WITHOUT« RELIEF, OPERATING BELOW EXPECTED WORKING CAPACITY «

PREDICTION: T-MAT BASE EARTH SUPERVISOR GIA KELLY WILL SEND « INVESTIGATIVE TEAM ■

PREDICTION ACCURATE: CONTROLLER OSGOOD HAS ARRIVED «

!!WARNING. WARNING !! «

THE OUTER AIRLOCK DOORS HAVE BEEN ACTIVATED. NO MOONBASE « PERSONNEL ARE ON THE EXTERIOR SURFACE «

CONCLUSION: ALIEN PRESENCE FORCING ENTRY. ALIEN PRESENCE NOW « WITHIN THE COMPLEX. COMPUTER DETECTING DEATHS OF PERSONNEL « THREE HUMANOID ALIENS NOW PRESENT IN CONTROL ROOM. OSGOOD « SABOTAGING COMMUNICATION EQUIPMENT LINK TO EARTH. OSGOOD « PROCEEDING TO SABOTAGE T-MAT CONTROLS. OSGOOD TERMINATED. « FEWSHAM HAS OFFERED TO REPAIR T-MAT DIRECT LINK TO EARTH CONTROL« BASE. FEWSHAM BEING GUARDED BY ALIENS WHILE REPAIR WORK IS « INSTIGATED ■

AUDIO NOTATION «

SUPERVISOR GIA KELLY ■

Commander Radnor has arrived and taken charge of the situation. I detect pressure from higher officials over breakdown of T-Mat. A possible solution to solve the dilemma has been found, but I must stress my concern over the use of obsolete space rockets.

Radnor is seeking help from a former colleague, Professor Daniel Eldred, a virtual recluse in

AIR
LOCK

15

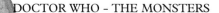

the remains of his History of Space museum. Government special observation sections report he has spent the past four years constructing a rocket. The device is our only hope of reaching Moonbase to ascertain what has gone wrong. I predict possible antagonism on Professor Eldred's part; his hatred for T-Mat is renowned.

It appears Special Observations overestimated the operational ability of Eldred's craft, which is by no means complete or space-worthy. Three strangers to my records, I assume they are friends of Eldred, have offered their help. Admittedly, the man called the Doctor displays a certain degree of knowledge in such matters, and the girl, Zoe, has a remarkable grasp of astro-physics theory. Unfortunately – and Commander Radnor concurs – the boy Jamie has an intelligence level that suggests he would barely qualify for the lower ranks of T-Mat security.

Nevertheless, I will start to requisition the appropriate technicians and materials. Take-off must happen within hours. We have to get to the moon, even if a miracle is involved to accomplish this!

DECODED COMPUTER OBSERVATION DATA«

T-MAT MOONBASE «

LIFE SIGNS INDICATE THAT TECHNICIAN LOCKE HAS BEEN TERMINATED BY «
THE ALIEN PRESENCE. TECHNICIANS FEWSHAM AND PHIPPS WITNESSED «
LOCKE'S PARTIALLY SUCCESSFUL ATTEMPT TO COMMUNICATE WITH EARTH «
CONTROL. PHIPPS HAS ESCAPED FROM CONFINES OF CONTROL ROOM. ALIEN «
GUARD HUNTING HIM DOWN WITH ORDERS TO TERMINATE LIFE. «
TECHNICIAN FEWSHAM HAS SUCCESSFULLY REPAIRED ONE OF THE T-MAT «
LINKS TO EARTH. ALIEN LEADER HAS INSTRUCTED THAT IT WILL ONLY «
RECEIVE TRANSPORTATIONS AND NOT SEND ■

AUDIO NOTATION «

SUPERVISOR GIA KELLY ■

Complaints are beginning to come through from national sectors. Civil unrest in the population is beginning to mount because of the breakdown of T-Mat.

There is now some sign of hope. The Doctor and his companions are currently just outside the outer hemisphere of the planet on their rocket journey to the Moon, aiming to land at the solar-powered fuel stacks, via its homing beacon.

Technician Fewsham has managed to open a T-Mat signal enabling personnel to travel to the Moon. I will travel ahead of the work party and initiate the repair programme.

DECODED COMPUTER OBSERVATION DATA «

T-MAT MOONBASE «

REPORT: SUPERVISOR GIA KELLY AND TWO TECHNICIANS HAVE ARRIVED AT«
FUNCTIONAL T-MAT TERMINAL «
STATUS: REPAIR WORK HAS COMMENCED ON T-MAT. RECEIVING T-MAT «
SIGNAL SHUT DOWN «
TRANSMISSION DATA: DETECTION OF SIGNAL EMITTING FROM WITHIN BASE «
ESTIMATED DESTINATION: HOMING SIGNAL FOR ROCKET TRANSPORTATION «
FACILITY CURRENTLY ORBITING MOON «
STATUS: T-MAT REPAIR COMPLETE «
FUNCTIONAL ANALYSIS: T-MAT ABLE TO SEND FROM MOONBASE TO ANY «

POINT ON EARTH «

REPORT: ROCKET TRANSPORTATION HAS SUCCESSFULLY LANDED «

SURVEY: ONE OCCUPANT HAS ENTERED MOONBASE COMPLEX «

SITUATION ANALYSIS: SUPERVISOR KELLY NOW HELD CAPTIVE BY ALIEN «

PRESENCE. ACCOMPANYING TECHNICIANS HAVE BEEN TERMINATED ■

MOONBASE TECHNICIANS' AUDIO-LOG «

TECHNICIAN PHIPPS ■

I've always hated this place and its echoey silence of nothing. The sound of a pin dropping at least reassures you you're not on your own. I now know why people crack under the pressure: it's the fact that it would be so easy to walk into a booth and return to Earth, but you can't do it because you'd lose everything.

Two days before my tour of duty was up, those creatures came. I cannot clear my mind of those things – their sheer reptilian power, their ruthlessness. Stupid Fewsham, the pressure was pushing him to breaking point. He only had a week left, but working with those creatures? Putting every life on earth in danger? All to save his own worthless neck.

The only weapon against the creatures appears to be intense heat. Solar amplifying lamps rigged up in the solar energy storeroom proved to have a startling effect on one: it simply evaporated into nothing, complete molecular disintegration through heat. Their shell-like armour seems to be resilient against any object; perhaps this is the only way to defeat them.

My SOS transmissions through a make-shift apparatus seem to have had partial success. I thought the rocket would be carrying an army of troops, but the only passenger appears to be a strange man called Doctor. Perhaps he is one of the fabled inventors of T-Mat – at tech-training we were always told these scientists were eccentric.

Our exploratory trek to the control centre was cut short by a confrontation with several of the creatures – Ice Warriors, the Doctor calls them. The Doctor managed to free Miss Kelly from the creatures but was captured; we have retreated to the solar energy room along with the Doctor's companions Jamie and Zoe. Our aim is to gain access to the maintenance tunnels.

If we can reach the control centre, we might be able to rescue the Doctor as well as turn up the heating to full power. The heat might subdue the Ice Warriors long enough for us to get help from Earth.

DECODED COMPUTER OBSERVATION DATA«

T-MAT MOONBASE «

LIFE SIGNS: THE ALIEN LEADER HAS ATTEMPTED TO TERMINATE THE LIFE OF «
THE HUMAN CALLED DOCTOR ■

ANALYSIS OF TERMINATION METHOD: USE OF SEED PODS CARRIED WITHIN «
MOBILE GROWTH CHAMBER. POD IS COMPOSED OF VEGETABLE MATTER. «
SECONDS AFTER CONTACT WITH OXYGEN, IT EXPANDS UNTIL PRESSURE «
RUPTURES THE OUTER SKIN. A CLOUD OF SPORES ARE EJECTED INTO THE «
ATMOSPHERE WITH IMMEDIATE EFFECT ON THE HUMAN RESPIRATORY «
SYSTEM. DEATH THROUGH OXYGEN DEPRIVATION RESULTS «

ANALYSIS: SPORES LIGHTER THAN AIR. TRAVEL TO GERMINATE TO NEXT «
STAGE OF LIFE CYCLE ■

PREDICTION OF NEXT STAGE: UNKNOWN. POTENTIAL RAPID GERMINATION «
THROUGH SPORES' ABILITY TO SPREAD QUICKLY THROUGH AIR-STREAMS ■

WARNING WARNING «

T-MAT OPERATIONAL ■

ALIEN PRESENCE TRANSPORTING POD TO EARTH TERMINAL, LONDON, «
ENGLAND ■

!!WARNING WARNING!! «

POTENTIAL DEATHS IMMINENT ■

MOONBASE TECHNICIANS' AUDIO-LOG
TECHNICIAN PHIPPS

After successfully dispatching another Ice Warrior with the solar amplifiers, the journey through the maintenance tunnels was, to say the least, a slow one. The added bulk of Jamie heavily restricted movement. Eventually, we reached the grille to the control centre: the sight that greeted us was not inspiring.

Fewsham appears to be working with the creatures, using T-Mat to dispatch some kind of pod to all the major cities of the Earth. The whole operation was being supervised by a sleeker version of the creatures.

Jamie and I only just managed to rescue the Doctor from the T-Mat cubicle before he was ejected into space. While Jamie tried to drag the Doctor back to the solar energy store room, I tried to reach the heating controls, but the grille was too small for me to climb through.

On my return, we realized the ideal person to get through was Zoe. It is with great reluctance that I've agreed to lead her back to the grille.

COMPUTER OBSERVATION DATA «

EARTH T-MAT CONTROL «

T-MAT MATERIALIZATION FROM MOONBASE: NON-HUMANOID, «
UNIDENTIFIED VEGETATION «

!!DANGER DANGER!! ■

REPORT: POD HAS EXPLODED. SEED PARTICLES DISCHARGED INTO AIR. «

SUCCESSFULLY EXTRACTED FROM ATMOSPHERE AND EJECTED INTO «

EXTERIOR ATMOSPHERE ■

REPORT: MASS SIGHTINGS OF PODS THROUGHOUT COUNTRYSIDE «

INFLICTING VEGETABLE BLIGHT IN FORM OF SPREADING PATCHES OF FOAM.«

RATE OF GROWTH: TEN SQUARE MILES PER HOUR, LIABLE TO INCREASE «

RAPIDLY ■

REPORT: WORLD CAPITALS UNDER SAME THREAT. COUNTRYSIDE INFESTED «

WITH SUBSTANCE ■

‼DANGER DANGER‼ «

ALIEN PRESENCE HAS ARRIVED IN T-MAT CUBICLE «

TYPE OF CREATURE: UNKNOWN ■

SECURITY EVALUATION: 100% FAILURE IN STOPPING CREATURE. CREATURE «

HAS LEFT CONTROL CENTRE, DESTINATION UNKNOWN «

SITUATION REPORT: THE TOTAL BREAKDOWN OF T-MAT HAS RESULTED IN «

CESSATION OF ALL WORLD SHIPMENTS AND DISTRIBUTION. TOTAL «

BREAKDOWN OF SOCIAL ORDER IMMINENT. EMERGENCY MEASURES «

PROVING TO BE INADEQUATE. SITUATION CRITICAL ■

AUDIO NOTATION «

SUPERVISOR GIA KELLY ■

It is with regret that I have to report the death of Technician Phipps, but he did not die in vain. His sacrifice enabled Zoe to reach the heating controls. Unable to withstand the higher humidity, the creatures have collapsed, enabling us to return safely to Moonbase control centre.

Fewsham appears to be redeeming himself after his efforts to save Zoe from an Ice Warrior. Suggesting that we all T-Mat back to Earth, he apparently lied about his intentions to follow us using the timing device on the T-Mat controls. The Doctor has found that it does not work; Fewsham is still trapped with those creatures.

Our return finds Commander Radnor under siege – the entire planet has been infested by the seed pods that Jamie and the Doctor have spoken of.

DECODED COMPUTER OBSERVATION DATA «

T-MAT MOONBASE «

REPORT: TECHNICIAN FEWSHAM HAS CONNECTED A COMMUNICATIONS «

DEVICE TO THE SOLAR BATTERIES ■

ANALYSIS: DEVICE IS A HOMING BEACON FOR THE ALIEN PRESENCE «

POSTULATION: MORE SPACECRAFT OF THE ALIEN PRESENCE WILL ARRIVE «

SHORTLY USING SIGNAL 'ICE LORD' COMMUNICATING WITH 'GRAND «

MARSHALL' ■

STATUS: TECHNICIAN FEWSHAM HAS OPENED COMMUNICATION LINK WITH«

EARTH UNDETECTED. ALIEN PRESENCE TESTING HOMING SIGNAL.«

RECORDING OF SIGNAL TAKING PLACE ON EARTH. INDICATIONS SUGGEST «

THE ALIEN FLEET IS LOW ON FUEL. ALIEN PRESENCE HAS DETECTED SIGNAL «

BEING SENT TO EARTH. TECHNICIAN FEWSHAM TERMINATED ■

AUDIO NOTATION «

SUPERVISOR GIA KELLY ■

Fewsham displayed a stroke of genius by opening the video link to Earth control, so we all witnessed the Ice Lord communicating data to his superior. The test signal for the homing beacon was successfully recorded before the broadcast cut-off. Fewsham may have supplied all the information we need, but it cost him his life.

The rocket due to launch the satellite to relay the T-Mat signals has had its take-off aborted. Professor Eldred has helped construct a transmitter to feed a fake homing beacon to the fleet of Ice Warrior ships. It will alter their flight path in such a way that they will get caught in the gravitational pull of the sun.

As far as the foam blight is concerned, the Doctor accidentally discovered the one thing that will destroy it is simply H_2O; water. This explains why the Ice Warrior that materialized on Earth was last seen at the Weather Control Bureau. It was obviously intent on stopping the production of any rain.

Jamie and Zoe had already left to investigate, and it was up to the Doctor to save them from the creature prowling through the bureau. The Doctor has managed to reprogram the controls and heavy rain storms are due. Apparently the foam would have absorbed all the oxygen from the Earth's atmosphere making it the same as that of Mars.

When the signal is transmitting safely from the rocket, the Doctor has announced that he intends to return to the control centre at Moonbase to close down the signal being sent from there. My thoughts go with him.

DECODED COMPUTER OBSERVATION DATA «

T-MAT MOONBASE «

T-MAT ACTIVATED: TRANSMISSION FROM EARTH «

LIFE SIGNS READING: DUAL CARDIOVASCULAR SYSTEM. ONLY HUMAN «
KNOWN TO SYSTEM WITH THIS READING IS THE DOCTOR ■
HEAT READING: AMPLIFIED SOLAR LIGHTS USED AS WEAPON TO DISPOSE OF «
ICE WARRIOR. ■
STATUS: ICE LORD NOW HOLDS DOCTOR CAPTIVE. SIGNAL TRANSMITTING «
FROM CONTROL CENTRE TERMINATED. APPROACHING FLEET OF SPACE «
CRAFT TRAPPED IN GRAVITATIONAL PULL OF SUN. FLEET'S TRANSMISSION «
HAS TERMINATED ■
SECOND HUMANOID ARRIVAL FROM EARTH: YOUNG MALE «
STATUS: ICE LORD TERMINATED OWING TO WEAPON MALFUNCTION. ALIEN «
TRANSMITTER USED TO TERMINATE REMAINING ICE WARRIOR. ALIEN «
PRESENCE ERADICATED. HUMANS HAVE RETURNED TO EARTH ■

AUDIO NOTATION «

SUPERVISOR GIA KELLY ■

The rain cycle programme has been implemented with 100% success, the foam is retreating rapidly. Estimates suggest only a few hours will be needed for it to be wiped out completely. The crisis is now over.

In future T-Mat must be centrally controlled from Earth; the risk of an assault on a base on the Moon could happen again. Professor Eldred's demands for a back-up force of rockets is invalid: the cost alone would make such a venture prohibitive.

I would have appointed the Doctor and his companions as technical advisers, but they appear to have vanished without trace.

The Mythology of Peladon

Passages taken from the sacred Books of Aggedor, volumes I, II and IV.

King Peladon looked down upon his Kingdom and wept

for he saw there were no more lands to conquer.

The Fall of the King, I.110

earsome winds of darkness tore into the very soul of the Castle of Royals, the night the mighty and noble King Peladon was slain in his final battle, for even those as strong in spirit as he cannot defeat the ominous spectre of death.

His dying wish that his chancellor, Torbis, should teach the young prince the knowledge of his power and the breadth of his domain. The kingdom of Peladon awaited the day that the new King would rise.

Alas, thoughts of evil and the longing for power can corrupt those of the purest heart and mind, for deep hatred lay growing in the soul of one man, a hatred that would shake the very foundations of the kingdom he coveted.

There will come a day, when the spirit of Aggedor will rise again to warn and defend his royal master, King Peladon. For on that day, a stranger will arrive in the land bringing peril to Peladon and great tribulation to the land.

The Curse of Aggedor

The Plan for the Future, II.1

Young King Peladon's desire to improve the lives of his subjects were more than wishful dreams. To gain wealth and prosperity to his world, the King sought membership of the Galactic Federation; its Committee of Assessment met to consider his plea. The chancellors of Peladon favoured this plan for the future, but the High Priest, Hepesh, and his followers grew uneasy.

The destruction of religious order and the loss of all that was sacred; the downfall of society and the nobility of Peladon was an ever-present nightmare for Hepesh, who railed at the idea of joining the renowned interplanetary council. He could not bear to contemplate his King's thoughts becoming more than a dream.

The Shadow of Death, II.4

Hushed voices whispered words of the spirit of Aggedor rising from the towering mountains. Enraged at his loss of respect, Hepesh knew his god would condone his every thought. The Curse of Aggedor fell upon Peladon, and Chancellor Torbis's life was taken by the god in his rage. Aggedor had returned to the Castle of Royals.

The Delegates from the Stars, II.9

The delegates from the Galactic Federation grew uneasy once rumours of the demise of Torbis reached them. Representatives from the world of Arcturus and Alpha Centauri, delegates Izylyr and sub-delegate Ssorg from Mars anxiously awaited the arrival of the chairman delegate from planet Earth.

The Earth Princess, II.16

The timely arrival of the Earth delegate came not without cause for concern: his craft suffered damage in the storm that raged outside the walls of the palace, causing it to crash in the lower region of the mountains. A rescue party was dispatched to retrieve the vessel from its rock-strewn grave.

Chairman delegate Doctor presented his royal companion before the assembled delegates: Princess Josephine of TARDIS, the official observer of the monarch of her world.

The Assassin in the Shadows, II.20

The vast stone image of Aggedor that for centuries had gazed from its carven balcony, fell from its lofty seat towards the delegates below. The lives of both Alpha Centauri and Izlyr were spared through the prowess of

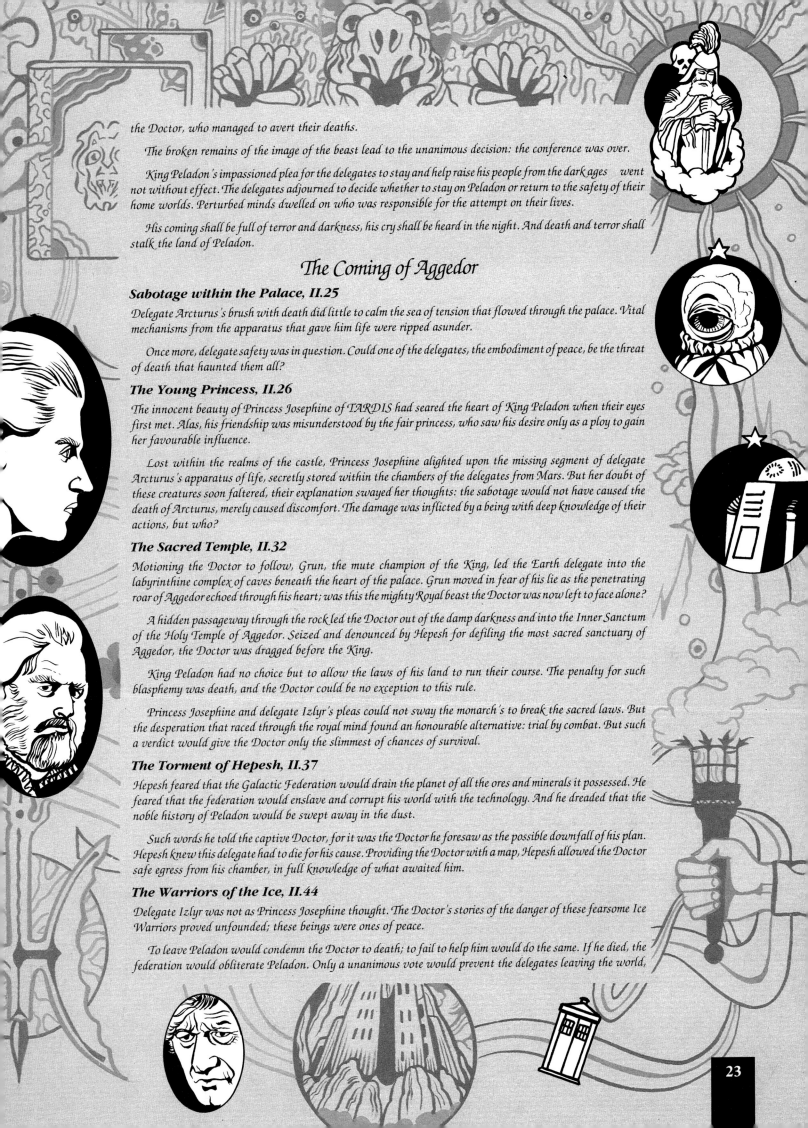

the Doctor, who managed to avert their deaths.

The broken remains of the image of the beast lead to the unanimous decision: the conference was over.

King Peladon's impassioned plea for the delegates to stay and help raise his people from the dark ages   went not without effect. The delegates adjourned to decide whether to stay on Peladon or return to the safety of their home worlds. Perturbed minds dwelled on who was responsible for the attempt on their lives.

His coming shall be full of terror and darkness, his cry shall be heard in the night. And death and terror shall stalk the land of Peladon.

The Coming of Aggedor

Sabotage within the Palace, II.25

Delegate Arcturus's brush with death did little to calm the sea of tension that flowed through the palace. Vital mechanisms from the apparatus that gave him life were ripped asunder.

Once more, delegate safety was in question. Could one of the delegates, the embodiment of peace, be the threat of death that haunted them all?

The Young Princess, II.26

The innocent beauty of Princess Josephine of TARDIS had seared the heart of King Peladon when their eyes first met. Alas, his friendship was misunderstood by the fair princess, who saw his desire only as a ploy to gain her favourable influence.

Lost within the realms of the castle, Princess Josephine alighted upon the missing segment of delegate Arcturus's apparatus of life, secretly stored within the chambers of the delegates from Mars. But her doubt of these creatures soon faltered, their explanation swayed her thoughts: the sabotage would not have caused the death of Arcturus, merely caused discomfort. The damage was inflicted by a being with deep knowledge of their actions, but who?

The Sacred Temple, II.32

Motioning the Doctor to follow, Grun, the mute champion of the King, led the Earth delegate into the labyrinthine complex of caves beneath the heart of the palace. Grun moved in fear of his lie as the penetrating roar of Aggedor echoed through his heart; was this the mighty Royal beast the Doctor was now left to face alone?

A hidden passageway through the rock led the Doctor out of the damp darkness and into the Inner Sanctum of the Holy Temple of Aggedor. Seized and denounced by Hepesh for defiling the most sacred sanctuary of Aggedor, the Doctor was dragged before the King.

King Peladon had no choice but to allow the laws of his land to run their course. The penalty for such blasphemy was death, and the Doctor could be no exception to this rule.

Princess Josephine and delegate Izlyr's pleas could not sway the monarch's to break the sacred laws. But the desperation that raced through the royal mind found an honourable alternative: trial by combat. But such a verdict would give the Doctor only the slimmest of chances of survival.

The Torment of Hepesh, II.37

Hepesh feared that the Galactic Federation would drain the planet of all the ores and minerals it possessed. He feared that the federation would enslave and corrupt his world with the technology. And he dreaded that the noble history of Peladon would be swept away in the dust.

Such words he told the captive Doctor, for it was the Doctor he foresaw as the possible downfall of his plan. Hepesh knew this delegate had to die for his cause. Providing the Doctor with a map, Hepesh allowed the Doctor safe egress from his chamber, in full knowledge of what awaited him.

The Warriors of the Ice, II.44

Delegate Izlyr was not as Princess Josephine thought. The Doctor's stories of the danger of these fearsome Ice Warriors proved unfounded; these beings were ones of peace.

To leave Peladon would condemn the Doctor to death; to fail to help him would do the same. If he died, the federation would obliterate Peladon. Only a unanimous vote would prevent the delegates leaving the world,

Izlyr placed his vote against leaving, determined to repay the Doctor in kind for saving him from the assassination attempt.

The King's Dilemma, II.50

Through accident more than chance, Princess Josephine found the Doctor within the catacombs beneath the castle. She was not to have known that the beast she valiantly frightened away was one of the fabled Royal Beasts, a creature long thought to be extinct.

Before the assembled delegates in the throne room, Princess Josephine and the Doctor presented their evidence to the King. But after a life of being taught that Aggedor does not exist, King Peladon had no choice but to denounce the Doctor's lies; the chairman delegate would have to endure trial by combat.

The Pit of Combat II.53

Champion and challenger descended on ropes into the oppressive air of the centuries-old pit. Both knew that only one of them could return.

Yet the Doctor had had his suspicions confirmed when Hepesh confronted him in his chambers and admitted that corruption lay within the heart of one of the delegates present on Peladon. The Doctor knew the foul traitor would be present to witness his demise, eager to see the single threat to his scheme vanquished.

As Grun lay defeated in the dust, his life spared in his hour of shame, Arcturus's attempts to destroy the Doctor with a laser weapon were intercepted by Ssorg, whose sonic device dealt a deadly blow to his fellow delegate. With the Doctor's ability to solve the mysterious circumstances of earlier events, the answer slowly came to light.

Hepesh had carried out the attack on the life apparatus of Arcturus, following the delegate's instruction as to what should be removed. The high priest, too, had placed the incriminating evidence in the chamber of the Mars delegates. And it was Hepesh who instructed Grun to push the statue of Aggedor from its balcony.

The high priest had discovered a few of the Royal Beasts of Peladon remained on the highest points of the mountains. He had brought one back and trained it carefully to respond to his instructions.

His collaborator, delegate Arcturus, came from a world without valuable mineral deposits. Arcturus and Hepesh made a secret pact whereby the delegate would gain all Peladon's minerals if the planet did not join the Galactic Federation. And if Hepesh were to accuse the Ice Warriors of plotting the death of Arcturus, an ancient feud would be resurrected and bloody battle would be joined.

A Retreat to the Catacombs, II.59

Tormented by the prospect of failure, Hepesh knew in his heart that the faith of the warriors of Peladon would remain true to their god, the god that he could manipulate. Every weapon would rise to support his valiant cause; even if civil war were the only solution, Hepesh was willing to risk it.

A Gathering of Force, II.70

Hepesh assembled his men and forced entry into the throne room. An ultimatum was presented to his King: if the forces of the Galactic Federation did not withdraw from the planet instantly, allowing society to return to the ancient ways he cherished, Peladon's reign would end abruptly on the point of a sword.

Victory was within the grasp of the High Priest, until the Doctor suddenly returned with Aggedor by his side.

The Return of Aggedor, II.72

Warriors, brave and true to the cause of Hepesh, fell on their knees in respect to their God. Enraged at the stupidity of men, Hepesh used fire to demonstrate the creature being no more than a trained beast. Alas, the might of the noble animal was too much for the old priest. High Priest Hepesh lay slain by the god he abused in his pursuit of power.

The dying words of many a man admit to mistakes of the soul, and so at the last Hepesh confessed he was wrong in his beliefs — perhaps the progress Peladon that required was the right path to take.

The Coming of War, II.96

Peladon flourished, proving everything King Peladon knew in his heart to be true; his world became a powerful

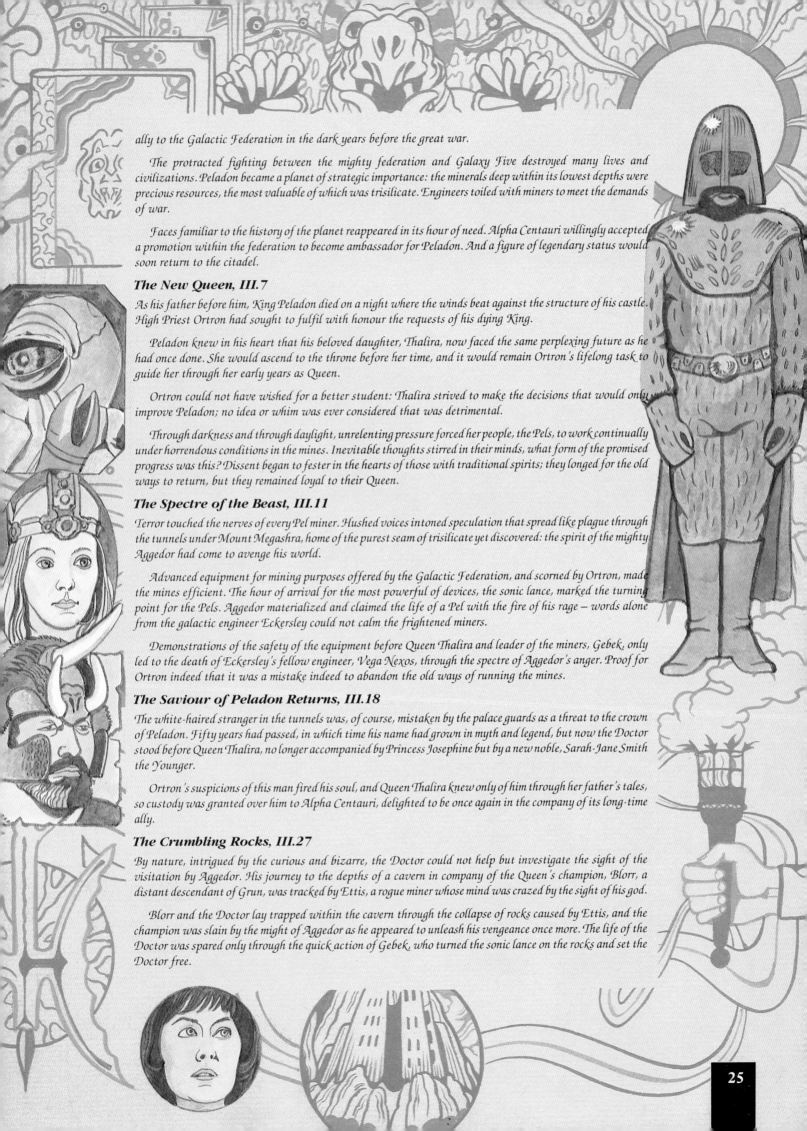

ally to the Galactic Federation in the dark years before the great war.

The protracted fighting between the mighty federation and Galaxy Five destroyed many lives and civilizations. Peladon became a planet of strategic importance: the minerals deep within its lowest depths were precious resources, the most valuable of which was trisilicate. Engineers toiled with miners to meet the demands of war.

Faces familiar to the history of the planet reappeared in its hour of need. Alpha Centauri willingly accepted a promotion within the federation to become ambassador for Peladon. And a figure of legendary status would soon return to the citadel.

The New Queen, III.7

As his father before him, King Peladon died on a night where the winds beat against the structure of his castle. High Priest Ortron had sought to fulfil with honour the requests of his dying King.

Peladon knew in his heart that his beloved daughter, Thalira, now faced the same perplexing future as he had once done. She would ascend to the throne before her time, and it would remain Ortron's lifelong task to guide her through her early years as Queen.

Ortron could not have wished for a better student: Thalira strived to make the decisions that would only improve Peladon; no idea or whim was ever considered that was detrimental.

Through darkness and through daylight, unrelenting pressure forced her people, the Pels, to work continually under horrendous conditions in the mines. Inevitable thoughts stirred in their minds, what form of the promised progress was this? Dissent began to fester in the hearts of those with traditional spirits; they longed for the old ways to return, but they remained loyal to their Queen.

The Spectre of the Beast, III.11

Terror touched the nerves of every Pel miner. Hushed voices intoned speculation that spread like plague through the tunnels under Mount Megashra, home of the purest seam of trisilicate yet discovered: the spirit of the mighty Aggedor had come to avenge his world.

Advanced equipment for mining purposes offered by the Galactic Federation, and scorned by Ortron, made the mines efficient. The hour of arrival for the most powerful of devices, the sonic lance, marked the turning point for the Pels. Aggedor materialized and claimed the life of a Pel with the fire of his rage – words alone from the galactic engineer Eckersley could not calm the frightened miners.

Demonstrations of the safety of the equipment before Queen Thalira and leader of the miners, Gebek, only led to the death of Eckersley's fellow engineer, Vega Nexos, through the spectre of Aggedor's anger. Proof for Ortron indeed that it was a mistake indeed to abandon the old ways of running the mines.

The Saviour of Peladon Returns, III.18

The white-haired stranger in the tunnels was, of course, mistaken by the palace guards as a threat to the crown of Peladon. Fifty years had passed, in which time his name had grown in myth and legend, but now the Doctor stood before Queen Thalira, no longer accompanied by Princess Josephine but by a new noble, Sarah-Jane Smith the Younger.

Ortron's suspicions of this man fired his soul, and Queen Thalira knew only of him through her father's tales, so custody was granted over him to Alpha Centauri, delighted to be once again in the company of its long-time ally.

The Crumbling Rocks, III.27

By nature, intrigued by the curious and bizarre, the Doctor could not help but investigate the sight of the visitation by Aggedor. His journey to the depths of a cavern in company of the Queen's champion, Blorr, a distant descendant of Grun, was tracked by Ettis, a rogue miner whose mind was crazed by the sight of his god.

Blorr and the Doctor lay trapped within the cavern through the collapse of rocks caused by Ettis, and the champion was slain by the might of Aggedor as he appeared to unleash his vengeance once more. The life of the Doctor was spared only through the quick action of Gebek, who turned the sonic lance on the rocks and set the Doctor free.

True allies in spirit, Gebek undertook a vow to return his perturbed miners to work if the Doctor worked on a solution to the mystery of the killer apparition.

The Arsenal of Freedom, III.34

Ortron's fear that the miners would revolt became a reality as Ettis used his guile and cunning to steal weapons war from the royal armoury, taking the Doctor's companion as a hostage of war.

Freed by royal guards, the young girl was brought before Ortron, whose temper raged at his loss of control. In the sacred temple he passed judgment of her fate, and the unexpected delight of the Doctor's arrival provided the high priest with two sacrifices for his god. The pit where the mighty Aggedor lay was opened to the daylight once more, and the lives of the Doctor and Sarah-Jane Smith were cast down into the darkness.

The Beast in the Darkness, III.18

Legend tells of how the mighty Aggedor's rage lay tamed by the kind spirit of the Doctor. Myths of the Royal Beast tell of his wise dispensation of justice to the wicked and kindness to the good; the spirit of Aggedor had not forgotten the Doctor. Ortron's amazement held no bounds as he saw his god crouch at the feet of the being he had offered as sacrifice.

Queen Thalira's outrage at her high priest's carelessness brought forth a storm of anger that only few had seen before, long, long ago in the body of her noble father, King Peladon.

Conferences of Power, III.46

Ettis had stirred hatred in the minds of his fellow miners; Gebek's words of peace fell on deaf ears. Through careful planning the rebel miners gained possession of the sonic lance.

Galactic Federation troops landed on the summons of Alpha Centauri, concerned about the security of supplies of trisilicate. Led by the Commander Azaxyr, an Ice Lord of the planet Mars, the Ice Warriors repelled an attack on the palace by miners under the control of Ettis.

Suspicion lay heavy on the Doctor's heart. Following directions supplied by Sarah-Jane Smith to the disused refinery in the mine, Gebek and the Doctor discovered an Ice Warrior within. How could this be, they reasoned: the mighty creatures had only just arrived on Peladon.

Wasted lives unite the fiercest of opponents. Ortron and Gebek, distraught at the deaths of so many Pels, joined forces to return to the ways of the past. Both knew that technology was bringing nothing but death and destruction to their land.

A Plan of Madness, III.40

The Ice Warriors guarding the miners found great weakness overcoming them; the Doctor had sabotaged the heating controls, making conditions unbearable to the creatures of the ice. Brave in heart and mind, Gebek charged forth with the palace guards that remained loyal to his cause and attacked the aliens.

All attention was on the battle when Ettis emerged from hiding. He sought to turn the sonic lance on the palace, even killing the miner Rima to advance his plans. Yet Rima lived long enough to reveal Ettis's intent.

Confronting the madman with only a steel sword as defence, the Doctor sought to stop Ettis. The madman's attack against his Queen, however, was doomed to failure: the sonic lance would self-destruct if fired. None the less, Ettis operated the device; as flames consumed the melting rocks, all thoughts turned to the end of the legend of the Doctor.

The Air of Life, III.47

Commander Azaxyr found nothing but pleasure in the knowledge that the meddlesome Doctor and the rebel Ettis had been destroyed through their own stupidity. His thoughts turned to quelling the rebellious miners, and ruthlessly he ordered that all the oxygen be drained from the mines. Survival would entail moving to the upper air-filled caves, where Azaxyr's Ice Warriors would be waiting for them.

Protestations from Queen Thalira and her high priest had no effect; they were to remain prisoner in the throne room with Sarah-Jane Smith, tortured by the knowledge of the inevitable massacre of the Peladonians. Alpha Centauri's information concerning Commander Azaxyr's plans of the conquest of Peladon, and the enslavement of all its people to work in the mines failed to inspire hope.

Plagued by defeat, Sarah-Jane Smith's brave-heartedly suggested sending a distress signal from the communication centre. Alas, the escape by all four prisoners was noticed, allowing only the Doctor's companion and Alpha Centauri to escape. Queen Thalira, devastated by the death of Ortron at the merciless hands of an Ice Warrior, remained on her throne to face the wrath of Azaxyr.

The Traitors Revealed, III.54

Combined in force and belief, Engineer Eckersley and Commander Azaxyr represented the secret forces of the might of Galaxy Five. Azaxyr craved the success he had failed to find among his own kind; his race was dedicated to maintaining peace throughout the universe, but his bloodlust for war led him to seek allegiances with other powers. Eckersley was motivated purely by financial gain.

The visitation of the mighty Aggedor were merely a technical trick devised by the engineer, using technology that was beyond the comprehension of the Peladonians. A hologram equipped with a directional heat ray projector enabled the spirit of Aggedor to take his revenge, vaporizing the innocent miners to nothing but ash.

The Battle in the Refinery, III.63

Accompanied by Sarah-Jane Smith and Gebek, who found his ally survived the explosion of the sonic lance, the Doctor barred the entrance to the refinery from within. The wrath of the hologram Aggedor was now on the side of Peladon. The Ice Warriors burning an entrance through the walls were quickly dispatched, allowing the Doctor to concentrate the device within the mines. The Pels at last saw their god fighting for them; his fiery wrath destroyed the Ice Warriors before their eyes.

Illusions and assaults on the mind, however, are the most damaging of weapons. Eckersley's attempts to turn these weapons against the Doctor failed to take instant effect, merely inducing a sensory withdrawal into his subconscious. Yet the engineer miscalculated; he assumed the Doctor was dead.

The Threat to the Queen, III.69

Gebek and his victorious forces scoured the mines and palace for the elusive leader of the Ice Warriors, fired by the righteousness of men who have seen god.

Beaching the barred doors of the throne room, Gebek found Azaxyr within, a death-giving weapon held to the Queen's head. Gebek had no choice but to fight for Queen Thalira's life. Years of mining gave him the strength he needed the strength to Gebek's arms he needed.

Azaxyr was no creature of weakness, but a blow aimed at Gebek by his guard, Sskel, destroyed him with the sonic waves of his weapon. The Ice Lord's dying reflexes triggered his own sonic gun, felling the mighty Sskel. The last of the creatures lay dead at the feet of Queen Thalira.

The Royal Beast of Peladon, III.72

The history of Peladon tells that Aggedor will defend the royal family of and slay all who threaten its members' lives. Though centuries old and aged to a degree where most creatures would die, the senses of the noble beast returned as he led the Doctor in search of his Queen.

Eckersley knew full well that his only chance of escape from the planet lay in gaining safe passage to his hidden space shuttle, with Queen Thalira his hostage.

Recovered from the assault on his mind, the Doctor released Aggedor from his sacred pit. The beast fulfilled the legends: he struck down Eckersley, but in turn the laser device of the engineer slew the mighty Aggedor. But the Royal Beast of Peladon had saved his Queen.

The Future of Peladon, III,80

The war against Galaxy Five was destined to be no more than a memory past. Everything lay with the success of Azaxyr's mission, and as news of failure reached commanding powers, a treaty came within a day.

Queen Tharila now faced years of prosperity and peace, with her new Chancellor, Gebek, at her side. And lo, the history of Peladon came full circle, the Doctor and his companion vanished as mysteriously as he had done with Princess Josephine before.

THE ZARBI AND THE MENOPTRA

The plague of darkness came, and all that was light died. The land, its roots, and the forests, all life that grew from soil died; only creatures of the darkness and shadows survived. That which survived was taken by the evil, the evil that now grew, feeding, taking all that had given the land life. The weak and the lame faded away; the strong fled to seek sanctuary from evil. Vortis withered to no more than a husk. Evil was victorious. Victorious until the time of the travellers who fell from the sky.

Menoptran inscription discovered on the planet Vortis

An unexplored world, inhabited long ago by a society composed entirely of insects, a species totally unlike anything seen on the Earth. Evidence of an evolving culture – cave paintings, carvings, inscribed monoliths. What a vast labyrinth of history: a race that seems to have been torn from its roots, but which fought back valiantly. There is a truly remarkable story waiting to be unearthed.

Audio notation by Professor Strontus, archaeological reconnaissance to Vortis

All that lay before the Animus fell victim to its greed. The day of great harvest came, yet no fruit or flower lived in the mighty forests. Then came then day that the light began to die and even the temples of light grew dark. We knew not of the Animus and the danger of the Caresnome. The eldest of the song weavers approached the Caresnome with offerings of peace. Never did he return nor those who sought to find him. No rock or tool could prise the Caresnome from the ground, nor metal cut the surface of its evil. We knew the Caresnome would grow, swelling until Vortis became Caresnome.

Menoptran inscription

It would seem that the terror in the words stems from a vast parasitic spore that had become embedded in the surface of the planet. Various spores capable of absorbing matter have been discovered, all able to gestate in the void of space, but the Caresnome seems to have possessed a structured form of intelligence, the Animus.

The first to encounter the parasite seems to have been the Menoptra, the surface dwelling indigenous species of the planet, and certainly the most literate of the four life forms present on Vortis. Carvings on rock monoliths illustrate the peaceful life cycle of these creatures, which was clearly devastated by the arrival of the Animus.

As man had his distinctive seven ages, the life of the Menoptra is divided into four:

The Age of Learning

Larval Menoptra are bipeds capable of movement on their hind legs. In a system almost comparable with an education, they are shown how to understand cycles of light, the meanings of colour and the wonders of the vegetation that once flourished in every open space of Vortis. Larvae are quiet and sedate, awaiting the time of transformation that will transform them to their adult form.

The Age of Understanding

Vast caverns house the larval Menoptra as their elders weave cocoons around their dormant forms. Their minds expand as their bodies change; when the season of harvest comes to Vortis, the larvae break free from their cocoons.

Once colourless bodies now display patterns of yellow fur, and the skin blemishes form delicate patches of black and white. The stumps on the back of a larva have now grown into vast wings of delicate skin, and the creatures soar into the sky trying to touch the lights in the sky. Their lives have meaning: they now know what it is to be a Menoptra and worship the gods of light in the sky.

The Age of Song

As the harvest of vegetation is complete, the Menoptra move to the temples of light – gigantic pyramids of delicate fibres in which patterns of glorious colour pulsate. Here the song weavers hold their fellow creatures enraptured by their words. It is a time of peace.

The Age of Wisdom

As the Menoptra age, they build more temples of light for the generations destined to follow them. The elders supervise the planting of flowers during the season of growth, and watch the young Menoptra fly towards the sun as they emerge from their cocoons.

As death overcomes a Menoptra, the creatures celebrate the life of the creature that has passed away. His body is entombed in a chamber of one of the temples of light, where his name and words of song will be remembered for ever, the spirit of his life preserved for eternity.

Three sub-species also existed at that time, but their lives were harmonious with the Menoptra – only the Animus changed that.

The Zarbi can be identified as a species of drone insect that foraged for food and which lived in vast tunnel systems in the hills of the planet. If Menoptra can be compared to the butterflies of Earth's ancient times, the black, six-legged Zarbi are comparable to the ant.

Manipulated by the Animus, the Zarbi turned into vicious predators. They guarded the Caresnome, attacking and hunting down any who dared to stray too close to it. Capable of great speed, they moved on their hind legs, allowing the front four legs mobility that they had not experienced before. With no other weapon than their unnatural strength, they relied heavily on the lowest form of life natural to Vortis, the Larva Gun.

A multi-legged grub protected by a segmented carapace, the Larva Gun possessed the remarkable ability to discharge concentrated amounts of electricity through its snout. It proved a lethal weapon against the Menoptra.

Under the caverns of the Zarbi, away from the light, a new species was destined to evolve.

> Blood of our kinsmen lay across the once fertile land. We knew not of the strength of Zarbi. The elders looked upon the sky, yet no light was there to offer guidance. The end of the Menoptra was near.
>
> Only one saw light for our future: the new moons of Vortis. With what energy remained, we departed for Pictos, the nearest of the three. There will be no more songs on Vortis, for Vortis is no more.

The last of the inscriptions tells of the desperate struggle the Menoptra faced as they tried to escape the wrath of the once benign Zarbi, fleeing to a rogue moon. Vortis has always been recorded as a planet without any satellites in geo-stationary orbit, yet the sheer power of the Animus drew three into a trapped orbit on the outskirts of the planets atmosphere.

The vast size of the Caresnome, the roots of which burrowed deep within the planet, could

possibly be attributed to the fact that it tapped the magnetic pole; untold amounts of energy energized it, and perhaps in turn created the malevolent intelligence at its core.

The slaughter of Menoptra was extreme. Evidence of mummified husks indicated that the wings of the creatures were torn from their backs. Such mutilation made it impossible for these creatures to escape the planet's surface; under the guard of the Zarbi, they were slaves on their own world.

> We live in eternal darkness; despair fills the air. My kinsmen die every light cycle. Vegetation once glorious in colour and taste, lies rank and dead. Water, fountains and jets are no more. Pools new flow with water that burns. The roots of evil spread through Vortis in burning water. We feed it without rest, and the Animus grows.

The captive Menoptra faced unending slavery, apparently providing nourishment for the roots of the Caresnome, which thrived on liquid sulphur and acid. Only a few Menoptra escaped slavery and found the lowest cave levels of the planet.

Darkness transformed the Menoptra. The elegant beauty of the language became distorted. The creatures' wings were unsuited to such restricted spaces, and over ensuing generations they became no more than stumps. Once-beautiful fur fell out, and the skin beneath turned to hardened scales, forming a shell along the spine. They grew limbs suited to the restricted space: eight stumpy arms. Adapting to the lack of light, their eyes became vast, and antennae developed into dozens of feelers.

The pronunciation of their breed name became more abrupt, Menoptra, Enoptra, Noptra and lastly Optera. Over a period of several hundred years, the once-elegant Menoptra became the slug-like Optera.

The Domination of Vortis

The Menoptra who fled to Pictos found survival was barely possible: the race became listless and its members souls, once full of song and beauty, hardened to the reality of war. The elders knew that they would have to fight if ever Vortis was to be theirs again.

Technology dawned on the race and a weapon became their hope – a weapon that could kill the Zarbi and allow them access to the Caresnome. Their hatred of the Animus must have been extreme: rock paintings show horrific images of the Animus as their minds imagined it, for no Menoptra had seen the parasite and survived to tell of the encounter.

At least two Earth centuries passed before the Menoptra returned to Vortis. In that time their monuments on Vortis crumbled, leaving unrecognizable pillars; the temples of light became buried in rockfalls. Whole generations of Menoptra had come and gone on Pictos; the sights and wonders of Vortis were now no more than race memories, stories passed on to the larva by the elders.

By far the most celebrated section of Menoptra history depicts their attempts to recover their world. Entire cave walls are covered in vivid images and the elegant lettering of the species. It is truly an extraordinary accomplishment.

And came upon the world of Vortis,
A being of wisdom, all knowledge was his kingdom,
The blue temple of his world is well,
His fellow breed within its shell.
The saviour of all Vortis.

The song of song weaver Prapilius

And lo, the chosen kinsmen make ready their souls. The way to Vortis will be paved by their courage. The elders predict that only few light cycles remain before the evil of the Animus consumes Vortis; they labour to find the key to freedom.

An isotope will destroy the Animus, taking the evil heart away from Vortis. All able Menoptra await the call for the final battle. The chosen few will move ahead – we await their word. And then we shall descend on the world that is the true domain of all Menoptra.

During the years on Pictos, a new bloodline developed, nurturing what can only be termed as 'natural aggression'. The race memory of the forced evacuation of Vortis turned from fear to anger, but not one of the species knew what Vortis would now be like.

In what was technically the first recorded instant of insectoid militaristic strategy, the primitive communications device that the Menoptra elders had constructed failed. During the ancient times on Vortis, the song weavers had discovered crystals natural to the Zarbi's tunnels, clear rock formations that resonated and projected any sound directed at them. What was once a musical instrument used for no more than amusement had been adapted; held in a structure of movable segments, it could be manipulated to send signals to and from Pictos.

The elders could not have allowed for the magnetic powers of the Animus, which jammed any messages they tried to send. The message of hope the Menoptra on Pictos longed to hear did not reach them; the invasion swarm had no way of knowing that the signal would have been a warning.

In various parts of the cave systems leading to and from the remains of the temples of light, objects have been strewn across the ground, long since forgotten artefacts from the time of the Animus. Curved in a shape similar to that of a wishbone, delicately built in mottled gold, what I at first assumed to be a fossil presented a perplexing mystery.

Images on the cave walls depict it being used on captive Menoptra by the Zarbi, hanging across the collar bone and over the shoulder. A slight registering of magnetic power still present within it suggests Animus influence; if this is indeed the case, it could have been used as a control device.

From descriptions in Menoptran broken text, it seems that the first Menoptra to return to Vortis encountered a being under such influence, simply because it wore a decorative item of gold, unaware of the consequences. There are no remains or physical signs to indicate that a fifth sub-species had evolved on the planet; the words of the Menoptra give an alarmingly close description to that of a female human, but this is hardly possible.

The Zarbi are beyond control. The Animus has increased their powers; their strength is greater than any Menoptra has seen.

Species they held captive, unseen before by Menoptra. Menoptra efforts to free her triumphant. No colour of any Menoptra is on her skin, no wings on her back, eyes are not that of any breed of Vortis. One kinsman thought her to be of the Animus. Her fear of Menoptra and Zarbi show this is not so. Arbara her name, not of Vortis blood. Fled she from our cave in fear.

Images depict the being, Arbara, leading Zarbi to the cave where the trio of Menoptra lay hidden, obviously recaptured and under the influence of the Animus. One of the Menoptra seems to have been slain by a Larva Gun; the female leader Vrestin managed to destroy the crystal communicator before escaping. The remaining Menoptra was subjected to the Zarbi's brutal torture; both wings were savagely torn from the bone sockets on his back.

I have managed to ascertain that the chamber/cavern where the Menoptra captives force fed the Animus had an ancient name. Centuries before, a natural formation of razor sharp crystalline rocks grew there in vast numbers – mica spars used to harvest crops. Now used by the Zarbi as weapons, and as excavation implements by the captives, the supply had obviously died out; only the name remained, The Crater of Needles. It seems that the surviving Menoptra from Pictos and Arbara were taken there.

The surviving Menoptra found the planet to be totally unlike the one she imagined: it was a desolate landscape of rocks and ravines; dust storms drifted across its cracked surface. Vrestin found the Caresnome. If the crater left on the surface of Vortis now is any indication of its size when living, the entity she saw was easily the size of the city. In a haze of protective web, the surface structure pulsated with a life of its own.

Heron spoke of the world of the Animus. Rescue him, I, from the strength of Zarbi. Knew he of fellow kin Arbara. Two more lay within the Caresnome, Dokotor and Iviki. Heron spoke of a temple of blue which carried their spirits to Vortis. Sought he Arbara, wishing to return her soul to the temple of blue. Our words and dreams fled from our thoughts, Zarbi and Larva Guns sought us. The routes and lands of Vortis were no longer the same as our elders spoke of. Sanctuary. Heron found safety in a cleft of mighty rock. Fell we to a world of darkness.

It is possible that Vrestin and being Heron rested on an air crater, covered by only a thin shell of soil and rock. Their combined weight caused it to give way. Whatever happened, evidence on the lower level caverns of the planet suggested that they fell a considerable distance. Vrestin had no concept of the fact that the creatures that confronted them were her distant ancestors.

The Optera feared all that came from the land above. Deep-rooted race memories stung their minds with fear at the prospect of ever ascending to the surface. They knew little of the Zarbi. The primitive creatures worshipped the image of the Menoptra – cave paintings show them in abundance. Perhaps these works of art were done by the Menoptra who fled underground centuries before.

The Optera's story tells of a day of revelation, when one of their sacred gods returned to them and spread the wings of knowledge before them. Obviously, Vrestin spread her own wings before the hostile creatures to convince them of who she was, with immediate effect: the leader of the Optera, Hetra, agreed to lead them to the roots of all evil – Pwodarauk, the Animus.

The level below ground that the Optera inhabited was at the same depth that the Caresnome roots had reached, and the creatures knew all too well of its existence. A protective, semi-toxic gas spread through their tunnel systems from the pores of the parasite's flesh. Led by Vrestin and Heron, they sought to find its source.

> No thought strayed from Vortis. All minds dreamed of times of the past returning: the time of peace; the time of love; the time of songs. Pictos heard no word of peace. The crystal transmitter remained silent. No choice remained: the spearhead invasion would fly to Vortis; the isotope would destroy the evil . . . the Animus.
>
> Menoptra of great breeding, Menoptra of great mind – all flew with the strength of generations. All flew to reclaim Vortis. We could only wait for word of success. Our hearts and minds waited . . . waited . . . waited . . . We knew not what fate the spearhead swarm would face.

Delicately etched maps show the point the Menoptra spoke of, the point on the Sayo Plateau where the invasion forces were destined to land. The plateau was one of the few remaining areas of land on Vortis that was not blighted by the Animus.

Legends says the Dokotor battled the intellect of the Animus, trapped with fellow being Iviki; the Animus used all forms of deceptions and mind probes to discover where the Menoptra were to land.

The Menoptra escapees and Arbara had no concept of the fate that lay ahead. The swarm leader of the Menoptra arrived to find that Zarbi forces were massing to slaughter his kinsmen. Graphic cave paintings show the vast number of Menoptra deaths, the weapons the elders had devised had no effect on the Zarbi. A single monolith stands on the plateau: a Zarbi is depicted stooping down over the inanimate carcass of a Menoptra.

Managing to escape from the Caresnome, the being called Dokotor found his fellow species type, Arbara, in the sanctuary of a wrecked temple of light. It seems that the Dokotor was given

the isotope by the Menoptra; it was their last hope of killing the Animus: the cell-destructor would destroy the molecular structure of the Caresnome.

The remaining group of Menoptra attacked the Caresnome. The creatures appear to have had the assistance of a Zarbi, under the control of one of the wishbone-like control devices. Its frantic signalling led the guard Zarbi to charge into the Caresnome, allowing access for Arbara and the others.

> Nestling in a chamber of hate, pulsating with light to the beat of its evil heart, the Animus waits. The tendrils of its soul reach out from its mind; it floats in an atmosphere of hate, destroying the minds of all who look upon it. Its heart lay bare below its mind, tempting futile attack. All beings wilt before the might of the Animus.

The Optera, led by Heron and Vrestin, broke through the surface of the parasite's skin, climbing up from the depths into the chamber where their fellow beings all faced death from the Animus. Arbara lunged with the isotope, killing the parasite instantly. Legends speak of its death scream echoing around the planet for many light cycles, haunting all who heard it.

Little is mentioned of the mysterious fifth sub-species of Vortis after that point. The Zarbi and Larva Guns became docile and passive, once the Animus died, as they had been centuries before.

The Menoptra returned and rebuilt their world. Lush vegetation now covers the entire domain of Vortis – plants of wondrous varieties, shapes and colour. But there are no signs of the Menoptra or other creatures, perhaps their world lives on but they died out long ago...

Audio notation

Professor Strontus

I find, to my amazement, that the creatures returned to building monuments. In the heart of a clearing of foliage, a rock statue stands of four figures – all look humanoid: an old man, a young girl and a mature man and woman. Menoptran carving shows names under each: Dokotor, Arbara, Iviki, Heron and Atrids. Atrids? My knowledge of Earth history is comprehensive, but the shape behind the figures, the blue temple the songs of the Menoptra spoke of, seems like an ancient police box. It's hardly possible . . . The phrase underneath their names, 'Heroes of Vortis', is fascinating.

Reading from ship's computer as Strontus ship broke gravitational pull of Vortis

LIFE SIGNS REGISTERING ON PLANET'S SURFACE. MASS READINGS. «

NUMBER UNKNOWN. POSTULATE MANY THOUSANDS OF LIFE FORMS. ALL «

ENTERING ATMOSPHERE OF PLANET. ALL FLYING ■

THE YETI

The Search for the Abominable Snowmen

Based on extracts taken from the expedition diaries and files of Professor Edward Travers, scientist, anthropologist and leader of the 1936 Everest venture. Other material has been drawn from his books *The Lost Gods of Tibet* and *The Reality of Legends: Man's Origins Through Myth*. The Royal Geographical Society Lecture extracts have been reprinted with permission.

> *Let us probe the silent places,*
> *Let us seek what luck betide us,*
> *Let us journey to a lonely land I know,*
> *There's a whisper in the night wind,*
> *There's a star, a gleam to guide us,*
> *And the wind is calling, calling,*
> *Let us go!*
> ### RWS
> ### Team motto, Everest Expedition 1936

Gentlemen, let me assure you that the body of evidence that has accumulated over the years is undeniable: the Abominable Snowman does exist! A form of anthropoidal life, creatures that are worshipped from afar, they are the Lost Gods of Tibet.

Gentlemen, I intend to find conclusive proof that they are the missing link to the questions we have asked for so long. They are the key to solving the mystery of our own evolution!

Excerpt from the lecture Professor Travers conducted to the Governing Board of Research Commissions and Grants, 5 November 1935

Professor Travers's Diary
5 January 1936
London

Alas, pride is indeed the downfall of many a brave heart. My own was foolish enough to be goaded into accepting the challenge of Professor Rubin Walters. Now my career and reputation are in jeopardy.

'My dear Travers, if you're so certain that this strange creature of yours exists, why don't you go and look for it?' O, those words were so simple for a mind that refuses to believe. I shall prove Walters to be so very wrong.

The question of finance has been, to say the least, a problem. The good will of one Josiah Hogan, editor of a newspaper of questionable repute, has solved the dilemma, in return for exclusive publication rights to any photographic proof we can produce on our return.

'Crook-a-dest' railway.

A grant from the Royal Geographical Society would have made matters easier, but Walters ensured that our only resort was to beg to the gutter press.

I continue with total faith in what I am attempting to do. Mystery has become a rare commodity in our lives, and I intend to bring it back with a bang!

26 January 1936
Portsmouth, England

Veteran Everestier and survivor of the 1920s expeditions, General Bruce, has sent messages of sympathy, advice and admonition. His stories of ailments that can afflict, and in many cases, kill you, have not had an all to inspirational effect on the meagre team I have assembled for the trip.

Budgeting has been restrictive; rations are at a minimum. Perhaps our sponsors are relying on our death from starvation if we fail, thereby getting at least one headline for their money.

We await the HMS *Leviathan*, due to dock two days hence.

Travers writes to his wife, Victoria, 31 January 1936

We are on our way, my darling. There is no turning back now.

Walters could not resist the opportunity of sending a farewell telegram. His suggestion that if I return empty-handed, I should grow a beard and masquerade as one of the creatures, seemed somewhat childish for a man of his standing and repute.

Travers's Diary
12 March 1936
HMS *Leviathan*

A mountaineer *par excellence*, Mervyn McKay has proved to be an excellent travelling companion on this intolerable voyage. His heart is ablaze with a passion for the unknown.

Nights of intolerable storms have been alleviated by drowning doubts and despair in liquor. Sometimes my mind wanders back to England, back to my home.

Today has given rise for celebration: the coastline of India has been sighted.

Extract from *The Lost Gods of Tibet*

Chapter Three: Arrival

The wondrous land of Siliguri: lush green jungles whose foliage runs with moisture, butterflies of bright and varied colours, creatures that howl and growl within the hidden depths of the forest. To breathe the air was to become part of the mystery.

The tiny 'Crook-a-dest' railway wound its way towards Darjeeling; in the distance, higher than imaginations dared to soar, was our Holy Grail: Mount Everest.

Travers's Diary
7 April 1936
East Sikkim

McKay is sick, his pallor is white; we have both fallen prey to altitude sickness. Hallucinations haunt our every moment. Victoria seems to be with me at times, yet I know she is safe at home. Logically we should turn back, yet I cannot contemplate such an action.

Travers writes to his wife, Victoria, 11 April 1936

We have entered the domain of the Yeti. Villagers speak of the creatures in hushed tones of reverence. If any doubt was left at the back of my mind, it is now truly eradicated.

They are here, Victoria. They are here.

Intricate tapestries made by Sherpas depict their image, crude paintings carry their likeness. I always reasoned they would be vegetarian, but these creatures are depicted as powerful, bear-like carnivores. Darkness surrounds their features, as though some terrible evil were present.

Travers's Diary
2 May 1936
First Base Camp, the Rongbuk Glacier

This infernal plateau of ice has withheld its secrets for close to two weeks. Sleepless nights are spent with howling winds trying to rip my tent from the ground.

The land of deathly white claims our spirits and souls one by one: McKay's Sherpa fell victim to a crevice; only three remain.

Everest looms overhead. There is no escape from its glare; a jagged jaw from the depths of hell, white and lethal.

McKay's weight loss is rapid; his breathing is difficult, and I fear for his health.

7 May 1936
Second Base Camp, the Rongbuk Glacier
Our ascent is slow, only 2,500 feet in five days.

A sighting at last! McKay has spotted a creature stalking across the darkened horizon for the past two nights; it glistens in the moonlight as only fur can.

I can hardly contemplate sleep, exhaustion forces me to do so. McKay is keeping watch, the light of day will be with us soon.

Extract from *The Lost Gods of Tibet*

Chapter Four: Haven

Tormented dreams tore into my mind, until the burning sensation of pain drew me back to reality. A crumbling stone-walled cell, riddled with damp and decay, was my new home. I had no idea how long I had been unconscious – days, perhaps weeks recovering from my wounds.

Alerted by the black smoke from Base Camp II's charred remains, the monks of the Det-Sen Monastery trekked across the glacier to assist. My saviours made no mention of what they found, but I was the only survivor.

Memories of the darkness slowly began to return. I saw McKay fighting for his life against savage fury; the Sherpas' bodies sprawled across the snow where they had fallen. Moonlight glinted against the vast creature's flailing claws; McKay's broken body fell to the ground.

The beast was too fast for me to use my rifle. I felt a sudden impact against my head and heard the echoing roar of triumph.

Was it a dream? My inability to move from my bed, and the heavy cloth dressings, made me realize the truth of the matter. McKay was dead; why I was still alive was a mystery. And the reason for the Yeti's attack was even more perplexing.

Travers's Diary
Date unknown
The Det-Sen Monastery

There is no doubt in my mind that the whole affair has been devised by Professor Walters. He has realized the truth of my words and plans to steal the glory. A rival expedition has meticulously followed our tracks, and under the cover of darkness, Walters's men attempted to terminate our quest.

I am no fool. McKay's death is Walter's responsibility.

I shall wait within the relatively safety of these walls. They will come, curiosity will overcome them, and I will be waiting.

The Det-Sen Monastery

One arrived this morning. A small, insignificant little man – he must be a reporter of some kind. Unbelievably, the fool had the very item of evidence that I needed to convince the monks of my story – my rucksack, lost in the carnage of Base Camp II. Yet he had the audacity to deny any knowledge of the attack.

I remember the fur of the assailant; this Doctor chap is encased in a thick fur coat that makes him appear twice his size. If he didn't look so harmless, I'd wager he was the guilty party.

The monks are insisting that he controls the Yeti – what arrant nonsense. A system has been devised to allow the monks to put their theories to the test: by stringing the Doctor up on the main

NED RAW TREALISKE '45

gates, their logic dictates that he's innocent if the Yeti turn up and kill him, but he is indeed their master if they try to rescue him.

Walters has obviously sent an innocent subordinate into the fray. There are doubts in my mind about leaving this poor fellow to his fate, but I must forge ahead. A reconnaissance of the immediate area is in order to establish the location of Walters' encampment.

Date unknown, day 10
The Ice Pinnacles, Rongbuk Glacier

Camouflage is an art I have never been able to master, but basic survival instincts told me to take cover under an incline of rocks. Something was charging down the slope ahead, but all the darkness would reveal were two human shapes.

The young chap in a kilt and a sweet young girl claimed they were travelling companions of the Doctor. I dutifully redirected them towards the monastery, implying that the Doctor was there and a reception would be waiting for them. I would have let them go on their way until, that is, the girl spluttered something about seeing a vast fur-covered creature.

Date unknown, day 10
The Det-Sen Monastery

Our arrival at the monastery was greeted by a barrage of rocks and spears. I was, to say the least, somewhat perturbed to discover that some of the damn fool monks thought a Yeti had taken on my form to gain entry to their fortress.

Happy reunions were the order of the day for the Doctor and his friends. I realize now that I've been terribly mistaken; Walters is not on the mountain, it is simply not possible. The Yeti are carnivores and McKay must have been murdered by one after all. There was nothing I could have done to help.

The earliest reports of any white man getting within fifty miles of Everest were of Captain John Noel's solo efforts in 1913, yet the Doctor claims to have visited the monastery centuries earlier. Altitude sickness must be getting to the poor fellow.

The monks of that era lost their holy ghanta, a small but ornate sacred bell. When the Doctor produced it before their eyes, you could have knocked the monks over with a feather.

I overheard a few words that the girl, Victoria – a name close to my heart, yet so distant – said to the Doctor, something about a cave with a pyramid of spheres.

Supporting the argument that the Yeti should, by nature, be benign and that their current lapse in behaviour must have an explanation, my speech to the Doctor inadvertently heralded the arrival of a squad of the creatures outside the fortress.

Extract from *The Reality of Legends*

Chapter Four: Effective Implementation of Traps

By far the most effective and efficient of methods, the systematic disorientation of the subject through elevation from ground level will render it motionless with all main functioning systems succumbing to immobility.

A structured rope net is spread across the ground, with the end of a rope secured to each corner, with the other ends being attached to a system of pulleys.

Once the subject is lured into the centre of the net, the pressure of weight exerted on the ropes will cause the net to envelope and capture the subject.

Travers's Diary
Date unknown, day 10
The Det-Sen Monastery

Examinations of this nature are difficult to define, but taking the apparent rigor mortis of the captive Yeti into consideration, autopsy might be an adequate description of the Doctor's current activity.

The concept of the Yeti as a metallic automaton was, to say the least, difficult to grasp. According to the Doctor, a chest flap of fur reveals an interior cavity that should house some form of spherical control apparatus. Exactly what remains a mystery, but it is proof that these creatures are not the real Yeti.

The real Yeti may be in the vicinity. Loyalty dictates that I should stay and help the monks, but my quest is more important. A certain degree of devious planning will be employed to leave this fortress, after that, there are certainly no plans for sleep on the agenda for the night ahead.

Night watch report

Taken from the expedition files

The Rongbuk Glacier

5.00 p.m.: The trek ahead through the ice pinnacles, towers of multi-coloured frozen algae and moss, should lead me to the cave system where Jamie and Victoria spotted the creature that pursued them.

6.45 p.m.: I have established a suitably hidden observation post, just under a steep incline of rocks, providing a certain degree of shadows to hide within.

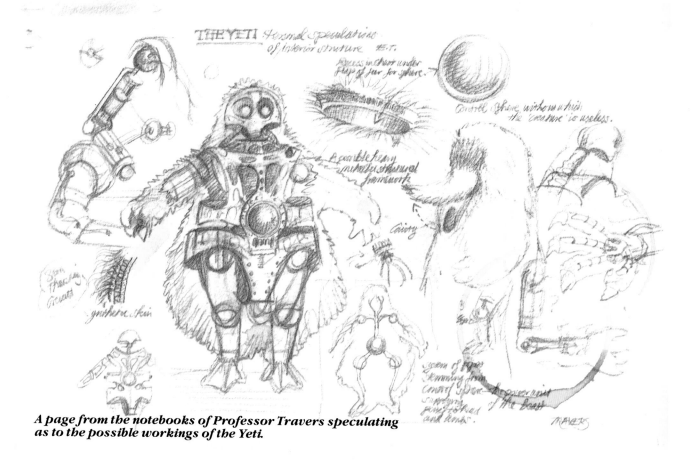

A page from the notebooks of Professor Travers speculating as to the possible workings of the Yeti.

10.07 p.m.: Three creatures of a similar persuasion to the captive at the monastery have arrived. They are simply standing, motionless, in front of a large boulder that appears to be blocking the cave mouth.

11.30 p.m.: The creatures have stirred but once. I am tempted to move closer, but McKay's fate reminds me how foolish that would be. I have taken the opportunity to sketch the creatures under the bright light from the full moon.

11.57 p.m.: A fourth creature has emerged from the darkness, accompanied by a human. Of all people, if I am not mistaken, it is Khrisong, the abbot of the monastery. The three spheres he carries are precious cargo indeed. Perhaps they are the same ones that Victoria spoke of?

12.00 p.m.: The Yeti remain on guard. A distant sound echoes through the caves, sounding distinctly like lightning! The strength of the creatures was demonstrated by the ease with which one of them moved the boulder, weighing several tons at least, allowing Khrisong to enter the cave.

12.30 p.m.: Khrisong and the creatures have left. I have decided to take the opportunity to enter the caves. As McKay always said, 'Embrace the adventure!'

12.41 a.m.: The mouth of the cave entrance is surprisingly warm. White light radiates from the far end of the tunnel – a simple structure supported by wooden pit props. I am about to enter the inner sanctum of the labyrinth.

Extract from *The Lost Gods of Tibet*

Chapter Seven: The Pyramid

The pyramid of spheres nestled within a hollow chamber. Intense white light beamed from every one, its hypnotic pulses searing my eyes. The room echoed with a pounding, pulsating beat, almost like a heart struggling to live.

My mind felt as if it would burst; it was filled with the knowledge of the universe. The greatest of intelligences explored my every thought.

Minute bolts of lightning skipped across the sphere on the summit of the pyramid. Cracks appeared; the essence of living intelligence bled from the wound, set free and hungry for knowledge. It sought to consume everything it touched...

I ran, sprinting faster than any of my best times at Cambridge. Muscles ached as I sped along the seemingly endless tunnel. I doubted I would ever get out.

Travers's Diary
Date unknown, day 11
The Det-Sen Monastery

My memory of events in the cave system are somewhat hazy, mainly because of the hypno-therapy the Doctor has apparently performed on me. The monks say that I was found outside the gates babbling like some damn idiot. Most embarrassing.

Owing to, I assume, some form of dispute, the Doctor and his companions, with myself and one of those monk chaps, are currently being held in one of those stone cells.

Date unknown, day 12
The edge of the Rongbuk Glacier

The sky is ablaze with the spiralling reds of a furnace, glowing pure evil. All I can do is sit watching from the glacier's edge. Surely the situation is beyond hope. The Yeti are everywhere, prowling through the night and guarding the fortress.

The light radiating from the cave illuminates the land, spreading through the entire area as the intelligence gains strength. The light is such that from where I shelter, I can write and observe the surrounding area.

After our release from the cell, the Doctor accompanied me on a return trek to the cave. Yeti, however, forced an abrupt about turn back to the monastery.

The Doctor's prowess at tact and diplomacy is beyond compare, as aptly demonstrated when he calmed the insurrection growing among the monks. They have now fled to the safety of the mountain's lower regions.

My stubborn pride has inevitably led me into danger again. I took it upon myself to try to destroy the pyramid, but the oozing mass is now bigger than I dared to contemplate. Everything it touches dissolves and decays. I pray that the Doctor's ingenuity does not fail him now. There must be a way to defeat this menace, perhaps he's the only man who can.

Extract from *The Reality of Legends*

Chapter Nine: Religious Communities in Tibet

The Monks of Det-Sen Monastery

The community of monks founded a new order at the abandoned Det-Sen Monastery during the late 17th century, led by Padmasambhava, the High Abbot of the Siliguri Monastery. Renowned for their peace and tranquillity, their world was nearly destroyed when Chinese bandits looted and burned the buildings to the ground.

As rebuilding work commenced, Padmasambhava taught his monks the art of warfare learnt in the desert during the holy wars. The brotherhood were soon being called 'The Warrior Monks'; their new monastery was a formidable fortress, and a sanctuary for the poor from warring bandits.

A force assembled to destroy the monks, and it was then that Padmasambhava is said to have made the sacred holy ghanta vanish in a blue box. The monks, however, emerged victorious from the savage battle.

Padmasambhava retreated to the inner depths of the fortress to meditate. He was never seen again; legend says he died from his wounds and is at one with his god.

Travers's Diary
30 June 1936
The Det-Sen Monastery

Enough time has elapsed for me to consider the events of the past few hours. The patrolling Yeti outside the monastery converged on the main gate; I followed their destructive trail as they charged towards the inner sanctum of the complex, an ornate chamber of worship that overflowed with relics.

Crouched in a grandiose throne, the withered, almost husk-like figure confronting the Doctor was apparently the root of the problem. I sensed the same brooding presence here as I had from the pyramid of spheres. Firing my rifle at the figure proved futile in the extreme. Caught by his hand like a cricket ball, the ammunition was simply thrown to one side.

Jamie, ably assisted by a monk, managed to uncover a secondary sphere within the chamber, which they proceeded to demolish with an admirable display of heroic enthusiasm. The effect was instant: the Yetis went out of control. Claws flailed wildly as they staggered, savagely striking anything in their path. The huge bulks of fur started dropping to the floor, collapsing with such force that the very foundations of the building seemed to rock.

Screaming and shaking with spasms of pain, as if the torment of an eternity of life were being released, the long awaited shadow of death passed over the husk-like figure, which slumped across its throne, quite dead.

Silence filled the air. It was over; whatever was out there had gone.

Notes from the expedition files

The 'Det-Sen' Monastery

Padmasambhava had survived through centuries. Eternal life forces flowed through him, preserving his decrepid flesh. A form of meditation was achieved by the monk that allowed him spiritually to pass through the plains of other dimensions.

The Doctor has explained that all forms of intelligences exist there, from the smallest of microbes to the greatest of intellects. It would appear that Padmasambhava was confronted with the greatest of them all. It plied him with offers of eternal life and access to higher plains of thinking in return for the use of his natural body.

Capitalizing on its new found physical freedom, the Great Intelligence maintained a benign exterior, using generation after generation of monks to construct robotic Yeti. Its intention was to consume the raw energy of the Earth, destroying the planet in the process.

The Doctor postulated that the second pyramid acted as a form of transmitter to the stack in the caves; when it was destroyed, everything the Great Intelligence represented simply vanished.

I must assume that it returned to its place of origin, but if not, where exactly could it have gone?

Travers's Diary
4 July 1936
The Det-Sen Monastery

They have vanished; the Doctor chap and his two companions have gone. I would have thought they would have at least joined me for my moment of triumph.

I saw a Yeti, not one of those metal contraptions, a real Yeti, resplendent in its flowing ginger fur and lemur-like face, I pursued it but lost the trail.

Travers writes to his wife, Victoria, 21 July 1936

My darling, I shall be returning to you soon. I have been unable to write for reasons of great complexity, but I shall endeavour to tell you the full story on my return.

There are just one or two items that remain to be packed and something that has to be sent to my dear friend, Professor Walters.

Memo issued to all members of the Royal Geographical Society

A collection will be taken today for the purchase of a small token of our sincere wishes, to be sent to Professor Rubin Walters, currently residing in Charring Cross Hospital.

It is understood that he will be absent from society meetings for some considerable time, owing to the severe shock induced by the arrival of what the constabulary describe a 'large bear, of somewhat deformed appearance', at his study in his home in Kent.

Professor Travers has asked for his best wishes to be passed on, and his sincere apologies for the accident caused by his gift to Professor Walters.

Travers's Diary
17 April 1949
Research Centre, Manchester

War restrictions leave me with no other choice but to close the base it has taken eleven years to establish. Part of my store of artefacts must be sold to compensate for losses, and finance the return move to London. There is, thankfully, an added joy in my life. Anne is now two months old; my time is torn between work and my daughter.

5 January 1969
London

Once again, the shadow of poverty breathes down my neck. With all connections severed, the RGS now seems to endorse the press's campaign of ridicule against me. Julius Silverstein has acquired all my memorabilia at extortionately low prices: four complete specimens were salvaged from the carnage in Tibet; his purchase of my final one will complete his collection.

He can open his Yeti Museum for all I care. I will bide my time concentrating on learning the secrets the last control sphere holds.

24 December 1975
London

I've done it, reactivation has started the damn thing signalling again – shrill staccato bleeps, just like they did in Tibet. Perhaps it can be used to control the Yeti: a demonstration of its mobility would at long last prove my accounts of the '36 expedition are not fictitious. The only obstacle is Emil Julius – the new curator has proved to be as obstinate as his predecessor.

I have searched everywhere to the point of exhaustion, the damn thing has simply vanished. If it reached the museum . . . Telephone communications with Julius is an exercise in futility; the man is too stubborn to listen.

Anne is late, I'll have to go there on my own. Julius will have to listen – if the Yeti is reactivated, the consequences could be disastrous.

The Yeti invasion of Greater London

Carry your gas mask at all times when travelling. Do not enter patches of mist where visibility is at a poor level. Inhaling the mist can cause serious damage to your health.

Government Health Warning, January 1975

Extract from coroner's report

Subject: Emil Julius

The spinal cord was snapped in two places: the upper and lower vertebra. A further dislocation is evident at the base of the neck. The entire backbone was effectively shattered. A blow to the centre of the spine, exuding a force at least one hundred times the strength of any man, would cause such an effect. Emil Julius was murdered by something far stronger than any human being.

Travers's Diary
30 December 1975
London

Why are my feelings for Julius so twisted with guilt? He was cantankerous and obstinate to an extreme, but he did not deserve to die like that. I tried to warn him, but the old fool just wouldn't listen.

The police had the audacity to hold me as a suspect. Anne's timely intervention with an alibi, and the police physician's announcement that I was incapable of such an assault, saved the day.

That creature is alive again, and it's out there... somewhere.

7 January 1975
London

After all this time, the RGS has finally acknowledged that I am still alive, with a courteous letter informing me that Professor Walters has passed on. There should be celebrations akin to the recent New Year festivities, but the manner of his death was too gruesome for that.

Walters walked straight into one of this strange patches of mist while out on his morning constitutional. The rumours that people are spreading are true: the next morning he was found, totally asphyxiated by some form of sponge-like web.

The web substance appears to float inside the mist. People walk into it as easily as they do a spider's web.

20 January 1975
London

I had to respond to the official summons from Whitehall. The government believes I'm the right man to devise a solution to the mist, which has spread across the entire capital. I can't see how they got that idea into their heads!

The government boffins have deduced that the mist is thicker below ground – it's effect has been devastating in the Underground – and they mentioned several reports that gigantic creatures have been spotted down there. Now, I can readily accept that the Yeti may have retreated down there, but these sightings claim as many as five in one group.

Goodge Street station had a kind of armoured fortress built into its structure during the last war, but it was abandoned shortly afterwards. I will have to refer to it as home from now on – it's been converted into a base to monitor the mist at close range, and I've been appointed scientific adviser.

Principal among my tasks will be the detailed analysis of the mist, the web and anything else the soldiers based down there throw at me. Written reports will have to be filed daily on my findings. Time to bring Annie in on this I think. She's turned out to be quite a little genius in her own right – and she can type.

Extract from Report 001

Subject: Analysis of Web Substance

The consistency and structure of the mist is most perplexing. The actual matter of the substance seems to consist of a network of fibrous strands, intertwined in such a way that the best definition remains a 'web'.

Lighter than air, it seems capable of drifting along air currents until it homes in on a target. I have instigated experiments to discover what attracts it to human flesh. Fibres of clothing and static electricity have so far been ruled out.

At the moment I must resort to base tactics to disperse the mist. Explosives have been set up on the Charing Cross station platform to try to break up one of the denser areas of web.

Travers's Diary
22 January 1975
Goodge Street Fortress

The Yeti are present in the Underground system, and in far greater numbers than Tibet. I cannot begin to theorize where they have appeared from, unless . . .

After the failed detonation at Charing Cross, a second one has been prepared. Detonation will take place at midday – I hope it provides the answers that have eluded me so far.

23rd January 1975
Goodge Street Fortress

Detonation has failed again. Captain Knight has taken his men on a return visit to the blast site. Since they've been gone, Anne has arrived with a vision from my distant past. The young Scots lad and the girl from Tibet, found wandering in the tunnels – Jamie and Victoria, how could I forget? Forty years have passed, and while time has taken its toll on me, they have aged but a day. I should not have greeted the Doctor's claims of owning a time machine with such scepticism.

The Doctor's the ideal chap to deal with the Yeti, but he's lost in the tunnels. I just hope he's nowhere near the blast site.

Extract from Travers' notebook

There is no doubt in my mind that the Great Intelligence has returned. Could it be possible that

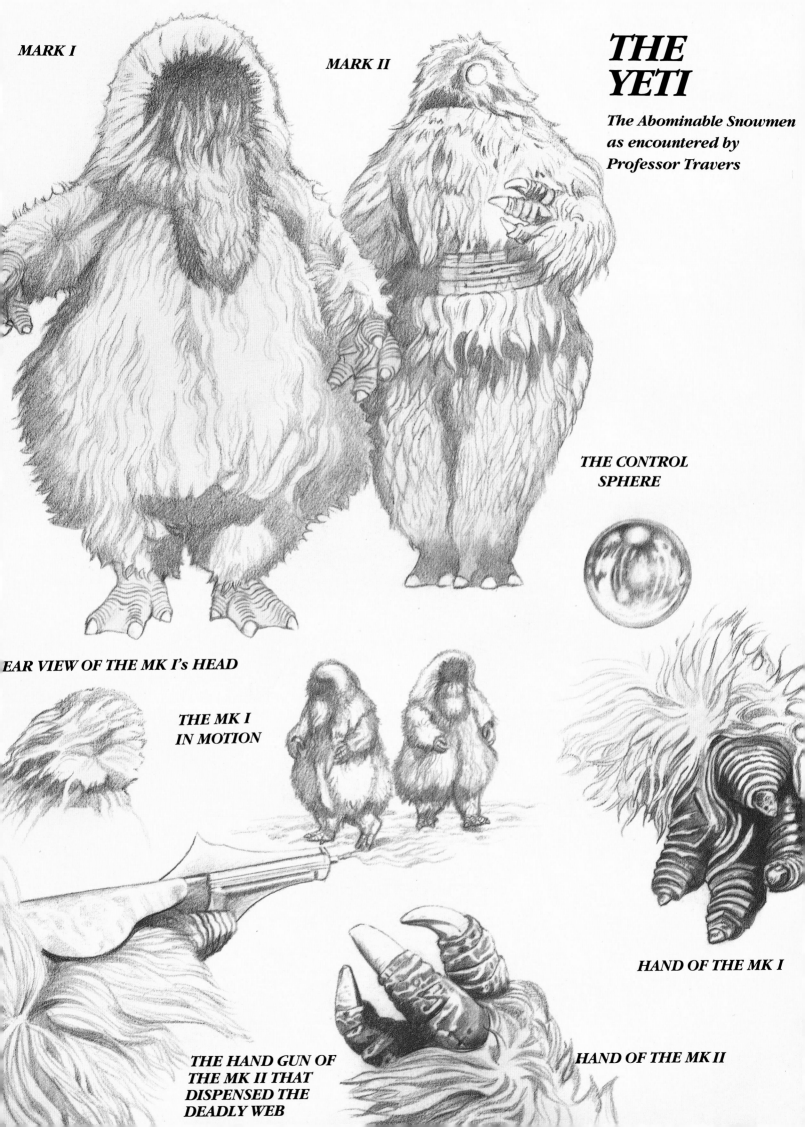

MARK I

MARK II

THE YETI

The Abominable Snowmen as encountered by Professor Travers

THE CONTROL SPHERE

EAR VIEW OF THE MK I's HEAD

THE MK I
IN MOTION

HAND OF THE MK I

THE HAND GUN OF
THE MK II THAT
DISPENSED THE
DEADLY WEB

HAND OF THE MK II

when it was dispersed from Tibet, it remained in the atmosphere, building strength as it waited for its chance to reappear? By reactivating the control sphere, I might have inadvertently opened the gateway it required. I can only wait and hope that the Doctor is safe. Without him, I fear there is no hope.

Travers's Diary
Notations
Goodge Street Fortress

An immaculate display of logic has impressed the military to such an extent that they are literally carrying out his every idea; it is so reassuring to have the Doctor subtly controlling things again.

The new commanding officer found him wandering through the tunnels. Strange chap, this Colonel Lethbridge-Stewart – he seems hell bent on blowing everything to pieces. Thankfully explosives are in short supply, with nowhere near the quantity his scheme would require. He seems to have formed an instant rapport with the Doctor though.

Consultation with the Doctor has led him to concur with my theories concerning the Great Intelligence. He feels certain that he has been drawn here as a part of some grandiose plan of revenge.

Apparently, the Yeti control the web. The Doctor saw them using some type of gun that sprays the stuff in a jet – the blasted mess was responsible for the explosives failing to detonate.

As I write, the Doctor is wiring a timing device to the last vestiges of explosives the army could muster. With the web advancing towards us, the apparatus will be strapped to a goods wagon and pushed in the direction the Yeti are heading. The explosion will block the tunnel, giving us a few precious hours while they find another route.

The Doctor has planted a thought worm in my head, a doubt that will grow as my mind realizes the potential of his words. The Yeti seem to know our every move – could they, as in Tibet, have a human agent among us?

Notations, later entry

All plans have been aborted as far as the explosives wagon is concerned. The Yeti penetrated the fortress security systems and attacked the stores – the entire stock of dynamite is cocooned in web.

The Doctor has left Anne and I with a minor, taxing problem to solve. Other than that, I must wait and bide my time until he returns. Strange noises are coming from the rooms nearby, I doubt that one of the creatures could still be here . . .

Presumably 24th January 1975
Piccadilly Circus station

Things are no better. I have but a single companion by my side, dear Victoria, while we are flanked on either side by Yeti. Obviously we are prisoners of the Great Intelligence. I just pray that the Doctor has some knowledge of our predicament.

My workroom was indeed subject to a Yeti attack, I remember the twisted remains of the guard outside the door, and I remember the Yeti closing in on me. The Yeti swung its claw and then the darkness came.

Our imprisonment has allowed Victoria to give detailed explanations of what happened next. It appears that I returned to the fortress, accompanied by two of those damnable creatures, with a pallor resembling that of a corpse; the Great Intelligence was now in my mind.

There is almost an aftertaste in my head, a sensation of dark thoughts, the lingering presence of evil. Headache aside, I feel as I did before, although I must still be of some use to the Intelligence, or I would most certainly be dead. Victoria is sure that the voice was one and the same as Padmasambhava's during his possession. My body was merely a voice box, enabling the Intelligence to make its demands known to the Doctor.

A veritable encyclopedia of universal knowledge and wisdom, the Doctor's mind is the object of desire. The Great Intelligence is prepared to go to any lengths to absorb it. Two basic options have been presented: either the Doctor willingly submits his mind to ingestion or he will witness the systematic destruction of every mind in the fortress.

At least I have the knowledge that Anne is safe for the moment – the Yeti wanted me, not her. All we can do is await the arrival of the Doctor.

Later

One of the soldiers, a considerably battered Sergeant Arnold, managed to slip past the platform unnoticed. He knows we are being held prisoner. I just hope he manages to alert the Doctor.

The Yeti have suddenly become rather active; they seem to want us to move towards the exit stairs at the end of the platform.

Later

For creatures of such a pendulous shape, the Yeti have displayed a remarkable agility in manoeuvring their considerable bulk up the escalators. Victoria and I have been deposited in the ticket hall, and I must admit that my blood ran cold on being confronted with the contraption before us.

Glowing radiantly, a pyramid of crystal-like glass, with an almost hypnotic glare, has been carefully constructed in front of the ticket office. What can be best described as a throne has been placed alongside it. Wires running from the pyramid seem to be connected to its glistening steel frame. An armature reaching out from the pyramid's apex hovers over the back of the throne. Its metal ring would fit neatly onto a human head...

The intelligence seems to be able to manipulate electric airwaves. It communicates with us through the public address system – could this indicate that it's an electrostatic form of life?

25 January 1975
London

I suppose it was to be expected. They went without so much as a goodbye in Tibet, and I suspected they would vanish mysteriously this time as well. One thing is for certain: without the Doctor, I very much doubt I would be alive to write these words.

Harold Chorley, incompetent reporter extraordinaire, was my immediate choice as the Yeti liaison. He had plagued me with imbecilic questions from the instant I arrived at the fortress, but when Sergeant Arnold was revealed as the culprit, I think I'm safe in saying that everyone was shocked. This epitome of British soldiering had betrayed our every move.

We could only watch helplessly as he led the Doctor to the throne and connected him to the pyramid. Unbeknown to myself, the Doctor had captured and reprogrammed several Yeti, which were controlled by voice activation through a microphone. With the device hidden in his pocket, Jamie took the opportunity to turn the Yeti against each other.

I raced to Jamie's assistance as he struggled to free the Doctor – the damned fool didn't seem to want us to. Lethbridge-Stewart and the others helped. Eventually succeeding, I was thrown to the ground, and in the next instant the pyramid exploded as Jamie threw the device into its heart. The agonized howl of the Great Intelligence scorched my mind.

As the smoke began to clear, I saw Yeti strewn across the floor, chest flaps smoking where control spheres had exploded. Devastation and wreckage lay throughout the Underground system, but the threat was gone, and so was the Doctor and his mysterious – what's it called – TARDIS.

28 January 1975
London

That Lethbridge Stewart chap telephoned: he wants advice. Of course, that is something I am qualified to give in excess, so I readily agreed.

It transpires that he wants to form some group, an organization of sorts, that would be prepared to combat such threats as the Yeti, should anything like that ever happen again.

I will give all the help I can, but I fear the post of scientific adviser is not for me. The Doctor would be the ideal man for the job, should he ever reappear.

My mind craves a different kind of stimulation. Anne is now my assistant, and together we shall now move to new pastures of study. Perhaps the Loch Ness Monster would be worth looking into.

THE WIRRN

WARNING, WARNING . . . YOU ARE ENTERING A DANGER ZONE. DANGER, DANGER... THE LIFE CYCLE HAS BEEN REACTIVATED. THIS IS A RECORDED MESSAGE. AVOID IMMEDIATE RANGE OF FIFTY QUADRANTS. REPEAT. KEEP AWAY FROM NERVA BEACON. WARNING, WARNING . . . THE LIFE CYCLE HAS STARTED AGAIN... ■

Broadcast transmission from Nerva Beacon recorded by the space freighter Nostromo III

This is the Earth High Minister. This is an instruction to all ranking med-techs. It is your duty to preserve all life, whether terrestrial or unknown, for the gathering of knowledge.

High-security access recorded message issued on space ark Nerva Beacon

DATA LOG, NERVA BEACON ■

The exact time of the Wirrn infestation is not known. Wirrn are a form of parasitical insect capable of sustaining life in deep space. The progenitor of the species lays her eggs in a separate living organism. It seems that the larva gestates within its host, feeding and growing. The larva infects the entire DNA structure of the host vessel with its own chromosomes, and eventually the host becomes the mobile form of the larva.

ACTIVATED AUDIO LOG

FIRST MED-TECH VIRA ■

I had not allowed for the possibility of any remaining eggs . . . another body was infested. I have sealed the inner chamber of the area where Kane's chamber was housed. The larval stage seems to have been trapped within the cryogenic chamber. It moves with a surprising mobility.

I had not realized how insecure it could seem within the chambers. The girl Sarah may not have survived our technology, and it was indeed fortunate that the traveller, known as Doctor, arrived with his companions.

The vast ark houses the vestiges of mankind. I dare not contemplate what the consequences would have been if the Doctor had not repaired the damage inflicted by the Wirrn.

The dying queen caused severe damage. Apart from technician Kane, technician Dune was infected. In this instance the resulting larva broke free from its chamber. Seeking energy from the solar stacks that power Nerva, the creature gestated and multiplied into further larvae. One of the larva infected prime unit Noah – the infection spread through him so quickly.

DATA LOG ■

The larvae can pass spores to human tissue. After initial contact, an infected limb mutates to a fungal sponge, breaking down all human cells and regenerating them into Wirrn chromosomes. Within several hours, human tissue is completely transformed.

ACTIVATE AUDIO LOG ■

The Doctor deduced that the Wirrn needed the entire populace of Nerva. Every cryogenically frozen human would act as a perfect host for Wirrn eggs. Tens of thousands of humans would have mutated into an entirely different species.

Kane's larva has become inanimate. I assume it has entered the cocoon stage. My study topic being Earth history, I deduce that it is a similar process to that of the insect butterfly, long since extinct, of course. Noah became the swarm leader for the creatures, supervising the gestation and guarding the cocoons of incalculable numbers of Wirrn. He displayed a symbiotic activism with the race. The race memory of the tortured history of the creatures now spreads through his mind.

I must move Kane while I can. A small automated trolley should be able to carry the chrysalis.

DATA LOG ■

The native habitat of the Wirrn stems from the planet Andromeda. They preyed upon the herbivores of the world for host vessels, creating vast colonies that dominated the tunnel systems in the planet's mountains. The hive queen lay in a central chamber with drone Wirrn catering for her every need.

Mankind's first encounter with Wirrn came as the early inter stellar dawn timers arrived from Earth to colonize Andromeda. The colonists sterilized the planet of the creatures. One queen, however, retreated to the regions of outer space. The time between her departure from Andromeda and her arrival on Nerva is incalculable.

ACTIVATE AUDIO LOG ■

I postulate that the cargo jettison pod is the best housing facility for the larva: it provides security and allows for observation. Unless I have underestimated its capability, the pod can safely be sent into space. As I wait for signs of activity to register, I feel a strange emotion spreading through my consciousness. Training on Earth base was meant to eradicate all traces of memory, yet I find myself longing to see Earth again. The planet should surely have recovered from the solar flares that forced us into cryogenic incarceration.

The idea was that Earth would regain its natural resources and flourish, becoming habitable again for the settlers from Nerva. It would be capable of supporting life – life that the Wirrn came so close to terminating.

The Doctor and his companions fought with honour to protect the storage chambers – a system of electrical wiring to the main entrances kept the Wirrn from entering. After cutting all power to the station, a power line was connected to the fuel supplies on board the shuttle craft on the docking bay of Nerva.

No more than a few of the Nerva populace had been revived. The Doctor made the logical deduction that the death toll inflicted if the Wirrn defeated our attempts to stop them would be considerable.

Technician Libri sensed something strange on his revivification. Noah showed no external signs of Wirrn infection at that time; his greeting to Libri caused severe neural anxiety. I postulate that Libri's semi-conscious state impaired his vision to an extreme degree – he saw Noah as a Wirrn, but his fear overcame his sense of logic. Overcome by the Wirrn influence, Noah killed Libri.

Technicians Rogin and Lycett came out of revivification unimpaired by neural damage. Lycett was terminated by a Wirrn larva that broke into the storage chambers. The ventilation tunnels running throughout the station seem to act as an ideal passageways for the larvae's movements.

DATA LOG ■

COMPUTER ANALYSIS ■

THE WIRRN DISPLAY A REMARKABLE ADAPTABILITY TO ANY GIVEN TERRAIN. COLONIES COULD EASILY BE ESTABLISHED ON ANY WORLD. THE NEED FOR OXYGEN REPLENISHMENT IS IMMATERIAL: THE SPECIES IS ADEPT AT STORING SUPPLIES OF OXYGEN WITHIN THE LUNG CHAMBERS OF THE BODY, ALLOWING THE WIRRN TO SURVIVE IN DEEP SPACE FOR GREAT PERIODS OF TIME. A SELF-INDUCED COMA ALLOWS THE TIME SPENT FLOATING IN SPACE TO PASS WITH EASE. ■

ACTIVATE AUDIO LOG ■

The Wirrn displayed a degree of tactical deduction that is quite remarkable for an insect species. The rocket was the source of power that was stopping them from gaining access to the cryogenic chambers, so their deduction was simply to storm the vessel in force. On such low power, I have to admit that visibility and reception on the exterior hull monitors was not up to the standard normally associated with Nerva technology. The sight confronting us, however, was undeniable in its authenticity. The entire swarm of Wirrn had space-walked across the surface of Nerva in order to reach the rocket.

Rogin sacrificed his life to preserve the populace of Nerva. He stayed under the rocket and unlocked the bracing mechanisms by hand. He was reduced to ash as the engines of the rocket caught him.

The Doctor and his companions, with the task of eradicating the Wirrn menace complete as far as they knew, departed in the transmat to Earth. Substantial repair work is needed for the mechanism to become fully operable again.

I long to be with my intended pair-bond Noah – I long to hear his voice again. The essence of humanity that was everything Noah represented was still within the creature he had become. The geostabilizers were deliberately unattended – the rocket was destroyed in an instant. Noah sacrificed his life to save us all.

A thought has struck my mind. Could he . . .? Logic dictates there is a possibility...

DATA LOG ■

COMPUTER ANALYSIS ■

SURVIVAL PROJECTION OF WIRRN SPECIES: ONE SURVIVING WIRRN WOULD TAKE ON THE ROLE OF PROCURATOR. ITS IMMEDIATE OBJECTIVE WOULD BE TO HUNT FOR A PROGENITOR – A FEMALE OF ANY SPECIES THAT COULD BE GENETICALLY ALTERED TO PRODUCE WIRRN EGGS. ■

PREDICTION: THE PROCURATOR WIRRN WILL SEEK OUT ANYTHING ADAPTABLE FOR THIS TASK AT THE RISK OF ITS OWN LIFE. NOTHING WILL STOP IT ■

ACTIVATE AUDIO LOG ■

The Wirrn that has emerged from the cocoon is unlike any of the other creatures that were ejected in the rocket. Infinitely taller with a heavier physical structure; the scales on its body seem to be of a stronger quality than the other Wirrn's. As if seeking nutrition, the creature digested the shell of the cocoon.

I should eject the pod and the creature instantly, yet I find a feeling stirring within me – a fascination. The Wirrn does nothing other than stand at the porthole of the pod, almost as though it were staring at me.

The thought has crossed my mind. Noah spoke of the race of creatures and their history; he had inherited the entire memory of every creature that had ever been part of the breed. I postulate that the essence of Noah is now part of the race memory. Could the creature that stands before me contain any of Noah within its psyche? Noah – we were to be pair-bonded. Could he stand before me now? I find myself strangely drawn to the airlock of the pod. It would be so easy to take one closer look before I eject it.

COMPUTER ACCESS DATA ■

COMPUTER OBSERVATION ■

CARGO POD EJECTED FROM NERVA BEACON. LIFE SIGN INDICATION ON BOARD REGISTERING. HUMANOID LIFE REGISTERING AS ONE OF SIGNALS... UNKNOWN SOURCE FOR SECONDARY SIGNAL ■

ANALYSIS: NO HUMAN LIFE REGISTERING ON BOARD NERVA. AUTOMATIC REVIVIFICATION OF NERVA POPULACE UNDER WAY ■

CONCLUSION: FIRST MED-TECH VIRA HAS LEFT NERVA IN CARGO POD. CORRECTION. ERASE PREVIOUS ENTRY. THE TWO LIFE SIGNS ON BOARD CARGO POD ARE NOW REGISTERING AS NON-HUMAN. BOTH SIGNALS ARE NON-HUMAN. ALL LIFE SIGNS OF FIRST MED-TECH VIRA ARE GONE. TWO UNKNOWN SPECIES ON BOARD CARGO POD ■

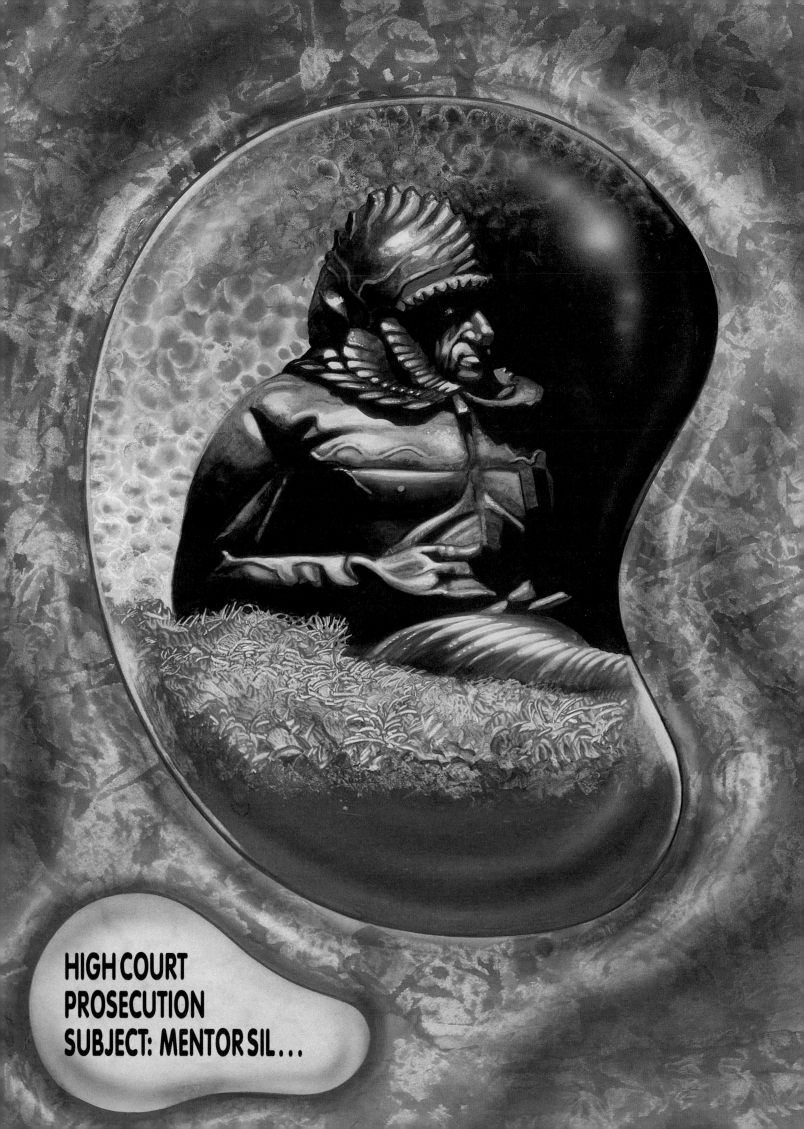

Sil and the Mentors

The inquest into the highly regrettable and tragic demise of Lord Kiv, mightiest and most financially erudite of all Mentors, now begins. The jury of fiscal adjudicators has decreed that the Mentor responsible for the disaster resulting in the crash of the intergalactic shares of the company Thoros Beta Enterprises Ltd will answer to these charges.

First, unequivocal responsibility for sending Thoros Beta, the Mentor homeworld, into receivership.

Second, total liability for failing to indicate the chances of fatalities occurring from the introduction of his business plan, which was intended to improve the economy.

Mentor Sil, you are charged as stated before the court. How do you plead? Economically iniquitous or comprehensively unimpeachable...?

From the trial of Mentor Sil

I promise to tell the truth of the situation and all it's apparent viabilities. The whole truth on an economically sound basis, and nothing but the truth of the profits available. So help me Morgo, god of financial wisdom.

Oath from the judicial system of Thoros Beta

Most honourable and wise members of the jury, before we begin, I feel that it would be most advisable to examine the file on the accused. Sil is a Mentor of a most cunning nature; it is easy to underestimate his capabilities.

Prosecution statement

High Court data file
Mentor Sil
Natural habitat

Sil was born as part of a spawning of fifteen inter-related Mentors, off the Eyelets of Tranmi, with parentage of a most questionable nature. There seems to be some indications that he is the son of a mere marsh-minnow fisherman, and that the highest position ever reached by any of his progenitors was that of a sub-level accountancy filing clerk. His claim that he is part of a long-lost spawn of Royal Mentors is to be ignored.

It is understood that the other Mentors of Sil's spawning have not been located. Claims that Sil sold them to the Neural Science Division of the capital's Medical Sector have yet to be confirmed.

It is theorized that one of Sil's earliest financial deals, for the purchase and acquisition of Minnow Farming Lakes near his home-marsh, may have some connection with the poverty and starvation that was induced in the community shortly thereafter. It has been speculated that the accidental deaths that occurred wiped out all traces of his surviving ancestors, making it impossible to gain first-hand information about his background.

Financial career

The exact time of Sil's entry into the realms of Mentorian accountancy remains unknown. Elder Mentors have given sworn statements to the effect that they recall Sil working as one of the sub-supervisors working in the water distribution refinery of Thoros Beta.

Advertising campaigns for 'The alcohol you can't taste or smell', with a further claim that all intoxicating ingredients had been removed, show how Sil gained the capital he needed to enter the ranks of high finance stock-dealing. He sold bottled water to planets with sub-Mentorian intelligence levels. A second sales campaign on the same planets was equally successful. The native population rushed to purchase 'The ice that never melts' for novelty value alone, while Sil requisitioned all the broken glass he could salvage from Thoros Beta to meet demand.

Records indicate that Sil next capitalized on the gullibility of tourists venturing onto the shores of Thoros Beta. His tales of ancient creatures that inhabited the outer marshlands long ago, were backed up by recently discovered remains presented on memorial plaques that were available on special offer. Several reports indicate that forests inexplicably disappeared from the planet's surface at that time; the connection is apparent.

Sil moved on from being a mere trader to being an acquisitions agent, eventually securing a position with the Galatron Mining Corporation. It is common knowledge that Mentors rarely venture off Thoros Beta for financial dealing, with the time-honoured tradition being to work from a computer terminal in a personal hydro-chamber. Sil broke new ground in this area and gained the respect of Lord Kiv for his sense, enterprise and initiative.

The phrase, 'Young upwardly mobile Mentor in economic stock-dealing', is believed to have been developed as a result of Sil's activities. Sil began to venture out on behalf of his clientele, bartering face-to-face with the various rulers and governors of mining communities, whose product he sought to pillage. During this time, Sil's character began to change, resulting in some startling levels of deception to achieve his ends. This came to a height on the planet Varos.

Members of the jury, before we enter into the exact nature of what occurred on Varos, it is perhaps advisable to examine the structure of the society and its industrial produce fully to understand what the long-term implications would have been had Sil's dealings concluded with success.

Prosecution statement

High Court data file
Planet Varos
Surface analysis

Atmospheric conditions effected by the diminishing orbit, rotating round two suns, have laid waste to the natural vegetation. Natural moisture in the surface land mass has simply evaporated, leaving arid basins of dry rock and sand. The methane content that has developed in the outer atmosphere gives the air a purple tint; methane clouds are believed to sweep across the land, mixing the toxic gas with a rain that has developed a highly acidic quality.

The unique conditions in question have proved to be one of the last crystallization growth areas for Zyton 7, an ore of vital importance in certain areas of stellar engineering, and essential to experimentation in inter-dimensional time dynamics.

Indigenous population

The first humanoid lifeforms noted as being present on Varos date back several hundred of their years, when the planet was colonized as a prison establishment for criminals from Earth. Analysis indicates that they are not ideally suited for survival in the atmospheric conditions of Varos; inhabitation domes proved vital.

The descendants of the criminally insane prisoners established a more peaceful regime, but the dominating militaristic judicial system came back into force, forcing the people to work in the planet's vast mines. The governing powers used an innovative form of mass pacification to keep the population happy: a morbid fascination became a product available in the home.

Through mass audio and visual link-ups to every home in the colony, the security forces of Varos broadcast all manner of summary executions and torture. It relaxed the aggression in the minds of the populace, and the anger at the conditions they were forced to live in subsided. Mining operations for Zyton 7 continued smoothly; the people were passive, but the economy was crumbling around them.

The economy

The Governor of Varos elected to power when Zyton 7 first began to be exported brought a previously unknown wealth to the planet: high-tech equipment was introduced to the mines and distillation planets, and for a while Varos knew the meaning of success. But the price of the ore suddenly plummeted, for no known reason, crippling the economy of Varos. The Governor was blamed for the starvation and poverty that followed, and a new system that gave the Varosians the power to vet his decisions was introduced.

The Governor would face his people over the televisual broadcast system; a 'yes' and a 'no' vote button were installed by the monitors in everyone's homes. If his decision did not meet with the approval of the viewers, the Governor would be submitted to a charge from a human cell disintegrator. His term of office therefore depended on the number of negative votes it would take to kill him.

Varos was fighting for survival. The harsh militaristic security forces kept the population in order, while the Governor fought against traders and dealers to raise the price they were willing to pay for Zyton 7. It was this situation that Sil sought to exploit.

The following statements have been drawn from various sources involved in Sil's activities, following his arrival of Varos, in an attempt to give a clear picture of the situation to the members of the jury. All statements have been taken without prejudice, and in no way set out to discredit the character of the accused.

Prosecution statement

I have always maintained that it is more than a mere dream that Varos can rise above the darkness that surrounds it. Our world will thrive. As long as there is energy within me, I shall fight to achieve this goal. The ore is the last remaining profitable export from the planet and, of course, all depends on the price paid by its buyers.

At first, Sil seemed no more than yet another trader, though it must be admitted that Galatron Corp always secured the largest orders. The speech-translator unit he wore malfunctioned constantly, but I never allowed myself to show my amusement at his eccentric attempts at communication. It was as soon as he realized the devastated economy could not lose any income that he started to manipulate the agreed price for the ore.

Threats to withdraw the Galatron contract continually arose. Sil offered to act as a sales export agent for our punishment videos, if we lowered the price for the Zyton 7. Sil relished the thought of taking images of slaughter to those outlying worlds that did not need to impose martial law on their populace.

I tried in vain to fight off Sil's merciless offers. But the vote to take a ten per cent cut in food rations to compensate for the lower price resulted only in a taste of the human cell disintegrator.

At that time, I failed even to suspect any deviation from the duties of my Chief Security Officer. I admit that had I been told he was taking payments from Galatron Corp to try to influence my thinking, but when holding a position of power you quickly learn there is no one person that can be trusted completely.

Statement of the Governor of Varos

Members of the jury, it should be noted that Sil did not relent from insulting and demanding agreement from a man who had nearly been killed. The Governor had little chance to defend himself physically or mentally, but the overriding thought remained that his people had to be appeased. This was his third time against the disintegration ray – no Governor who preceded him had survived a fourth molecular bombardment. It was inevitable that his thoughts would now turn to the inevitability of his own death, and that to prevent it he would have to meet Sil's demands. The rate stood at seven credits a unit. Sil realized this was the moment to bring his plan into action...

Prosecution statement

High Court data file
Sil

Sil had come to an agreement with his superiors on the executive council of Galatron Mining Corporation to seek out mining planets under a weak state of government. After establishing the state of the populace and military resources, Sil was to send word to his superiors for a vast colonization force to be sent to the relevant planet. The populace would live under the rule of the company, and Sil would act as ruler of the planet, with the power to exploit and drain all natural resources. The precious nature of the ore Zyton 7 could be used to gain control of worlds other than Varos; thoughts of total dominion filled Sil's mind. He was determined that nothing would stop him.

So as you can see, there were no longer mere plans of acquiring raw ore for the company he worked for. It is clear that world domination lay in Sil's heart.

Several facts must now be drawn to your attention. The Governor instigated the execution of the rebel leader Jondar to appease his people, but this was averted by the arrival of a mysterious stranger in the punishment dome. The humanoid called Doctor, with an assistant Peri, became a firm favourite with the viewing Varosians, as he unwittingly became part of a macabre broadcast, as the guards of the dome hunted him down.

It became apparent that Sil's paranoia was growing considerably, and his conclusions drew him to the fact that the Doctor was a rival ore trader. Therefore, it was with an alarming degree of relish that Sil watched the pursuit of the Doctor on viewing monitors. But the Doctor did not die. While the rebels he freed were taken to termination cells to await slaughter, the human female that accompanied him was brought before Sil and the Governor, who had unsuccessfully tried to gain access to the unidentified blue space vessel that brought them to Varos.

Prosecution statement

I realized that Sil's fears of insider dealing were justified, but I had to know what the girl knew of Zyton 7. Her stories that both she and the Doctor were travellers through time was of little consequence, and I had to submit to the Chief Officer's demands that she and the wife of the rebel leader Jondar be submitted to the rehabilitator. The chief maintained that a massive alteration in the girl's molecular structure would force her to reveal the truth of her presence on the planet. I have to admit I was revolted at Sil's delight at the prospect of seeing the women mutate in a process developed from discoveries made in the mines. I never fully understood the exact nature of the system, but miners had been discovered with growths of fur and claws on

their hands after certain radiation in the lower tunnels started to mutate their metabolic structures.

The cell mutation has two basic results: subjects who feel unworthy of their life change into reptilian forms, while those who long to break free and escape to a new life become birds.

The Doctor had been recaptured, and with the rebel Jondar, an execution based on the methods of ancient times was arranged: a hanging. I found it odd that the Doctor demanded to know the exact nature of Sil's business on Varos before he went to the scaffold, and as I suspected, he revealed the fact that Zyton 7 is in fact of greater value than then price demanded by the delegate from Galatron Corp. Sil's attempt to silence the Doctor failed; his bodyguards tried to operate the scaffold trap doors, but I had ensured that the ropes were not connected to the overhanging beams. The Doctor and Jondar merely fell to the ground below unharmed. I had staged the whole operation to gain the information I needed from the Doctor.

I was now free to discuss facts with the traveller, who requested that the two women be freed from the rehabilitator. Although I was more than happy to oblige, I had not counted on the intervention of Sil.

Statement of the Governor of Varos

I would now like to draw your attention to the following sequence of events, which illustrate the vicious cruelty that the accused is capable of inflicting, and the results that his natural incompetence brings down upon him.

Prosecution statement

High Court data file
Sil

Assisted by the Chief Officer, Sil ensured that both women remained in the tissue transmogrifier and were subjected to the full process. The Doctor, however, destroyed the main control mechanisms of the machine and reversed the process before the mutated cell structure of the female humans stabilized; their natural metabolisms gradually reasserted themselves.

In the hours that followed, a state of near revolution occurred on Varos: the Chief Officer tried to depose the Governor, but his attempt was vanquished with the assistance of the Doctor. The Governor was free to regain control of his domain, but he had no knowledge of the plans laid by the accused for an invasion force to take over Varos. It is fortunate indeed that the plans backfired as drastically as they did.

Sil's megalomania reached its peak; as far as he was concerned he was triumphant. Varos was his. He saw worlds before him that were his to conquer. But as with the dreams of all dictators, his vision was shattered. The invasion was aborted when news came through of the discovery of Zyton 7 on the asteroid of Bio-Scalptor.

Sil's bargaining power was immediately withdrawn. Sil's orders were now to meet any price that was asked for – the Governor opened bidding at twenty credits a unit. The wealth and good living that Varosians had dreamed of for so long were on their way. Although here would be hardships ahead, they would be nothing compared with those under Sil if he had succeeded.

There are other instances of Sil's activities dealing with other species throughout the galaxy, but few records of these remain. His dealings with the notorious warrior race, the Ice Warriors, nearly laid a planet to waste. He is ruthless to an extreme that our society has seldom seen. Sil is a being who longs for conquest and will stop at nothing to achieve his aims, as the death of Lord Kiv clearly demonstrates.

Members of the jury, I have chosen not to dwell on the incidents that concluded with the aforementioned death; the evidence speaks all too clearly for itself on that matter. I have attempted to show you what Sil is capable of, and why he must be stopped. There is no place on Thoros Beta for the kind of Mentor that Sil is, and there is only one way to stop him carrying out any other actions such as this. Suffice to say, it would

be fatal. I leave the decision in your wise and fiscally erudite hands. I rest my case.

Prosecution statement

Members of the jury, you are informed that the accused has requested that he present his own defence. Mentor Sil, you are called before the jury to state your defence. Your time starts now.

Members of the most honourable, principled, trustworthy, upright and understandingly virtuous jury, before we begin, might I, if of course you agree without any hesitation, draw your attention to the High Court data file on the planet Krontep. The facts will inform your radiant minds of the nature of the population, whose valuable commerce I attempted to bring to this world of ours. Please inform me if the brightness of the viewing screen is too intense for your shrewd, and uniquely understanding eyesight . . . Let the screening commence.

How do you turn this microphone off? Will no one help me! May the curse of Rashadon fall upon your tail ends! May the mighty Baugarondo see fit to... <click>

Defence statement

High Court data file
Planet Krontep
Surface analysis

Generally regarded as one of the most uninhabitable oxygenating planets in the charted universe. The land masses are continually on the move, bringing hurricanes, volcanic eruptions, heat waves, and ice storms. It's the annual kind of weather that the thriving population have come to expect.

Indigenous population

Reports indicate that the natural inhabitants of Krontep, male and female alike, are warriors, specialists in all manner of warfare, death and destruction. Some of the most formidable fighters in the history of Krontep have been the female of the species. The royal blood line of the planet has always ruled, with the King or Queen leading the people to war.

The economy

The main source of wealth for the inhabitants of Krontep comes from the spoils of unending war. No known trade exists on the planet.

An agent on behalf of Thoros Beta Enterprises offered to plough financial resources into the planet so that certain scientific progress could be made and certain industries formed. The King of the planet knew only how to form war pacts and declarations of genocide, so it was decided that, in company with his guard, equerry Dorf, King Yrcanos would make the journey to Thoros Beta to open contract negotiations with the Mentors.

Of course, members of the most wise and knowledgable jury, the first thing I instigated upon the arrival of King Yrcanos was that his brain should be pacified. Dorf was of little consequence, O noble jurors, so I saw that he was handed over to the science division. Perhaps, and I say so guardedly as to not to offend to magnanimous intelligences of you all, it would be of some value to review the data on the arrival of the head of science, Mr Crozier. The data is on view. Would any of the jury care to partake of a marsh-minnow, freshly caught today and still squirming. Only the choicest of morsels, would I dare offer to such a refined set of palates as . . . <click>'

Defence statement

The screening of the data was delayed while court officials took the vocal unit from the defence council and examined the marsh-minnows. They were found to contain sugaouts, a drug that opens the mind to suggestions, in this case, Sil's claims of innocence.

High Court data file
Mr Crozier

The scientist Crozier won acclaim on Thoros Beta's twin world, Thoros Alpha, for his research into complete organic brain transference and enhancement. Lord Kiv hired the services of the scientist to expand the capacity of his brain, to allow for more complex financial deductions and economic analysis. The brain of Lord Kiv responded exceptionally well to the operation – too well. The Mentor's mind was continuing to expand beyond its capacity and a body with a larger cranial cavity was needed to allow the inevitable acquisition of knowledge to take place.

The first experiment to take place involved the brain of a security hybrid, the Raak, to be enhanced and expanded. If the tissue rejection failed to take place, Crozier knew it was safe to operate on Lord Kiv.

With the brain of the barbarian king more, shall we say, pliable, terms of contracts would be much easier. It was more convenient for Lord Kiv's delicate conditions, if such talks were untroubled by the bloodshed that would have inevitably taken place, should there have been a slight disagreement with King Yrcanos. Equerry Dorf, O perceptive and judicious ones, was chosen by Crozier as the first subject for cross-genetic trans mutation – into a being that was half-wolf.

I, my humble and gracious self, knew nothing of the demise of the Raak until Crozier came to impart the news. Intruders had terminated the creature's life. I had not realized the consequences of such an action: the life of the mighty Kiv now depended on one question. If the Raak had attacked the intruders, it must have regressed genetically, thus indicating that the operation on Lord Kiv may fail. And as you will immediately appreciate, O fiscally conversant ones, a crisis of the most profound nature then occurred. The intruders had to be located and questioned without loss of time.

Lord Kiv had announced that the pain within his cranial chamber was intense – Crozier had to know why the Raak was killed. Members of the jury, I ask you to take note that it was Kiv who put me in charge of the search for the intruders, such was his trust and faith in his self-effacing servant.

(Bearers, water me. I grow hot with the knowledge of my victory ahead. Water me!)

On seeing who the intruders were <click> I knew immediately that they were guilty, for I had acquaintance with this Doctor and Peri on Varos <click>. They were located in Crozier's lab <click>. What is happening with this micro——

Defence statement

The defendant was removed from the court to the medical centre in a state of unconsciousness. Water sprayed by his bearers had shorted the microphone. The court computer related the facts of the defendant's case on his behalf until he had recovered.

To extract the information required on the demise of the Raak, Sil ordered the Doctor to be restrained, and for Crozier to use the pacification helmet on the Doctor to open his mind to interrogation. King Yrcanos recovered as the Doctor was undergoing treatment; he laid waste to the lab as his fury and destructive abilities were demonstrated, freeing the Doctor and Peri and leading them into the cave systems of Thoros Beta. The main transformer in the lab facility was damaged during the escape, releasing the mind control on Thoros Alphan slaves, opening their minds to thoughts of rebellion.

The continual increase in pressure on Kiv's skull forced him to announce his ultimatum: he would allow only one more day for Sil to capture the Doctor and for Crozier to prepare for the operation.

Reports of the fugitives next arose from the Thoros Alphan immigration induction centre. An attack on the guard by King Yrcanos and Peri was foiled by the Doctor, who alerted the guards to the imminent attack. The Doctor joined forces with the Mentors; later analysis concluded that his brain had been affected by the pacification helmet. The Doctor readily assisted Crozier in repairing the equipment for the operation on Lord Kiv. The Doctor gained the confidence with Crozier and Sil with a vicious display of hatred of his companion, Peri, when questioning on her behalf of the Mentors.

Computer statement on behalf of the defendant

Most forgiving and wise members of the jury, to continue. I made every conceivable effort to ensure that a suitable body was found to house the monumental intellect of Lord Kiv. Candidates of a suitable breed and stature in society were, however, few and far between. A fisherman from the eyelets of Brak, almost certainly from the spawning mire of his magnificence Lord Kiv, was found and prepared for the operation. The body would house the mind of Lord Kiv until a more suitable candidate could be located. The resulting operation, of course, was a success.

Defence statement

The judge questioned the validity of the last statement made by the defence. The defence asked for it to be struck from the court records.

All right, all right! The operation was not as successful as I said, but no deceit was intended. Our most humble lives were under threat of death should the Mighty Kiv have perished. Crozier fought with all his medical expertise to keep the brain alive, alas, some of the donor's original memories began to infect the new genius that lay within its head. O most benevolent jurors, it became vital that a new body should be found.

The barbarian King Yrcanos had, most unsuccessfully, tried to incite rebellion among the Thoros Alphans, but now the rebel leaders and the royalty of Krontep lay imprisoned in a cell.

I would have most willingly submitted myself as a new body to house the might and wisdom of Lord Kiv. Alas, I feel that I am not worthy of such a privilege. But I was all too willing to assist in the search for a suitable candidate. The Doctor proved unsuitable, as did the leader of rebels, but the girl Peri was an ideal choice on both physical and health levels. Crozier felt most confident that a complete neural transfer would work with such a fine specimen. Members of the most prestigious jury, I draw your attention to this point: it was Crozier's decision to carry out the operation, not mine.

If I might draw your attention to the screens, other activities were afoot.

Defence statement

High Court data file
The Doctor

The Doctor freed King Yrcanos and his equerry Dorf, now termed Lukoser – part man, part wolf. The transformer controlling the minds of the enslaved Thoros Alphans was destroyed by King Yrcanos: the Thoros Alphans went into a state of catatonic shock, and wandered through the tunnels of Thoros Beta unable to control their movements. It is at this point that the Doctor is believed to have left Thoros Beta in his time vessel TARDIS. The reason is unknown. It is calculated that an outside force took him before he could free Peri.

The shaven head of Peri was a most noteworthy improvement on her previous appearance. Her brain no longer existed, Crozier had been triumphant, and I ask you to note, members of the jury, that Crozier insisted the mind of the girl no longer existed. The new shape of Lord Kiv arose majestically, feeling the energy and vitality surge of a youthful body once more.

No Mentor could have predicted what happened next. Nobody knew that Yrcanos and the Thoros Alphan rebels were armed and would attack the lab.

The first blast killed Crozier and his assistant, the second disabled my mobile conveyance unit. It was then that Yrcanos turned on Lord Kiv. The girl had been intended as his bride; his barbaric mind could not comprehend the sight of the magnificence that confronted him, and he opened fire. But that is not how the mighty Kiv died.

Members of the most sentient jury, I have gathered evidence to prove that the blame lies with Crozier, not with me. King Yrcanos knew nothing about the weapon he was using; the blasts aimed at Lord Kiv were stun blasts. The impact, however, was enough to eradicate the brain of Lord Kiv, allowing the intelligence of the girl to reassert itself. King Yrcanos carried the body away, leaving the carnage behind him. Lord Kiv's mind had been ejected into nothing due to Crozier's lack of competence.

As to the fate of the girl, she is now known to be Queen Peri, King Yrcanos's lady of the Krontep Empire. I therefore submit a plea of 'comprehensively unimpeachable'. Members of the jury, the blame lies not with me, Sil, but with the late Crozier. I rest my case.

Where have my marsh-minnows gone? What scum took them <click>?

Defence statement

The verdict of the jury was reached in favour of the Mentor Sil a unanimous vote of 'without guilt'. The Varos evidence was not taken into consideration on the decision of the judge, who declared it to be of little consequence to the trial in progress.

It should be noted that only hours passed before the nature of the bribes offered to the jury by Sil were discovered. The bribed judge has been denied the opportunity to defend at his next trial for perversion of the course of justice. Sil is quoted as being concerned about the evidence that will be produced.

For the honour of the empire of Sontara, I pledge allegiance to the might of the Sontaran Army Space Corps, and all planets that lie in its domain. Through the time-honoured laws of warfare, I submit myself for trial through simulated combat, as judgment of my worthiness for promotion. I call upon the mighty warriors of the past, so I might learn from their tactical prowess and wisdom, discovering the route to the ultimate glory of victory.

Sontaran cadet pledge, recited on entering the battle computer simulation facility, Sontara strategic HQ.

THE SONTARANS

The art of war does not only depend on the triumph of victory, you must understand the very nature of death and defeat. That is truly a victory in itself.

General Pelk, pre-battle speech, Galactic War III

BATTLE COMPUTER ACTIVATED ■

CADET ASSESSMENT PROGRAMME ENTERED AND RUNNING. CADET JAGO NOW SECURED WITHIN SIMULATION CHAMBER. SENSORY DEPRIVATION NOW IN PROGRESS. PHYSICAL RESPONSES REGISTERING NORMAL. TACTICAL SIMULATION NOW IN PROGRESS ■

TOTAL NUMBER OF SCENARIO PROJECTIONS FOR ASSESSMENT: FOUR. ■

OBJECTIVES FOR CADET: OBSERVE COMBAT RECORDS OF SELECTED SINGLE WARRIOR DEFEATS AND ASSESS VIABILITY OF VICTORIOUS ALTERNATIVE SOLUTIONS ■

EVIDENCE PRESENTED: VISUAL AND CEREBRAL DATA UNITS, RETRIEVED FROM V-CLASS SPACE VESSEL DATA BANKS ■

LIST SCENARIOS: ONE – COMMANDER JINGO LINX; TWO – FIELD MAJOR STYRE; THREE – COMMANDER STOR OF THE SSSS; FOUR – GROUP MARSHALL STYKE. RUN AUDIO INSTRUCTION TO CADET ■

Warning to cadet. The strategic value and technicality of certain references within the data may cause confusion. Help is available in these instances. Known explanations and assumptions will be displayed. The assessment starts now.

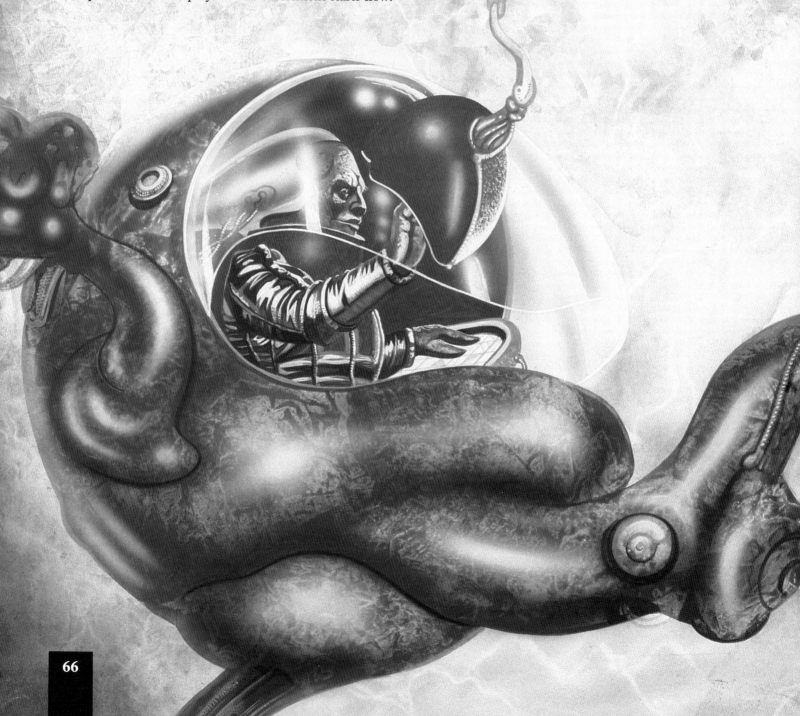

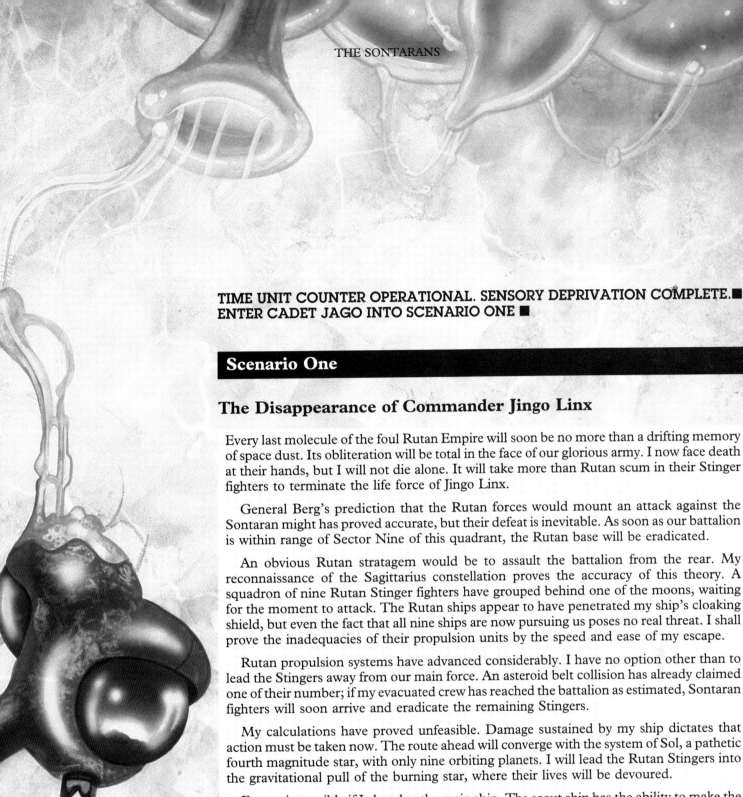

TIME UNIT COUNTER OPERATIONAL. SENSORY DEPRIVATION COMPLETE.■
ENTER CADET JAGO INTO SCENARIO ONE ■

Scenario One

The Disappearance of Commander Jingo Linx

Every last molecule of the foul Rutan Empire will soon be no more than a drifting memory of space dust. Its obliteration will be total in the face of our glorious army. I now face death at their hands, but I will not die alone. It will take more than Rutan scum in their Stinger fighters to terminate the life force of Jingo Linx.

General Berg's prediction that the Rutan forces would mount an attack against the Sontaran might has proved accurate, but their defeat is inevitable. As soon as our battalion is within range of Sector Nine of this quadrant, the Rutan base will be eradicated.

An obvious Rutan stratagem would be to assault the battalion from the rear. My reconnaissance of the Sagittarius constellation proves the accuracy of this theory. A squadron of nine Rutan Stinger fighters have grouped behind one of the moons, waiting for the moment to attack. The Rutan ships appear to have penetrated my ship's cloaking shield, but even the fact that all nine ships are now pursuing us poses no real threat. I shall prove the inadequacies of their propulsion units by the speed and ease of my escape.

Rutan propulsion systems have advanced considerably. I have no option other than to lead the Stingers away from our main force. An asteroid belt collision has already claimed one of their number; if my evacuated crew has reached the battalion as estimated, Sontaran fighters will soon arrive and eradicate the remaining Stingers.

My calculations have proved unfeasible. Damage sustained by my ship dictates that action must be taken now. The route ahead will converge with the system of Sol, a pathetic fourth magnitude star, with only nine orbiting planets. I will lead the Rutan Stingers into the gravitational pull of the burning star, where their lives will be devoured.

Escape is possible if I abandon the main ship. The scout ship has the ability to make the journey back to Sontara.

Intense heat has disabled parts of the scout ship; the loss of the gyro-stabilization units makes the journey back to Sontara an impossibility. To effect repairs, I will have to land on one of the planets. A small oxygenated blue world is in closest proximity. The atmospheric readings indicate the possibility of an indigenous hominid population ideal for adaptation as slave labour. Their technology level can be assessed on landing.

Q: NATURE OF BLUE PLANET AND HOMINID INHABITANTS? ■

Planet referred to as Terra or Earth. Atmosphere combines high levels of oxygen and low levels of carbon dioxide. Hominid creatures based around cellular and muscular growth on hardened bone calcium and marrow structures. Development is through solar cycles understood to progressively age tissue cells. Considered highly ineffectual. Two distinctive breeds existent within social structure. Opposite sexes: one is theorized to carry young of

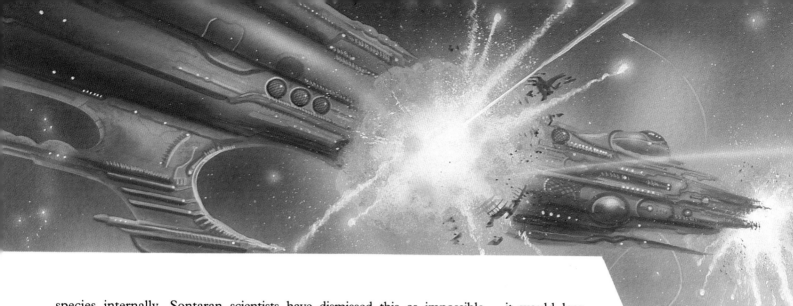

species internally. Sontaran scientists have dismissed this as impossible – it would lose incalculable hours of fighting time.

Cadet Jago

Assessing the damage to the scout vessel, I realize total repair to an operational standard required by Space Corps regulations will entail many light cycles of intense labour. I must establish a work force of servile hominids quickly.

A small unit of hominids has chosen to approach my ship, their meagre intelligence no doubt overawed by Sontaran technology. I had not allowed for the possibility that these creatures might be bipeds, or for the hideous nature of their physical appearance. A simple staser could easily slice through what is obviously an attempt at effective metal body armour. I estimate that it is constructed from raw ore. Summary: the hominids are generally repulsive, pitiful and inept.

Protocol dictates that I must formally inform the hominids that their planet is now under Sontaran martial law, and that all technology and resources should be instantly placed under my command. Communication through my dual translator will make it bearable to converse with their foolish primitive tongues.

Q: NATURE OF SONTARAN MARTIAL LAW ANNOUNCEMENT? ■

Speech recited upon the conquest of an inferior culture. 'By virtue of the authority as an officer of the Sontaran Army Space Corps, I hereby claim this planet, its moons and satellites for the greater glory of the Sontaran Empire.' Aliens questioning the validity of this statement are liable to summary execution.

Cadet Jago

Hominid Irongron has enough blade-brandishing warriors to overpower me. I have come to a strategic compromise; for the moment I am submissive. The shelter provided by his fortress will have adequate space and facilities to store the scout vessel. Irongron seems unable to comprehend the logic that the stone structure is impractical – its mobility factor is non-existent.

In return for his assistance, I will provide this fool with weapons far beyond their understanding. The sight of his forces eradicating his enemy will provide an interesting diversion and allow assessment of the species' fighting capabilities. Although base and primitive, there is a certain raw energy within these hominids that could be developed, given the right weapons and training.

Upon my departure I will consider leaving the scout vessel's sonic cannon for them to experiment with. A future study is worth entering on the effects of a primitive society when high level technology is induced within it. I speculate that the results would prove interesting.

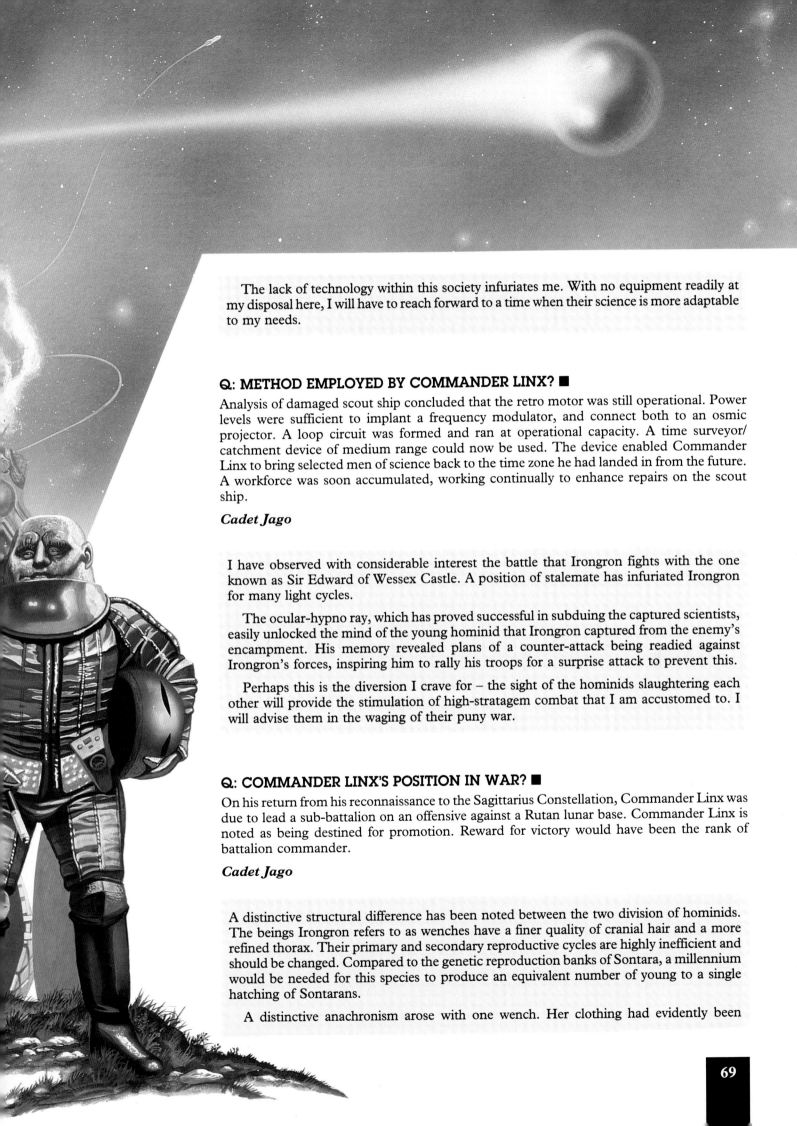

The lack of technology within this society infuriates me. With no equipment readily at my disposal here, I will have to reach forward to a time when their science is more adaptable to my needs.

Q.: METHOD EMPLOYED BY COMMANDER LINX? ■

Analysis of damaged scout ship concluded that the retro motor was still operational. Power levels were sufficient to implant a frequency modulator, and connect both to an osmic projector. A loop circuit was formed and ran at operational capacity. A time surveyor/catchment device of medium range could now be used. The device enabled Commander Linx to bring selected men of science back to the time zone he had landed in from the future. A workforce was soon accumulated, working continually to enhance repairs on the scout ship.

Cadet Jago

I have observed with considerable interest the battle that Irongron fights with the one known as Sir Edward of Wessex Castle. A position of stalemate has infuriated Irongron for many light cycles.

The ocular-hypno ray, which has proved successful in subduing the captured scientists, easily unlocked the mind of the young hominid that Irongron captured from the enemy's encampment. His memory revealed plans of a counter-attack being readied against Irongron's forces, inspiring him to rally his troops for a surprise attack to prevent this.

Perhaps this is the diversion I crave for – the sight of the hominids slaughtering each other will provide the stimulation of high-stratagem combat that I am accustomed to. I will advise them in the waging of their puny war.

Q.: COMMANDER LINX'S POSITION IN WAR? ■

On his return from his reconnaissance to the Sagittarius Constellation, Commander Linx was due to lead a sub-battalion on an offensive against a Rutan lunar base. Commander Linx is noted as being destined for promotion. Reward for victory would have been the rank of battalion commander.

Cadet Jago

A distinctive structural difference has been noted between the two division of hominids. The beings Irongron refers to as wenches have a finer quality of cranial hair and a more refined thorax. Their primary and secondary reproductive cycles are highly inefficient and should be changed. Compared to the genetic reproduction banks of Sontara, a millennium would be needed for this species to produce an equivalent number of young to a single hatching of Sontarans.

A distinctive anachronism arose with one wench. Her clothing had evidently been

machine produced, an achievement beyond the understanding of this species' current level of technological achievement, and her facial features were not as heavily formed as the others of her kind within this stone fortress. The ocular-hypno ray overcame her reluctance to communicate; as I suspected, she is not from this time period.

Her ignorance of inter dimensional travel added weight to her claim that she was merely a passenger with a far greater intelligence, a mind that has traced me back from the twentieth century to this period: Doctor John Smith. Knowledge is evidently present that should not exist until, I estimate, the 45th century. This hominid is a threat, it must be eradicated.

My countenance is displeasing to Irongron's eye. I suspected his basic nervous system would react in such a way; I find the shape and form of these creatures aesthetically unpleasing. To avoid inducing hysteria through over-reaction to my physiognomy, I shall continue to wear my battle helmet while imprisoned on this world. I must continue to placate Irongron.

Q: METHOD EMPLOYED TO PLACATE HOMINID IRONGRON?

Commander Linx constructed a low-capability battle-android. Structure encased within primitive body armour to protect circuits. First task: perform summary execution within fortress grounds. Execution order aborted through destruction of remote control unit. Commander Linx's presence required to shut down mechanism. Assailant unknown: Linx deduced assault carried out with knowledge of android engineering not present in time period. Conclusion: Doctor John Smith involved in assault.

Cadet Jago

It was inevitable that the one enemy within this hominid race that I face would soon be my captive, but the mind of this Doctor does not warrant instant eradication. His obvious mental capabilities are far more astute than those of many of the scientists I have taken from the future, suggesting an altogether alien intellect.

The truth has become apparent: he is a Time Lord, a member of a race renowned for its skills in inter spacial engineering, yet with no martial knowledge. This Doctor had the audacity to threaten me, a Sontaran commander, to keep my forces away from the planet. On my return to Sontara, I shall instigate pre-conquest research into the suitability of Gallifrey for colonization. For the moment, I will keep this Doctor and use his knowledge to enhance repairs on the scout ship.

I should have realized that a mere electro-shockwave helmet would not keep a being like the Doctor captive for long. On my return from delivering a redesigned batch of breach-loading weapons to that fool Irongron, the Doctor had escaped. My instincts insist that he will have retreated to a haven somewhere in the immediate vicinity, but my lack of ground knowledge of the surrounding area has prevented me from deducing where.

To confirm my suspicions that he has retreated to the enemy encampment, I shall accompany Irongron and his hominid barbarians on an assault of Sir Edward's castle.

Q: NATURE OF BATTLE AT WESSEX CASTLE? ■

Commander Linx and the hominids were deceived with the illusion that Wessex Castle was manned with a full squad of soldiers. Non-living replicants constructed from primitive suits of armour and wood created this effect. On deducing this fact a full-scale attack was launched. It was repelled with primitive smoke and scented bombs that caused distress through the nasal passages. An immediate retreat was instigated on the command of hominid Irongron. Conclusion: the Doctor was involved in the counter-attack.

Cadet Jago

The imbecilic Irongron still maintains that I am under his control. His strength is no match for my prowess at physical combat. If he does not heed my warning of the fate of his castle on my departure from this world, he will die along with the rest of his followers when the scout vessel breaks through the shell of the fortress.

I knew that the Doctor would return. He has the arrogance of a pacifist protester, wanting to find solutions to dilemmas a Sontaran is trained to answer with a phaser. He demands that I destroy the rifles I constructed for Irongron and free the scientists under my control. At last my chance has come to destroy this fool; I shall relish the sound of his every bone breaking under my grasp.

Q: OUTCOME OF COMBAT WITH DOCTOR? ■

Commander Linx was disabled before he could conclude the fight victoriously. It is believed that one of the scientists present in the cellar housing the scout vessel administered a blow against Commander Linx's probic vent. After consciousness was regained, Commander Linx remained bound and unable to effect an escape until the hominid Irongron released him. The hominid called Doctor had been successfully captured by Irongron. Commander Linx accompanied Irongron to confront the Doctor again.

Cadet Jago

The agility of the Doctor has been noted. He seems able to anticipate where the bullets being fired at him will hit. Irongron's men are poor shots, and I debate whether I should arm them with lasers. It would be easy for them to follow a target with a laser beam until it was incinerated. Before my chance to demonstrate how to kill effectively with one of the primitive firearms, a bracket on a chain swung towards the Doctor, enabling him to swing overhead and make good his escape.

Hominid Sarah Jane Smith's assistance in the escape was not unnoticed. If there is time before my departure, I will ensure that both she and the Doctor share an equally decisive demise, from which there will be no escape.

That barbaric idiot Irongron will not heed my warning – his fate is sealed within this castle. I shall make no effort to save his life; he and his men are worthless and of no strategic value. In less than one of their light cycles I shall be further away from this planet than their minds could ever comprehend. At last, I am free to leave this damnable planet.

Q: RECORDS END. WHAT HAPPENED TO COMMANDER LINX? ■

It is believed that a final confrontation between Commander Linx and the Doctor took place in the fortress cellar housing the scout vessel. Irongron returned to confront Linx. Linx obliterated Irongron. Commander Linx left for his ship knowing that the Doctor and all the hominids would be killed in the heat of the scout vessel's engines.

A bowman known as Hal, a weapons expert proficient in the use of firing wooden shafts with curved wood and hide, fired an arrow at Commander Linx as the hatch to the vessel closed. The arrow became embedded in the probic vent at the back of his neck. Commander Linx's final actions set the take-off mechanism in motion. The scout ship was retrieved near the Nebula. Mind probes indicate Commander Linx's last sight was the escaping forms of all the hominids, led by the Doctor.

Conclusion: Commander Linx honoured with first-class battle service and loyalty to Sontara merit notations. His body was ejected into space with full military honours. The battle that destroyed the Rutan base in sector nine was named Linx War to commemorate his valiant service to the Sontaran Army Space Corp.

Cadet Jago

Q: SUBMIT VIABLE VICTORIOUS ALTERNATIVE. ■

Eradicate Doctor at earliest opportunity.

Cadet Jago

COMPUTER ACCEPTS ANSWER AS CORRECT. ■

Scenario Two

Field Major Styre's military assessment survey

I have never heard of humans before, let alone the galaxy they inhabit, but I appreciate the strategic importance that their sector represents, and that this Earth is ideally positioned for a central battalion headquarters.

It will be interesting to test the pliability of a new race's anatomy and genetic structure, minds that can be manipulated and twisted by the lowest level of psycho-weaponry that the armaments division has produced. Of course, the fact that the Earth has been laid waste by solar flares poses no real problem: human colonists are known to be exploring the area. A simple lure will bring all the subjects I need for the experiments.

Q: NATURE AND REASONING OF EXPERIMENTS? ■

Field Major Styre was commissioned by the Grand Strategic Council to experiment on the inhabitants of Earth. Rutan forces were reported as heading towards the sector. Sontaran domination of the galaxy would prove of strategic value. Advance information was needed about the strengths and weaknesses inherent of humans. Field Major Styre was given total authority to carry out any tests. Only limited time was available before the Sontaran battle fleet would have to move in.

Cadet Jago

I find the peace of this planet unsettling. Records indicate that once a thriving civilization inhabited this world, but only foliage-strewn wastelands remain. Solar flares effectively removed all signs that they had ever existed.

After establishing a landing bay housed within an incline of rocks, the tractor beam energy was damaged in a rock-fall. Only enough power remained to draw one freighter down towards the planet's surface. Unfortunately, some humanoid tissue survived the impact, but certain samples of their technology remained undamaged. Radar monitors have detected what appears to be a military ship from their world answering the distress signal I am projecting into space with the retrieved equipment.

It is a primitive tracking signal, easily detectable on the lowest form of radar equipment. As soon as the ship has touched down, I shall obliterate it. The crew will be fighting against the elements of survival, but it will be in vain. As soon as the Scavenger is operational, they will be hunted down. It will be of interest to note how many survive the tests I have devised.

Q: NATURE OF THE SCAVENGER? ■

An adapted security surveillance robot commonly used at military bases and capable of traversing all terrains. The robot has the capability to capture and restrain life forms, subduing them with electric shockwaves. Field-Major Styre used the Scavenger to capture humans from the space vessel that responded to the distress signal. The machine had the capability to hunt during the time periods of darkness and light. Infra-red detection scanners made evasion impossible. It is not known how many torture implements Field Major Styre equipped the Scavenger with.

Cadet Jago

I have observed these humans. Some time has passed since their ship exploded; paranoia, fear, angst, self-doubt, anger and vulnerability have all been displayed with remarkable profusion since they realized there is no escape. I will allow them a brief period of time to recover from their fatigue, so their strength is at maximum capacity for the tests. There is a leader among them, a man of powerful mind and body for such an inferior species. I will note how he maintains these attributes as the extreme pressure and stress builds on the nine survivors.

Vural is a human who ranks as a major in the military ranks of the Galsec colonists. My deductions have proved accurate concerning his powers of perception – he found my scout vessel and was held by the Scavenger until my return. His obvious fear did not block his instincts for survival, with immediate offers to spy on his crew in return for his life. A simple micro-observation unit attached to the neck of his uniform will avoid him betraying his cover by reporting to my ship continually. I have programmed the Scavenger to release him should he be captured.

Mobility tests for the Scavenger will commence shortly. As soon as the light returns, I will send it to capture the first subject for testing.

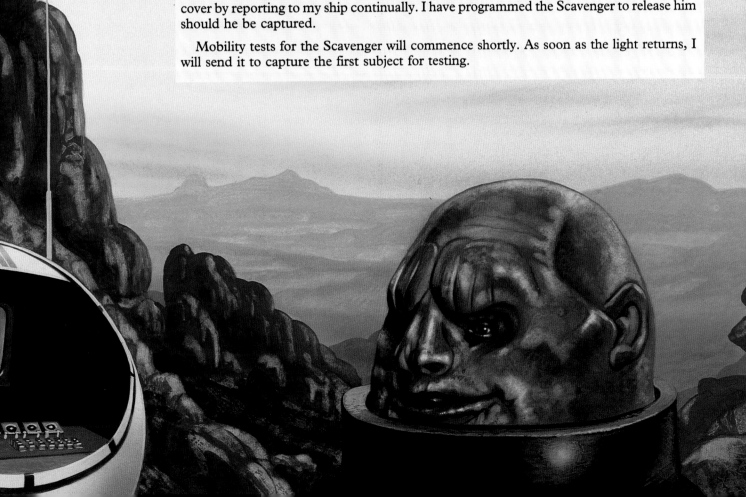

Experiment One
Assessment of durability of human tissue and bone structure

After an initial test with a strontium blade, it became apparent that the tissue surrounding the human bone structure can be removed with little effort, falling away easily with the application of any sharp object. The bones snap with only the mildest physical pressure. It should be noted that the chest area is particularly vulnerable. The subject of experiment one survived having large areas of his exterior tissue removed, but died when a shattered rib penetrated its cardiovascular organ.

Experiment Two
Assessment of effects of staser/laser beams against body

The mobility of the human body when moving at speed is effective, but the removal of any of the lower limbs with a simple laser beam results in the subject being unable to continue moving. The heat of the laser effectively seals the wounds inflicted by the weapon, but a certain degree of trouble is caused should the subject be needed for questioning. It is advised that some form of transportation for the captive should be organized in these instances.

Experiment Three
Assessment of effects of intense heat/cold against body

When a human life form is enclosed within a confined area at sub-zero temperatures, the fluid pulse rate round the body slows considerably. It is estimated that only a few hours in such an environment would result in death, with the body freezing into a solid state shortly after that. The reverse occurs with intense heat; the application of concentrated flames against the human tissue effectively cooks it. The eyes, breathing systems and limb mobility cease after a relatively short time on fire. Of the two, I conclude that intense heat is by far the speedier of the two methods.

Experiment Four
Assessment of physical immersion in H_2O liquid

When the upper half of a human body is forcibly submerged in the liquid they term water, the main organs that seem to act as oxygen pumps in the breast cage flood with it until asphyxiation occurs. Conclusion: a highly effective execution method.

I have set experiment five in motion. It will be interesting to observe what total deprivation of the H_2O substance will induce. The tissue texture is porous, suggesting that a certain degree of natural moisture is needed to maintain its flexibility. I was once fortunate enough to observe a Sugra execution, where the accursed creature was subjected to intense heat. Its physical substance dried until it became brittle. I await the results of the human test to see if the same effect is produced.

The monitor attached to Vural's clothing material shows a humanoid face I have not seen before. He is obviously of higher mental capabilities than the other beings I have tested to date – he recognized the advanced technology of the monitor. It is hardly possible that another craft has landed undetected, I shall send the Scavenger to retrieve this human called the Doctor.

Q.: NATURE OF THE DOCTOR? ■

Records indicate that the Doctor is the same man as that encountered by Commander Linx. Time Lords are understood to have the power of complete physical regeneration. The Doctor was physically different from Commander Linx's assailant. Two other humans are noted as accompanying him: a female called Sarah Jane Smith and a male called Harry Sullivan. Communication between the two beings is understood to have consisted of code names. The code name for Harry Sullivan remains unknown; the code name for the female is 'Old Thing'.

Cadet Jago

Audio devices planted round the encampment of the humans have revealed the possibility of another presence on the planet, explaining my observation of the one called the Doctor.

They claim three travellers from a space station termed Nerva Beacon transmatted down to the surface of the planet to carry out repairs to the teleportation facilities. On my descent through the cobalt atmosphere of this world, my detectors showed no indication that any such satellite was in geostationary orbit. I await the return of the Scavenger, perhaps there will be more interesting humanoid material to be tested.

Sontaran G3 military assessment survey
Audio report
Assessment of female human species number one

There appears to be no specific function for the female to serve; there is no military justification for her existence. The bone structure obviously differs from that of the human male; muscle development is of a weaker quality and makes her redundant for any combative work. She should not be present on this world.

The being is now held in a rock alcove, imprisoned by a force barrier and shackles. I shall devise a test for her mind.

The male of the species who escaped from the psychological tests of experiment six has been retrieved by the Scavenger. He has been drained of all potential value; I shall record the decay process for human tissue. He appears to have been known as Roth, and of some assistance to the girl. There is no one to help her now.

The Marshall is growing impatient; he fails to see the importance of my work. There are so many forms of death and torture to be devised for those pathetic, puny creatures. Their bodies are some of the most susceptible to pain that I have encountered. Their spirits are so easy to break.

They are dependent on chemical and organic intakes for nourishment, I have to know how this helps them function. Sontarans merely need a power recharge through the probic vent at the back of the neck, an efficient and energy-saving method compared with the digestion of organic matter.

Hundreds of Sontaran fighters will lay waste to this galaxy; I must know everything about these creatures before that happens. I need only a few more hours of experimentation.

Experiment Seven
Assessment of female human's resistance to fear

The female has been secured so that there is no movement of her limbs. A hallucinogenic inducer has been attached to her forehead. It will project images of her deepest fears; there is no way she can defend herself against them. Initial thought-exploration readouts show a fear of a reptilian creature called a snake, rockfalls and being physically engulfed by a substance called mud. I estimate that few of her senses will be left in a functioning capacity when the experiment concludes.

Any problem that the Doctor posed has been eradicated. His attempts to free the female from the experiment failed. He showed that audacity to attack a Sontaran Field Major, but he was dealt by a simple photon blast received on the back of the breast cage. The internal organ displacement would have killed him instantly. Now that any further trouble can be avoided from him, I shall instigate the final experiments on the remaining humans. A group experiment would be interesting to observe.

The Scavenger has returned with three humans, including the one called Vural. Their shock at discovering their leader to be a traitor shows the possibility that the planting of mis-information alone can stir anger within their ranks. I have devised a test that will involve all three of them.

Experiment five has been a success: water deprivation proved lethal, as expected. The human died after nine days. The need for liquid on a regular basis can be exploited in future confrontations.

Experiment Eight
Assessment of resistance to pressure on the human breast cage and assessment of physical muscular strength

The human Vural has been chained to a slab of rock. His two companions are holding a gravity bar over his breast cage at a minimum weight of forty pounds. Both men have been betrayed by their leader, and it will be interesting to observe whether their desire for revenge causes them to terminate Vural by dropping the bar on him.

An increase in weight to two hundred pounds showed signs of physical stress: the muscles in the forearms of both men went tight.

At three hundred pounds the bar has lowered and is difficult for them to support. Four hundred pounds: the two men can no longer hold the bar above Vural's chest; the main body of it is now resting on his breast cage. Five hundred pounds: the bone structure of the breast cage is beginning to crack . . .

Experiment suspended owing to incoming communication from the Marshall.

I must continue with the experiments at an increased rate of analysis. The Marshall claims that there is growing alarm among my superiors about the time needed for my experiments. I had to draw the Marshall's attention to the fact that I am working under the orders of the Grand Strategic Council. I have agreed to draw the tests to a close as soon as possible.

Returning to experiment eight, it was terminated by the intervention of the Doctor, whom I assessed as being deceased on our earlier encounter. He claims that the humans I have experimented on until this point have been of a sub-class – the inherently weak slaves of this planet. The Doctor claims that he is of the warrior class of the planet and has challenged me to a duel to the death. My energy is low – I need a recharge at my ship – but this will be of little consequence. The Doctor is hardly a threat to my superior skills of physical combat; he will be easily defeated.

Q: NATURE OF WHAT HAPPENED TO FIELD MAJOR STYRE? ■

Field Major Styre did not allow for the agility of the Doctor. The human called Sullivan sabotaged the energizing unit of Field Major Styre's vessel while the combat was in progress. When energy drained from Field Major Styre, he retreated to his ship with some urgency to replenish it. The machine reversed its process, Field Major Styre was unable to feed off the energy – the energy fed off him and liquified his physical structure. The vessel exploded and ejected the records of what happened into space. A V-class Cursitor retrieved them on the outskirts of the galaxy.

The science-tech division of Sontara research honoured the memory and battle history of Field Major Styre with the instigation of the Styre Assessment Programme, a set programme of experiments to be carried out on any species that is discovered in the process of universal conquest.

The Earth has been designated 'unworthy of conquest'. A communication between the Marshal of the invasion fleet and the Doctor took place after the death of Field-Major Styre. It is apparent that the humans represent more of a threat than Sontaran tacticians predicted. The tacticians in question have since been executed for making this grave miscalculation.

Cadet Jago

SUBMIT VIABLE VICTORIOUS ALTERNATIVE. ■

Eradicate the Doctor at the earliest opportunity.

Cadet Jago

COMPUTER ACCEPTS ANSWER AS CORRECT. ■

Scenario Three
Commander Stor's final SSSS invasion campaign

At last I have total power. My campaign against the Rutan base on the moon of Ragna gave ample proof to the Strategic Council that I am capable of establishing an elite fighting espionage force with the aim of developing and instigating plans for inter-planetary invasions, capitalizing on lesser species' lust for conquest and using them as expendable shock troops.

The plan is simple: the Sontaran Special Space Service will establish links with military forces of other species, use them under a false alliance that would convince them to make the first attacks of an invasion, and allow Sontaran forces to move in after the initial forces are wiped out. After eradicating both parties, the Sontarans emerge victorious. No alliance with our race means anything – Sontarans are the supreme beings.

Planets can be drained of all resources. The might of the Sontaran army will grow. There are countless worlds that will vanish in the wake of our forces, but only one could pose any threat to our universal rule: Gallifrey, the planet of the Time Lords.

S • S • S • S

Q: NATURE OF PLANET GALLIFREY? ◼

Located in the constellation of Kasterborus. The indigenous inhabitants are known only as Time Lords, and are believed to have perfected inter-dimensional travel with crafts known as TARDISes. Preliminary reports suggested that the race was of little consequence, puny and of no military value, but information from Commander Stor's special agents revealed that a power existed on the planet of far greater strategic value than had been estimated. The governing hierarchy termed as the High Council has access to the matrix through the Panopticon in the capital city of the planet. The matrix represents the sum total of knowledge of the universe. Other evidence showed that when combined with artefacts – the Rod of Rassilon, the Sash of Rassilon and the Key of Rassilon – the sum total of Time Lord power was formed. Stor realized the value of this to the Sontaran Empire. The search commenced for the race that would act as his storm troopers.

Cadet Jago

The Vardans are a most intriguing species. They are of humanoid appearance, yet have a natural ability to display the most effective form of camouflage that the War Science Division has seen. I am informed by scientist Teal that the principle involves the ability to break down the molecular components of the body, and transport them along any wavelength, be it air, electricity or the thought waves of the brain.

A neutral agent with access to Gallifrey has to be found – a being that not only has the capability to negate the seemingly impenetrable force barrier surrounding the world, but who also has free reign of mobility through the central dome that houses the main city of the Time Lords, and access to the heart of Panopticon.

The Vardans have entered negotiations with a free agent of the race known only as the Doctor, who holds the right to claim ascendancy to the title of Lord President of Gallifrey. His task is simple: the force barrier has to be shut down; the Vardans will then lead their invasion force on to the surface of the planet and combat any resistance that faces them.

Our battalion will be in geo stationary orbit round the perimeter of the next galaxy. As soon as the Vardans have landed we will move forward and eradicate their fleet, leaving Gallifrey open for Sontaran conquest.

Q: NATURE OF THE GALLIFREYAN TERMED THE DOCTOR? ◼

Visual identification confirms that the Doctor is the same being that Field Major Styre encountered on Earth. His appearance had altered between scenario one and scenario two – a complete physical and molecular restructuring unique to the race of Time Lords. Commander Stor received orders from the Strategic Council to eliminate the Doctor as soon as landing forces arrived on the planet's surface.

Cadet Jago

A hole of considerable size allowed the Vardan ship through as we had anticipated, but the Sontaran battlecruisers will need the force barrier to be neutralized. I shall lead a small attack force of scout vessels down to the surface of the planet and ensure that the operation is carried out successfully. Betrayal by the Vardans must be avoided. Our battle tacticians postulate that the hole in the barrier could be closed, denying the Sontarans access. We will use the Vardans to achieve this before eradicating them.

Our problem of effectively killing the Vardan Troops has been solved by one of the Time Lords. Our detectors indicate that the co-ordinates of Vector 3052 Alpha 7 14 Span no longer hold the Vardan's planet in orbit of its galaxy's sun – a time loop has been formed round it, sending the planet into a never-ending orbit throughout infinity, from which there is no escape. The Vardans are a casualty of war – in the event the species would only have been wiped out by Sontaran forces.

Eight units of my warriors have split up throughout the capital city. I shall lead an assault squad into the Panopticon.

The Doctor is present; he escaped from the Panopticon with his group of allies. My men have been dispatched across the immediate area to hunt them down and eradicate them on sight. I had not correctly estimated the size and labyrinthine nature of the Time Lords' domain. The force barrier must be neutralized to allow the main battalion to land.

Sergeant Darb's life reading has been terminated – a blade of steel was inserted at speed into his probic vent. The fawning Time Lord that has readily offered his assistance to the Sontaran Empire indicates that there is a companion assisting the Doctor, a Leela, whose savage tendencies indicate that she was responsible for Darb's death.

This Castellan Kelner, a meek hominid of weak stature and strength but of some use, has declared with certainty that the Doctor will be heading for his chambers, a presidential office, which he has used as his headquarters since he took power on Gallifrey. My men have orders to kill the Doctor's followers on sight. He, however, must live – until he has handed over the Key of Rassilon.

After numerous attempts to batter the doors down, I find that the room is empty. My men are tracking the Doctor and his group through the corridors several levels below this area.

Time is running out. I have to dismantle the force barrier. The battalion is under orders to return to Sontara should the shield close, but problems have arisen that I had not anticipated.

Q: NATURE OF TACTICAL PROBLEMS FACING COMMANDER STOR? ■

The force barrier had to be widened or shut off completely. To achieve this, the president had to wear a circlet about the cranium to be able telepathically to instruct the matrix to carry this out. The Doctor was the president, and he had evaded capture. To bypass this, the Great Key of Rassilon was needed – and the Doctor had the Great Key.

Dilemma: the Doctor and Cardinal Borusa, a high-ranking Time Lord ally of the Doctor, had taken refuge in the Doctor's TARDIS. Two of Commander Stor's best warriors failed to gain access to the vehicle. Staser blasters failed to cause any damage to the hull. In effect there was no way of getting the Doctor out of the TARDIS or gaining access to it.

Cadet Jago

The accursed Doctor is creating havoc with my plans. We are behind schedule; the battalion cannot wait much longer. The main defence barrier has been linked to the computational facilities within the TARDIS. The Doctor is using it to close the hole in the force barrier. If this cannot be stopped in time, the reinforcements I have sent for will be unable to enter the planet's atmosphere, and the battalion will turn away. Kelner has presented a viable solution, which had better work . . .

Q: NATURE OF KELNER'S SOLUTION? ■

By reversing the central stabilization banks present within the power engineering planet on Gallifrey, the TARDIS would be ejected into a black star, destroying all living matter within the vehicle. The fail-safe switch to prevent this was operated within the TARDIS. The TARDIS was effectively stabilized for eternity with nothing being able to alter this externally – the Doctor was trapped within the TARDIS. Entrance probes were used by Kelner to gain access to the central control room of the TARDIS. Commander Stor entered the vessel.

Cadet Jago

I find the so-called technology of the Time Lords obsolete and without any strategic value. The empty spaces within the control room alone could house an ample weapons supply. Sontaran engineers pack every empty nanometre with the most sophisticated technology they can create. I am informed that this model of TARDIS was taken out of service by the Time Lords centuries ago it is outmoded even by their facile standards.

My plans to destroy this TARDIS have been aborted. The Doctor has removed the primary fraction tube from the fail-safe control unit; with the circuit broken, nothing can destroy it. I cannot destroy the TARDIS; the Doctor cannot escape: we are at a stalemate.

The destruction of the ineffective barricade the Doctor mounted to try to prevent Sontaran forces entering the inner chambers of the TARDIS has successfully been carried out by Corporal Surl. My tracking device fails to work in this environment, some form of biological barrier has been set up that prevents it from detecting humanoid life forms. The corridors of this craft are infinite, and the search will be endless unless the barrier is destroyed.

My immediate plan to return to the central control room and dismantle the relevant equipment has been aborted. Time Lord Kelner has sworn allegiance and will disconnect the ancillary generator that powers the mechanism. The generator is some distance away; I had not appreciated the skills that these beings possessed in dimensional engineering.

They have been sighted. Corporal Surl is in pursuit – nothing will stop Surl now he has them in sight. Their immediate retreat to the sick bay of this craft failed to throw off my men, although their tactical prowess allowed them to evade capture at this point. Kelner is doggedly obedient, perhaps his usefulness will not end as suddenly as I thought. We will join Surl to execute the prisoners he has no doubt apprehended.

A simple trick and Corporal Surl was taken in. The one called Doctor led him through deception of noise into a carnivorous plant. The acidic digestive juices that it used to try to break down the physical molecules of Corporal Surl had no effect – the strength of Sontaran uniforms is shielded against such attacks and it released him.

I have dispatched Kelner and Surl to deactivate the power source.

Q: NATURE OF KELNER AND SURL'S SUCCESS? ■

The generator was successfully deactivated. Life signs immediately registered on Surl's monitoring equipment. Kelner accompanied him to an area of the TARDIS termed workshop. No reports indicate exactly what happened to Surl – Commander Stor lost all life signs for the corporal. It was as if Corporal Surl had been taken out of time.

Cadet Jago

No other stratagem remains. Total destruction of Gallifrey is the only militarily sound option that can be accepted. The Time Lords cannot be defeated with so few warriors. I shall destroy the world and all its puny inhabitants. A fusion grenade will trigger a chain reaction: the power of a black hole lies within the generators of the planet and once it is released the entire galaxy will be destroyed. The battalion will suffer the same fate, but it will be for the glory of the Sontaran Empire.

The detonation will take place in mere seconds. I will trigger the grenade on the central dais of the Panopticon. The Doctor presents little threat; whatever weapons he holds, it represents no threat to me. It is too late for him to stop me now.

Q: NATURE OF WHAT HAPPENED TO COMMANDER STOR? ■

All data and terminates at this point. Scientists postulate that the weapon Commander Stor saw the Doctor carrying terminated his life. Corporal Surl met the same fate. The legends of the Time Lords speak of a mighty weapon, the D-mat gun, capable of taking beings out of time. It is known that the Key of Rassilon is needed to construct such a device. The Doctor had the key to Rassilon. The battalion suffered no further losses and returned to Sontara when monitor detected the closure of the force barrier. Commander Stor's acclaimed battle record and history of strategic victories have been commemorated with the designation of a memorial adjacent to the Central War Headquarters on Sontara.

SUBMIT VIABLE VICTORIOUS ALTERNATIVE. ■

Eradicate the Doctor at the earliest opportunity.

Cadet Jago

COMPUTER ACCEPTS ANSWER AS CORRECT ■

ADDITIONAL DATA ■

Commander Stor should be noted as the instigator of Sontaran fighter patterns. Ships fly into battle in formations derived from ancient weapons: the spear, the arrow, and the blade. The battalion leading the invasion attempt of Gallifrey flew in the arrow flight pattern.

Scenario Four

Group Marshall Stike's Androgum alliance

Glorious victory lies ahead, a confrontation that will be decisive and final, the Rutan forces will never recover. My battalion will form at the Madillon Cluster and I will lead them into a battle that will change the course of the war. There will be, however, a slight deviation to my plans. I will take a trio of battlecruisers to space station J7 in the Third Zone. If the claims that this Androgum makes are not true, she will pay for her failure with her life.

Q: NATURE OF THE CLAIMS MADE BY THE FEMALE ANDROGUM? ■

Androgums are known to be a race of low-intellect hominid biped, of a heavier bone structure than humans. The biogeneticist and head of projects on the research centre, a Joinson Dastari, succeeded in technologically augmenting a female serving Androgum.

Scientists on the research centre had succeeded in breaking through the barriers of time. Several Androgums had been sent into the time vortex but were not retrieved. Research indicated that the Time Lords had an inherent genetic element in their DNA structure that allowed them to travel in time without fatalities. Androgum Chessene desired the power of time travel and contacted the ninth Sontaran Battle Fleet, offering Group Marshall Stike the unlimited power of time travel in return for the use of his forces.

The Time Lords were known to be preparing to send an emissary to stop the scientists, Kartz and Reimer, experimenting with time travel, fearing disruption to the time continuum. As soon as the Time Lord was secure on board the centre, Chessene would let the Sontaran forces land in the main docking bays.

Cadet Jago

The humanoids proved weak. The security forces were quickly and effectively wiped out. Never have I seen instances of death where total obliteration was so deserved – these beings display no urge to fight whatsoever. The Androgum slaves proved a more interesting challenge – some managed to withstand up to four Photon blasts before their molecular structure showed signs of disintegration.

As predicted, a Time lord is present on board the centre, a being called the Doctor. Major Varl will accompany the Androgum Chessene and her assistant Shockeye to the planet Earth, conveniently situated near the Madillon Cluster, so that I might return to lead my forces to victory at the earliest opportunity. The scientist Dastari has been spared from the slaughter in order to perform the operation on the Time Lord that will single out the chromosome the Sontarans need to conquer time as well as space.

No sign of Sontaran weaponry will be left – the carnage will look as if the Time Lords carried it out. It is widely known that they were demanding that the time experiments should stop, and this, therefore, will be a sign of Gallifreyan retribution.

I will pilot a scout vessel to the Earth and join Major Varl there.

Q: NATURE OF THE OPERATION ON THE TIME LORD? ■

The Time Lords are known to have a symbiotic nuclei within their genetic structure that enables them to pilot time vessels though the outer dimensions. If this element could be distilled, the vessel constructed by Kartz and Reimer could be used by any being implanted with the link. The molecular stabilization in Sontarans would enable them to travel through time itself.

Dastari would proceed to dissect the Doctor cell by cell until the relevant data was discovered. The Doctor would die in the process and remain conscious throughout the operation.

Cadet Jago

Major Varl has sent several reports to me on my flight path. It seems they have landed in a place called Andalusia on an Earth terrain termed Spain. The Androgum Shockeye has displayed a brutal ability to dispose of humans, killing an elderly specimen of the species to gain entrance to the building she inhabits, which is now confirmed as the base for operations. Shockeye is also displaying an insatiable desire to taste the flesh of the humans.

Varl has set up a homing beacon, I land within the hour. I understand from reconnaissance reports that there is sufficient weaponry within the society present on Earth to inflict damage on the scout vessel, therefore I shall shield it with an invisibility barrier on landing.

The Doctor has tried to provoke my anger, challenging me to a duel and casting aspersions on the supreme, infallible name of the Sontarans. He will not succeed, I see that he is trying to gain time and trying to stop the operation.

My impatience grows: time is of the essence and all Dastari seems to do is move medical equipment around the cellar of the building we are stationed in. If I do not return to my battalion soon, there is the chance of a Rutan ambush, which is unthinkable. The operation must take place.

Yet more delays have occurred. A female human has arrived that Chessene detects as having knowledge of the Doctor. This is hardly possible; the human male companion of the Doctor was left for dead on station J7.

Another Time Lord; the same Time Lord! A future incarnation of the Doctor with the human companion I had calculated to be dead on the space station. Whatever the case may be, the other Doctor has inadvertently revealed that Kartz/Reimer time vessel needs to be used only once by a Time Lord for the genetic code we seek to be imprinted on the circuits of the machine, enabling anyone to use it safely after that point. Merely threatening the life of the human companion known as Jamie made the Doctor prime the machine.

I have to kill them: the Jamie human attacked, wounding my leg with a knife, and both of them escaped. Chessene has now been outwitted – the time machine is primed and ready for Varl and myself to return in triumph to the battalion.

This pathetic world will be laid to waste in the wake of our departure, the self-destruct mechanism will be set on the scout vessel and the resulting blast will devastate the surrounding area. A message is being sent to the Sontaran High Command announcing our success. Varl has collected photon cannons from the ship. Before anything else happens, we will hunt down the Doctor of the future and the one called Jamie. Dastari has informed us that they have been sighted in the tunnels leading to the cellar. We will ambush them from behind.

Q: NATURE OF OUTCOME OF ATTACK ON THE DOCTOR AND JAMIE? ■

The attack was an ambush on Group Marshall Stike and Major Varl. Chromic acid gas was used and Major Varl fell in battle. The Androgum Chessene was believed to be responsible. Group Marshal Stike tried to get to the time vessel. The Doctor had tricked him: his attempt to travel back to the battalion failed. The effects of the gas were enhanced. Group Marshall Stike tried to get back to the scout vessel, but succeeded as the self-destruct trigger fired; he was atomized in the resulting blast.

Both Doctors and their relevant companions are believed to have survived the ensuing battle with Chessene. Chessene, Shockeye and Dastari were killed. It is believed that Chessene met the same fate as Group Marshall Stike. Her life was terminated on trying to operate the time vessel, and her physiognomy reverted to that of pre-augmentation.

A Sontaran scout vessel found the bodies of all three figures from the space station. The remains of Group Marshall Stike and Major Varl were ceremoniously burned with full military honours. The battle in the Madillon Cluster is acclaimed as one of the greatest victories of the war to date. Records now refer to the battle as Stike's War.

Cadet Jago

SUBMIT VIABLE VICTORIOUS ALTERNATIVE. ■

Eradicate both Doctors at the earliest opportunity.

Cadet Jago

COMPUTER ACCEPTS ANSWER AS CORRECT. ■

Cadet Jago, you have surpassed all estimations that your battle trainers and instructors gave on your ability to pass the computer tests. The Sontaran High Command has great pleasure in awarding you the ranking of First Officer with the Fourteenth Sontaran Battle Fleet. Your first mission, should you choose to accept it, will be to seek out and destroy the being responsible for the death of the Sontaran warriors whose demise witnessed during your tests. He is known only as the Doctor, and is to be regarded as the second highest-ranking enemy of this race, below the accursed Rutans. You will seek him throughout all known sectors of the universe, and travel to the points that have not been explored by the Sontaran race. Do not let us down.

Speech given by General Pelk

The military graduate induction ceremony

For some unknown reason, First Officer Jago was witnessed by many cadets banging his cranium against the surface of his new battlecruiser.

THE ZYGONS

Gentlemen, there is an undeniable need in all our minds for the creatures of myth and legend. Without them our imaginations would be sterile and dry. The Abominable Snowman, Sasquatch and Bigfoot are all readily dismissed by narrow-minded men, but for other men they are the centre of a vast and complex mystery. There are mysteries, too, closer to home – creatures within these very isles. What of the Loch Ness Monster?

Extract from 'The Forgotten Species', a lecture delivered by Professor Edward Travers

The Royal Geographical Society, December 1980

I have been asked formally to acknowledge that the Ministry of Defence, MI5 and MI6 recognize the public concern about reports of a creature of considerable size in the vicinity of the River Thames. Government scientists have discovered a hallucinogenic fungus in the drinking water for that area.

Government statement, late 1980s

The darkness of night enveloped the very soul of my being. Only the eternal blackness was my companion as I moved to the Chapel of All Prayers, in praise of our mighty Lord. Brother Robert's behaviour in days recent past has brought thoughts of concern to all our minds. When I came upon him that very night, lain face down in the muddy pools below the chapel steps, much despair passed through me. I knew a most fatal accident had befallen him. Never have mine eyes seen such wounds upon a man.

I saw something inhuman, gigantic about the belly and brow, and with line upon line of small craters stretched across his skin of a vile red hue. I fled as fear flowed through my soul. Could this being Brother Robert be? I know not, nor shall I ever know. Fleeing to the nearest shore, Brother Robert was consumed by the depths of his own will.

Abbot Douglas of the Monastery of Loch Ness

Translated from the monastery records – 1518

Moonlight provides a perfect source of illumination for my concealed troops as they wait by the ruined monastery on the shores of Loch Ness. I pay no heed to the ridiculous tales of sea monsters and ghostly monks spread by the peasants – their stories are but cover for Charles the Pretender, the Bonnie Prince himself.

Two figures emerged from the shadows of the building, but Corporal Banks's impetuous desire to succeed caused him to fire his musket too early; the other soldiers took this as the signal to attack and moved in. Both figures stood frozen as the gunfire shattered the relative peace of the night air. Then they tore at their cassocks, revealing the full horror of the creatures beneath. They had heavy dome-shaped heads that were covered in hollow boils; the screams of agony from the lead figure chilled the blood. Its squat hands tried in vain to cover its seeping wounds.

As my men reloaded, the unharmed figure dragged its injured companion towards the water and sank to the depths of the loch. Their bodies did not emerge again.

Account given by Captain P. Stewart

7th Redcoat Battalion, November 1746

The waters were as calm as I'd ever seen them, and that old moon was watching me row; I'd never been one to believe in the gossip about Nessie, so them waters were mine.

The odd bit of dynamite fishing here and there is an ideal way to stock the duke's larder for anything up to a month, and what with no fisherman daring to go near the loch, them fish were mine for the taking. First stick of dynamite brought hundreds to the surface; the second stick surely tripled the number, but that wasn't all that it brought up.

Some stupid devil out swimming must have got caught by the blast. Couldn't figure out for the life of me what he was doing swimming in the middle of the night. I struggled to get my boat alongside him, didn't help with the clouds coming over and blotting out any moonlight. I got him in the boat all right, but there was something odd about him. Best get him to a doctor, I thought.

I ran to get Dr Lennie when we hit the shore. When I returned with enough light to see by, I saw what I had rescued.

It was curled up like a sleeping child, and it wept as death overcame its ghastly body. Riddled with suckers, it was, like some octopus or squid. Its swollen body was tinged with the colours of fire.

It was odd how the man faded away, leaving only stains of water to show he'd ever been there, and even they soon vanished.

The diary of James McRanald

Gamekeeper to the seventh Duke of Forgill

Estimated date: 1914–18

Professor Travers's diary
Loch Ness, Scotland
Those damn fools at the Royal Geographical Society don't question any of my motives now. Any submission requesting a research grant appears in full. So many years have passed, and yet it is only now that I find I have the power to pursue any quest that I desire. The legend of the Loch Ness Monster is the most accessible to me.

The tenth Duke of Forgill, a terribly nice chap, has proved to be most accommodating to a total stranger, allowing me access to his vast library, which in the most part details sightings of the aforementioned creature. Wondrous volumes dating back to the eleventh century line the shelves, from monastic records to the diaries of the duke's late father. But something far more interesting has arisen from my studies.

Another form of creature seems to be present within the loch. It is the same shape and apparent size as a human, yet totally unlike anything known to man. An abundance of sightings exist, all meticulously recorded over the centuries. My mind is full of the intriguing possibilities that now present themselves.

Research study notes

The creatures of Loch Ness

From the relatively demure manta ray to the most vicious of predatorial sharks that roam the depths of the ocean, creatures of a considerable size can sometimes be found to be reliant on ones up to ten times smaller for survival. Is it possible that such a relationship could exist between these beings that have been sighted, and the famous Nessie?

Common assumptions about the Loch Ness Monster tend to avoid its gender. It is believed to be the last of its kind, but is this any reason to rule out the possibility of it being a female? It might be that these other creatures are but the young of the monster.

Whatever their relation with Nessie, it would seem highly likely that they are a semi-aquatic life form. Several accounts of sightings describe the skin coloration as varying from deep red to bright yellow – perhaps they are more reptilian by nature. The presence of what appears to be suckers spread across their entire body would indicate this fact.

All sightings concur that the entire physical shape is similar to a human foetus, underdeveloped and immature. Could these creatures be only at an early stage of their development?

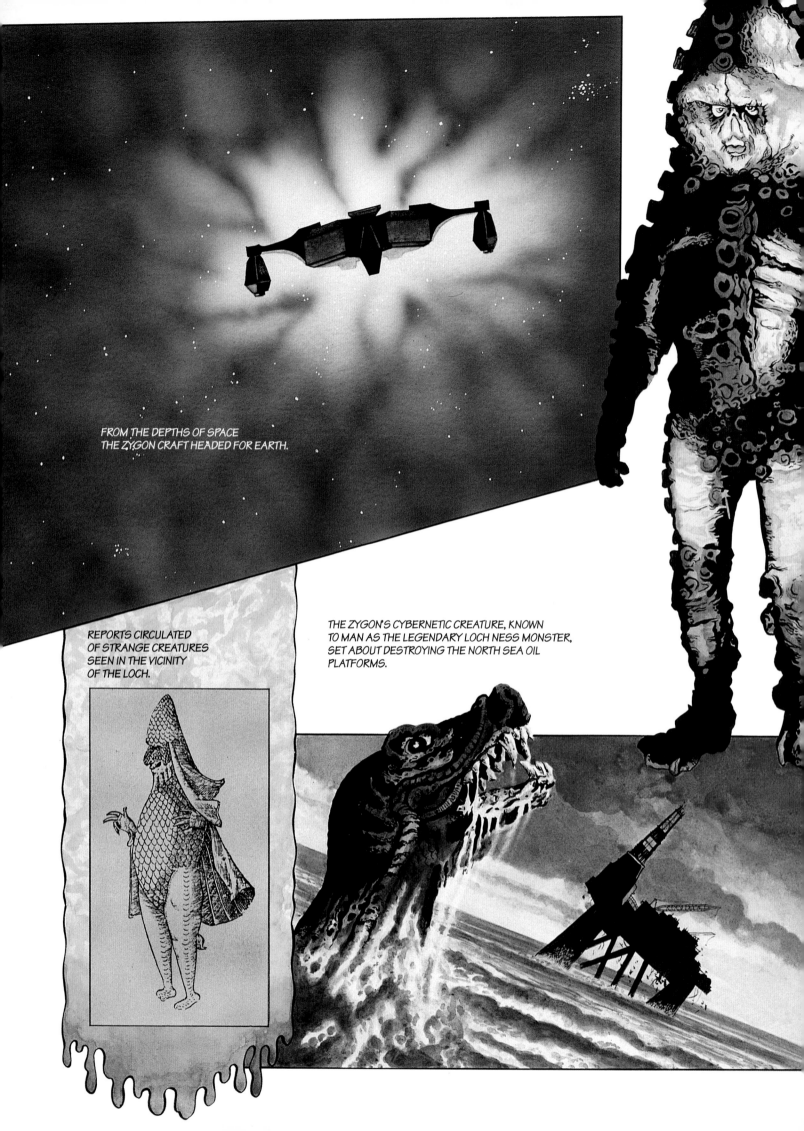

FROM THE DEPTHS OF SPACE
THE ZYGON CRAFT HEADED FOR EARTH.

REPORTS CIRCULATED
OF STRANGE CREATURES
SEEN IN THE VICINITY
OF THE LOCH.

THE ZYGON'S CYBERNETIC CREATURE, KNOWN
TO MAN AS THE LEGENDARY LOCH NESS MONSTER,
SET ABOUT DESTROYING THE NORTH SEA OIL
PLATFORMS.

CENTURIES AGO THE SPACESHIP CRASHED INTO THE STILL WATERS OF LOCH NESS.

FOLLOWING THE DESTRUCTION OF HIS SPACESHIP, THE ZYGON LEADER, BROTON, CAME FACE TO FACE WITH THE DOCTOR FOR A FINAL CONFRONTATION.

Professor Travers's diary
Forgill Castle, Loch Ness
That damnable servant of the Duke's, Caber, seems to follow me everywhere. Keeps muttering about never trusting anyone again. I don't know what could have stirred such hatred in the   man's soul.

Nobody will be drawn to speak on the subject, all I can ascertain is that something happened here a few years ago. As to what? That remains a mystery.

With the Duke and the Caber absent for the day, I shall take the opportunity to examine the journals kept by the Duke. There appears to be an inconsistency in a volume from the mid-1980s – whole months are missing. What could have led to this?

The journal of the Duke of Forgill, volumes IV–VI
August
Several of the groundsmen have alerted me to their growing concern about damage to the foundations of the castle. It is now just over three months since the American mining operation arrived in the area, against my strongest protestations.

Huckle, the man in charge, is arrogant to an extreme. He sees it as the natural right of progress to defile my lands. A certain degree of disturbance is something I could appreciate being part and parcel of such a giant operation; setting up a dozen or so oil-rig platforms in the sea does take time and equipment. However, the looting, poaching and litter that the 'roughneck' workers he has chosen to employ leave in their wake is intolerable.

Underwater detonation to clear rubble for site construction is playing havoc with the castle foundations. With the assistance of the Caber, I shall venture down the old monastery tunnels and see if water has broken through at the lower levels. I must admit that I had no knowledge of the passageway behind the library bookshelves, I have seen no record of it in any of my forefather's journals. I wonder what's down there . . .

Professor Travers's diary
Forgill Castle, Loch Ness
Alas, my time with the Duke has come to an end, I return to London with so very many questions left unanswered. Why was the Duke's journal cut off at that point? Did something happen down the tunnels? There is a gap of months before the entries resume and they make no mention of anything significant. But the biggest mystery of all came as I left the grounds of the estate.

A package, a simple parcel of brown paper and string, encrusted with dust and addressed to me, was found by the Duke as he sorted out the books of his collection. Well, it may provide an interesting anecdote, but it's hardly going to be the material I need to write a bestseller!

I wanted a conclusion, an end to my life of solving the mysteries of the unknown and myths and legends – something to help me go out with the proverbial bang! I doubt very much that this will be it, though.

Taken from the internationally acclaimed, award-winning bestseller by Professor Edward Travers: **The Reality of Myth and Legend**

The Mystery of the Creatures of Loch Ness

Disasters at sea

Drilling for mineral ores and oil in the depths of any ocean is a perilous job at the best of time. It appears that the first ten years or so of operation for the America International Mining Corporation were indeed particularly prosperous, and quickly established the company as the leading light in its industry. The Middle East and the outback of Australia were theirs to conquer, and conquer them they did.

It seemed an all too obvious move to establish a mining operation in the heart of the North Sea, an untapped reservoir of resources. Within seven months, the most structurally indestructible fleet of drilling platforms that had ever been seen stood proudly facing the elements. But three days after operations commenced, the first disaster struck.

The total obliteration of the Neptune rig was regarded by the world press as an unfortunate fluke. The oil slick clinging to the water was the only reminder of Neptune's existence. AIM, with a somewhat cavalier attitude, consoled itself with the fact that although the loss in finances and lives had been heavy, the other rigs under their command were still operational. A week later, the aptly named Atlantis rig vanished. Within a month of the first disaster, a third rig, the Bonnie Prince Charlie, met the same fate.

Panic set in at AIM. An external force was obviously responsible, but there was no way of knowing what it could be. Recorded transmissions from the Bonnie Prince Charlie demonstrated the speed of attack. Speaking to a radio operator at the Hibernian On-Land Headquarters of no more than trivial matters, for solitude can drive men of the bravest of hearts to gossip, an audio assault suddenly cut across the airwaves.

Mere minutes passed before the same on-land operator received a report from a helicopter returning from another rig. Hibernian control was informed that only an oil slick remained. The attack had taken place over no more than two or three minutes, and more importantly, the two- hundred-and-fifty-foot platform had been dragged underwater in the same amount of time.

United Nations Intelligence Taskforce

Specialist help of a most unusual nature was required. Only a handful of operational rigs were now let, and the workforce on each one was understandably less than willing and more than hesitant to remain in AIM's employ. Immediate assumptions ranged from extreme sabotage to acts of terrorism by a rival company.

When MI5 and MI6 feel that a situation is too extreme for their capabilities, an international organization moves in: UNIT, the United Nations Intelligence Taskforce. Speaking from my own personal experiences of working with them, Brigadier Lethbridge-Stewart was certainly the right chap for the job – he's a decent sort of fellow really, but does tend to get a bit carried away with firepower when diplomacy is really required.

Even UNIT, however, got nowhere in its investigation until its scientific adviser was called in. He's not an official operative for UNIT, you understand, but does the taskforce the odd favour by solving unsolvable mysteries now and again.

This adviser likes to be known as the Doctor. He's a terribly nice chap – I've worked with him once or twice myself – who tends to have assistants of varying intelligence quotas. The Scots lad and the sweet girl I met had gone by now; some reporter girl, Sarah Jane Smith, and a Surgeon Lieutenant Sullivan arrived with him at the Tulloch Inn.

Tulloch Moor

Parish records detail mysterious events as far back as the 1600s in this lowland pastoral area. Skeletons in the proverbial closet abound. There are tales of workers and normal villagers disappearing without a trace as thick mist descends upon the village.

A sparse cluster of houses sit on the edge of heather-strewn moorlands, where patches of marshland and steep rock inclines are as equally dangerous as the rumours of prowling wild beasts and creatures of the night that the local inhabitants happily try to chill your blood with.

Owned for centuries by the Dukes of Forgill, the community was shattered by the arrival of the AIM workforce. The small farmlands and cottage industries overseen by the Duke faced incalculable damage. The older villagers quietly sat and watched the community they had strived to preserve, the dignity and nobility they had fought to keep alive, crumble as modern society invaded their lives.

Dismissed as lies and stupid folk tales by the Americans, the myths of Tulloch Moor had no place in the minds of the roughneck workers, and it would be true to say that there was little sorrow in the villagers' hearts as news began to filter through of the disasters the company faced. Questions were asked: did anyone know what could be causing the accidents with the oil rigs? Some people had theories in their heart of hearts, but nobody spoke of them.

The early clues

The inevitable meticulous investigation of the little evidence that was available began, only to be greeted by the disheartening news that a fourth rig had met the same fate as its predecessors The Ben Nevis had total communication breakdown – only a vast oil slick indicated that a rig had ever been in the area. A state of near mutiny was beginning to grown in the ranks of the AIM workers at sea; the workers were well aware that another rig could go down at any second, but the question that preyed on all their minds was 'Will it be ours?'.

UNIT patrol boats began to sight more lightweight pieces of wreckage heading inland, estimating that they should reach the shoreline within hours. The grisly sight of bodies already lining the sand dunes was not expected; bodies had not been recovered from the previous disasters. Fleets of lorries ferried the corpses to the morgue of a nearby hospital, where local doctors tried to find clues to the nature of the accident.

On the Doctor's instigation, Sullivan was despatched to assist them owing to his wide variety of experiences at sea. Journeying by jeep along the coastal road, Sullivan apparently spotted another body on the shoreline, but this was one from the Bonnie Prince Charlie and he was still alive.

It seems that this Sullivan chap was shot at this point: he was only grazed across the skull by the bullet, but it still comes as a bit of a shock. The Duke of Forgill had given ample warnings to the AIM management that his gamekeepers were instructed to shoot intruders who might be poaching. Although Sullivan survived the bullet fired by one such gamekeeper, the rig man was killed.

Of the three main support legs of the Ben Nevis, little remained apart from sizeable chunks of metal, roughly the size and shape of a small boulder. Once particular piece bore the imprint of two large holes, one considerably larger than the other. With the assistance of some plaster of Paris, a mould was produced that accurately showed what had made the holes.

To the mere layman, it was obvious that it was a tooth, but one of gigantic proportions: a spiked molar with a lower-case incisor at the rear of the tooth, similar to the ones found at the back of the jaw of a shark. But that was where the similarity ended. The distinct possibility arose that the assaults were being carried out by a creature, but those of the size required to inflict such damage died out during the late Ice Age.

All thoughts of industrial sabotage vanished when it was realized the threat was far more serious. It was the Doctor who brought a rather more alarming fact to light. It was hardly possible that four attacks within such a short period of time could be random; whatever it was that was making the attacks, it was being controlled by something or someone.

The Zygons

The infamous stretch of land surrounding a lake by the name of Loch Ness lay no more than seven miles away from Tulloch Moor, which was by far the closest community to it. Centuries of sightings, documented in great detail, tell of the Monster of the Loch and the lesser known humanoid creatures that have been seen on the shores. It was only now that the truth of the stories became apparent: they were not speculation or myth as many had scoffed in disbelief; the creatures were all too real and alien.

A squat, heavily built breed, the Zygons are bipeds whose sinuous sponge-like muscular growth allowed them to exert great force owing to the heavy gravity of Earth. A porous lung structure would seem to be evident from the descriptions of their laboured breathing, which is at ease only in a damp atmosphere. With the air above ground lacking much natural dampness, it seems logical to postulate that intense heat may well have proved to be fatal to them.

All descriptions note the suction cups that run along the main bone outlines of their bodies; the cups diminish in size as they spread across the surface of the body. Perhaps these cups are used to absorb moist air, taking it directly into their lungs. An educated guess would point

to the newt as the Earthbound equivalent of such creatures. There is also a slight chromosomal similarity to the chameleon, but the Zygons have far greater abilities than just the ability alter the colour of their skin.

The Loch Ness Monster

It became apparent that great care was being taken to ensure that something could pass by the village without being seen: the Doctor and Sarah Jane Smith had been trapped in a decompression chamber at the hospital by unknown forces while a white mist flooded through the moorland village. Delicate gas seeped into every home and building, sending everyone in the vicinity into a deep sleep.

UNIT had not considered the possibility of this happening. When the Doctor returned, he concluded that whatever force was responsible for the rig disasters was now closing in on them. He had not been trapped in the decompression chamber by accident, Sullivan had disappeared from his hospital bed, and it seems that the trap was a diversion allowing whoever it was who took him time to make good their getaway. It was a damned cunning scheme.

Although tedious to an extreme, a search of all other segments of rig wreck was carried out, if only to determine whether any other teeth marks were present. The operation was more successful than anyone anticipated: in among the barnacles and limpets, a strange organic growth was removed, totally unlike anything the AIM marine biologists had ever seen. It was decided that the Doctor would perhaps be able to identify it.

Organic in structure, with a central mechanized core, it was, in essence, a homing beacon; it was certainly one of the methods employed to summon whatever creature it was that had destroyed the rigs. Further evidence of a recent encounter with the beast was found out on the moors – a UNIT soldier had been crushed to a pulp under the weight of the creature.

That odd contraption – the trilanic activator – started signalling: it was calling the creature. The Doctor took it upon himself to head towards the moors. If the creature moved through the village hunting for the device, the death toll and damage would be truly horrific. If my encounters with the man was anything to judge by, the Doctor has a habit of putting his life at risk, but perhaps even he was surprised to come out of this encounter alive. A creature of prodigious size did, it seems, pursue the device. Trapped in bracken and unable to move, the poor Doctor thought his time was well and truly up, but the device suddenly stopped signalling and the creature returned to its natural home, vanishing into the mists once more. It was not until much later that the cause of this became apparent.

A case of duplication

It was the girl, Sarah Jane Smith, who first encountered the Zygons' ability to transform themselves into an entirely different persona. Exact bodily characteristics, down to every tone of vocal inflection, had been reproduced to an amazingly authentic level. This ability enabled them to gain the confidence of anyone; they could appear as friends or associates, and the one that confronted Sarah took the shape of Sullivan. The Zygons seem to have used this disguise in an attempt to recover their trilanic activator, but the resulting pursuit of Sarah and UNIT troops proved to be fatal. In the throes of death, the figure of Sullivan reverted to its natural form and disintegrated.

Later accounts related by Sullivan for UNIT records related how the transformations were achieved. Any captive human need only be placed inside an alcove and subdued by the creatures' organic technology in order to transfer a body print of the human to any given Zygon. The transformation not only alters the genetic structure of the body, but accommodates for the clothing the captive wears as well, thus completing the illusion.

Sullivan bore witness to the fact that the Zygons held several human captives prior to his own capture: the Duke of Forgill, his servant Caber, and a nurse from the local hospital. This would explain the apparent disappearance of the Duke for several weeks. Exploring his castle's lower crypts for damage from subsidence, he obviously stumbled across the Zygon stronghold. It would seem that his castle had been infiltrated centuries before, with access tunnels from their own base into the building established when the monastery still existed.

The mystery deepens

There had been some concern for a considerable time over the fact that whatever plans UNIT laid, they were discovered and sabotaged with alarming speed. But the untimely death of the landlord of the Tulloch Inn, UNIT's operational headquarters, revealed the root of the problem. A stag's head had been presented to the inn several weeks previously by the duke, which the landlord had accepted with great pride and put on prominent display in the bar. This position allowed the Zygon monitor concealed within the head ample access to all UNIT's plans and deliberations. Fearing that it would be discovered, it was hastily removed when the landlord realized there was something decidedly odd about it. He died as a result of his curiosity.

With the false duke exposed, the Doctor deduced that he could lead them to the Zygons. It seems that the Smith girl was left in the castle, managed to find the passage to the Zygon base below the loch and free Sullivan, damn clever of her. Unfortunately, the Doctor's confrontation with the Duke led to his capture and the poor fellow was whisked down to their base. There was nothing the Brigadier could do about that, and predictably in an act that I find typical of the military mind, he bombarded the loch with depth charges in an attempt to destroy the Zygon base.

The crab ship

What little information that exists on the interior of the Zygon spaceship suggests an entirely different structure from Earth craft of alloys and steel. Zygon technology seems mainly to consist of organically structured tendrils: nodules act as controls, hardened leathery tissue forms walls and chambers, and fluids act as power conductors. The exterior of the ship had all the qualities of a crustacean, to such an extent in fact that it seemed in shape somewhat akin to a vast crab.

The Zygon leader Broton, having repaired his ship sufficiently to make short flights, decided the only course of action, now that he knew his home planet had been destroyed, was to colonize Earth. Its polar caps would be melted away and the temperature and humidity increased to a level more suited to the Zygons. His plans would be helped by the Loch Ness Monster, a creature called the Skarasen that was native to his home planet. Its natural life span had been enhanced by cybernetic implants, and it was now a nearly immortal cyborg.

Broton dared to stretch his spacecraft's power to the very limit as he undertook the flight to the capital of England, London. All detection of the vessel was cut off, with Zygon technology jamming all power throughout the land; the Skarasen followed by sea, homing in on the trilanic activator. Sullivan had proved how easy it was to jam it, distracting it during its pursuit of the Doctor, allowing him to escape.

It's assumed that the Doctor somehow managed to break the blackout signal, allowing a brief transmission to register on the radars UNIT had established at the Post Office Tower in central London. The craft was located in a disused quarry in Brentford, and the order was given to move in.

The heavy artillery was not needed after all; from various vantage points round the sight, UNIT soldiers sent reports in of the Doctor emerging from the portals to one side of the ship. More figures were reported to be emerging from the damp confines of Zygon technology – the Duke of Forgill, the Caber and a nurse. Whatever sabotage the Doctor had inflicted, it was most successful, for the ship's implosion sent shockwaves over a forty-mile radius. The papers, of course, labelled it the 'Brentford Earthquake'.

The Zygons were dead, their hostages recovered alive, but Broton had escaped with a trilanic activator. Still in the form of the Duke of Forgill, he was intent on making a last-ditch attempt to show the world his power.

The creature in the Thames

With the Duke of Forgill acting as the head of the Scottish Energy Commission, and due to speak at the Fourth International Energy Congress, Broton had access to what was perhaps the largest gathering of international powers in the country for that decade. By directing the Skarasen towards Stanbridge House, untold damage and innumerable casualties would result. The repercussions would result in war, perhaps global, weakening the planet prior to a Zygon invasion.

Cornered in the generator room in the building, Broton reverted to his natural form and viciously attacked the Doctor. A simple bullet, however, brought about the Zygon's end. The trilanic activator was thrown to the Skarasen as its head reared from the foaming waters of the Thames; the object of its torment was now destroyed and the creature was free to return to being one of the myths and legends of Loch Ness.

But what of the Zygon fleet that Broton spoke of? Perhaps it will remain drifting in space for eternity, searching for Broton's homing beacon. But nobody really knows what will happen, although it'll be interesting to wait and see . . .

SHOP WINDOW ATTACK PUBLIC

Shop-window dummies throughout the UK. Ani have been patrolling str counter.

The seemingly harmles broke out through shop wi yesterday morning, dress thing from immaculate b to pyjamas.

As mysteriously as t began, however, they app stopped. The dummies

MAN FROM SPACE HELD IN RURAL HOSPITAL

A man believed to be from the stars was being held in the critical ward of an Essex hospital last night.

Blood tests have proved the man is an alien. Medical staff at first thought the samples were animal

A DAILY CHRONICLE EXCLUSIVE REPORT

blood, substituted for the real samples as a practical joke.

Under examination, however, the man has been shown to have two hearts, a discovery that has baffled the medical world.

Top military authorities are believed to be speeding to the hospital to investigate.

U.N.

23rd June, 1911

My Darling Doris,
How are you, its been so busy
...UNIT recently, what with
...had

xxx

![U.N.I.T logo]

UNITED NATIONS INTELLIGENCE TASKFORCE

OFFICIAL REPORT CLASSIFIED AS: TOP SECRET
SUBJECT:

THE AUTONS

REPORT BY OFFICER COMMANDING UNIT FORCES,
UNITED KINGDOM

NHS PLAG
ME COUN
...e beginning to materialize
...mysterious disease were spr
...old, healthy
...es, with
...ries Ltd is donati
...its latest promot
...e research facili

...CHBRIDGE COTTAGE HOSPITAL
ATTENTION OF DR HENDERSON

ACKNOWLEDGE YOUR REPORT OF DISAPPEARANCE OF PATIENT UNDER UNIT GUARD. PATIENT NOW
IDENTIFIED AS DOCTOR OF UNIT SCIENTIFIC STAFF. BELIEVED TO HAVE UNDERGONE ACCIDENT THAT
AFFECTED YOUR EQUIPMENT READINGS, LEADING TO FALSE INFORMATION. DISREGARD AND DESTROY
ALL MEDICAL RECORDS OF PATIENT. NO INFORM...

The all-new revolutionary product of tomorrow. Plastic – it's economic, reliable and resilient. Probably the most flexible friend you'll ever have! Fact: damaged wood is costly to replace. Fact: rusting metal is dangerous and ugly. Plastic is here to replace them all! Plastic replaces the need to worry! All household and industrial goods can be replaced with ease! And it's cheap too! Use plastic now, before it replaces you!

Advertising campaign, January 1970

After extensive research and testing, we can confirm the viability of plastic for use in industry, schools and the home. Contrary to press speculation we can foresee no danger in the use of plastic.

Government endorsement, January 1970

'I'm picking up signals on the radar. Repeat, a formation of meteorites has broken through the outer atmosphere. They did not burn up. The meteorites are heading towards the surface. Geneva has confirmed they are in line with England. Their current speed and heading will bring them down in the North Sea. Just a minute! The meteorites appear to be slowing down. Repeat, the formation of meteorites has decreased speed. It's almost as if they were coming in to land.'

Recorded transmission from UK-based UNIT tracking station

The initial offensive of the Nestene forces
Material drawn from UNIT files and media coverage

Reports last night of a meteor storm over the area have yet to be confirmed by official sources. Numerous sightings of lights in the sky over Essex were filed to the news offices last night, claiming a diamond formation was clearly visible. Further reports suggest the meteorites actually landed in the area, with several sightings narrowing the area down to Oxley Wood on the border of Ashbridge. The area has been cordoned off by soldiers. A government official, when asked about the reason behind this, said it was 'merely operational manoeuvres, no more than that'.

South Essex Times

'This is Captain Munro. UNIT soldiers have searched every sector of Oxley Wood. There are no signs of any meteorite debris yet. There is something strange, though: a police box in the middle of the woods with some chap in strange clothing lying unconscious by its doors. Under Brigadier Lethbridge-Stewart's orders, he's been taken to the Ashbridge Cottage Hospital.

UNIT mobile radio transmission to UNIT HQ

MAN FROM SPACE HELD IN RURAL HOSPITAL

A man believed to be from the stars was being held in the critical ward of an Essex hospital last night.

Blood tests have proved the man is an alien. Medical staff at first thought the samples were animal

A DAILY CHRONICLE EXCLUSIVE REPORT

blood, substituted for the real samples as a practical joke.

Under examination, however, the man has been shown to have two hearts, a discovery that has baffled the medical world.

Top military authorities are believed to be speeding to the hospital to investigate.

'This is Corporal Holmes to UNIT HQ, over. Report for the Brigadier. Private Martin and I have found a poacher, Sam Seeley he calls himself, prowling near the police box. He claims he was only trying to find his animal traps, so we cautioned him and let him go. He claims no knowledge of seeing or hearing about the meteorite landings.'

Mobile radio transmissions to UNIT HQ

UNIT report: For the attention of Brigadier Lethbridge-Stewart

17:00: Orders received to supervise immediate transportation of patient under UNIT guard to UNIT Headquarters, London.

17:14: Dr Henderson, supervisor of treatment to patient, found unconscious in patients quarters. Patient missing.

17:16: Captain Munro discovers ambulance leaving hospital grounds at speed. Presuming the missing patient was within, UNIT troops opened fire on vehicle's tyres, to no avail.

17:18: Missing patient spotted strapped into out-of-control wheelchair speeding down the road to Oxley Wood. Patient gagged, apparent kidnap attempt by unknown parties now unsuccessful.

17:19: Reports received from Corporal Holmes and Private Martin. Opened fire on missing patient, unaware of who he was. Patient believed to be heading for police box where he was first found.

17:30: Patient returned to Ashbridge Cottage Hospital. Dr Henderson's diagnosis shows no more than superficial head wound.

18:00: Police box in Oxley Wood transported to UNIT HQ for safety. Guards increased at hospital.

18:30: Press photographs taken at the hospital returned for UNIT clearance. Captain Munro identifies leader of kidnap attempt on patient. Search through UNIT files instigated for identification. Sections of meteorite retrieved in Oxley Wood sent to UNIT HQ for analysis.

Conclusion: The identity, motivation and current location of the kidnappers remain unknown. Patient now stable.

Analysis of meteorite segments
UNIT Science Division report

The curved shaped of the meteorite fragments suggests they are part of an outer shell. Certainly, the whole object was spherical, with a smooth surface texture. Slightly flattened swellings appear to give it an aerodynamically sound flight ability. The shell itself appears to consist of a resilient plastic, one that could survive the heat of re-entry to the Earth's outer atmosphere.

There was certainly something within the shell, presumably something that dissolved on contact with the Earth's atmosphere when the shell that housed it broke.

'Repeat, receiving your signal. Brigadier Lethbridge-Stewart is unable to take your transmission. He is in conference with General Scobie. Over.'

'There's been an accident. The meteorite found in the wood was on its way to UNIT HQ by jeep. The driver has been killed; the jeep crashed head on into a tree. The meteorite has been taken from the wreckage. Repeat, the meteorite has gone. Soldiers scouting the area found a tramp, intoxicated and apparently terrified, claiming to have seen a man in blue who leapt in front of the jeep and later took a box from the back and fled. But the tramp says the man had no face. Repeat, he says he had no face, over.'

Communications between mobile UNIT forces and UNIT HQ

TELEGRAM

TO ASHBRIDGE COTTAGE HOSPITAL

ATTENTION OF DR HENDERSON

ACKNOWLEDGE YOUR REPORT OF DISAPPEARANCE OF PATIENT UNDER UNIT GUARD. PATIENT NOW

IDENTIFIED AS DOCTOR OF UNIT SCIENTIFIC STAFF. BELIEVED TO HAVE UNDERGONE ACCIDENT THAT

AFFECTED YOUR EQUIPMENT READINGS, LEADING TO FALSE INFORMATION. DISREGARD AND DESTROY

ALL MEDICAL RECORDS OF PATIENT. **NO INFORMATION TO BE DISTRIBUTED TO PRESS.**

Classified UNIT file
The statement of witness Ransom

Note: Ransome was found in the vicinity of Oxley Wood, where he sought help from the staff of the mobile UNIT HQ at the perimeter of the woodland. His state of panic warranted attention of the on-site UNIT physician, who provided large doses of sedative to calm the man down. His story was thought to be of sufficient importance for the attention of Brigadier Lethbridge-Stewart.

Channing — part owner of Autoplastics Ltd. — revealed to be an advanced version of an Auton.

Autoplastics Ltd was established under the directorship of Ransome and his business partner, George Hibbert, joint shareholders and investors. Autoplastic's breakthrough in the coloration of the raw substance found particular success in the toy industry. With a tone of pink dye crossing with yellow and white dye, a formula was created that produced a plastic whose colour was remarkably similar to that of human flesh.

Toy dolls and soldiers were exported all over the globe. Ransome left England for a promotional sales tour of America, but his return to the company six months later appears to have been greeted with several shocks. First, all his carefully selected workforce had been sacked to be replaced by automated machinery. Second, Hibbert had gone into partnership with another company that had bought out Ransome's shares. Ransome was effectively sacked on the spot.

Determined to recover his personal possessions, Ransome broke into the factory. It seemed that the entire building had been altered, with high-tech equipment installed in every available space. None of the machinery seemed relevant to the plastics-producing processes that Ransome knew.

He observed the apparent product of the new company: life-size humanoid wax figures, taller than the average man. The facial features were distorted, with no definition, and the head and visible limbs were totally without hair. The eye sockets on the heads had been left empty, presumably awaiting implants of false ones. The figures wore a navy boiler suit, a scarf and heavy boots.

Miss Shaw and the Doctor investigate the replica of General Scobie at Madam Tussaud's.

Investigating the nature of the main apparatus, a form of glass tank in the centre of the workshop, Ransome was attacked by one of the wax figures. The hand of the figure, five-fingered and flesh-toned, dropped down on a hinge just above the wrist. A form of firing mechanism moved forward from within, firing what appear to been concentrated bolts of electrical energy. Ransome described an echoing sound, similar to a rocket launch, before the ammunition scorched the metal surface of the apparatus at his side.

Conclusion: Confronted with such evidence, Brigadier Lethbridge-Stewart instigated immediate investigation, with the assistance of his scientific advisers, the Doctor [name deleted] and Miss Shaw.

'UNIT mobile division to UNIT HQ. Message from Captain Munro. One of the local villagers from Oxley Wood has come forward with information about another meteorite. It seems that he retrieved it from the woods shortly after it landed. His name is Sam Seeley. We await the arrival of the party from UNIT HQ, an investigation of Seeley's premises will be carried out as soon as possible.'

UNIT mobile radio transmission to UNIT HQ

TELEGRAM

TO UNIT HQ

INVESTIGATION OF SEELEY HOUSE. FIRE EXCHANGED BETWEEN SOLDIERS AND FIGURE ATTACKING HOUSE

FIGURE TRYING TO RETRIEVE METEORITE CONCEALED IN SEELEY'S OUT-BUILDING, SEELEY'S WIFE

INJURED BY FIGURE. FIGURE RETREATED AT SPEED. METEORITE HAS BEEN RETRIEVED BY THE DOCTOR

AND MISS SHAW. UNIT PARTY RETURNING TO HQ.

Analysis of complete meteorite
UNIT Science Division report

The substance within the sphere is hard to identify, but the cerebral activity monitor used to detect movement showed an alarming response. There is an active intelligence within the shell. It is conceivable that the sphere acts as one small part of a vast intelligence, spread throughout the meteorites. When grouped together the power could be devastating.

For such an entity to take on physical form, a shell that could be manipulated by its thoughts would be needed. Autoplastics Ltd specializes in full-size plastic figures, the perfect housing for the minds. If an accurate replica of any particular person was made, and part of the intelligence housed within, an effective duplicate of the human in question could function undetected.

Brigadier Lethbridge-Stewart has requested permission to use more troops to investigate Autoplastics Ltd, previously owned by International Electromatics. General Scobie has turned down all requests for more soldiers in the UK. General Scobie is reported as leaving UNIT HQ with the meteorite, destination unknown. Alert the Brigadier.

Inter-headquarters UNIT communication

The Doctor investigates the activities of Autoplastics Ltd., — discovered to be the Autons's base of operations.

Report of reconnaissance to Madame Tussaud's

Replica of General Scobie in place in museum. Theory of Doctor correct. Museum used to store replicas of politicians and heads of military forces prior to replacement of real counterparts. Paralysed body of real General Scobie stored in museum; the activated replica is at large. The Doctor warns of possibility of imminent attack by Autonoton (Auton) forces.

Officer commanding UNIT forces, Brigadier Lethbridge-Stewert with scientific advisor Miss Shaw.

SHOP WINDOW DUMMIES ATTACK PUBLIC

A DAILY CHRONICLE EXCLUSIVE REPORT

Shop-window dummies have wreaked untold damage and slaughter throughout the UK. Animated dummies armed with lethal weaponry have been patrolling streets and massacring any civilians they encounter.

The seemingly harmless dummies broke out through shop windows early yesterday morning, dressed in anything from immaculate business suits to pyjamas.

As mysteriously as these events began, however, they appear to have stopped. The dummies reportedly dropped to the ground in unison, becoming no more than inanimate plastic once again.

A government cover-up has made the most basic of facts near impossible to obtain. Apparently a top-secret organization prevented the disaster getting beyond control.

UNIT report
The Autoplastics factory

Successful confrontation with Auton forces in factory grounds, 12 wounded UNIT soldiers, 27 dead. Auton defeat came from apparent collapse of power, the Autons reverted to no more than crude plastic dummies.

Assisted by a high-power ECT apparatus, a signal could be generated of sufficient power to neutralize the intelligence present with Autons. Operated by the Doctor, the Auton General Scobie was neutralized and the main gathering of Auton intelligence confronted, the Nestene Consciousness. Apparently protected by the new partner of the factory company, Channing, the meteorite spheres had been gathered en masse in a gestation facility, forming their own single life form to operate from. Both Channing and the Nestene Intelligence were successfully neutralized.

Come, see all the wonders of the circus! The greatest show on Earth! The circus of Luigi Rossini, Maestro of Merriment, King of all Clowns – the Emperor of Entertainment. Come, meet the master of the one and only Rossini Circus.

Advertising campaign, January 1971

The wonders of plastic will never cease. Anything can be made out of plastic – wood, leaves, grass are all easily copied. Even the delicate daffodil!

Advertising campaign, January 1971

Exhibit 301: A Nestene Sphere
National Space Museum tour

Recovered by the United Nations Intelligence Taskforce from Oxley Wood in Essex, this is the one remaining sphere from a swarm of fifty that landed there twelve months ago. Believed to hold part of a vast alien intelligence, it has remained inactive since the rest of the spheres were destroyed.

Future in Space exhibition brochure
Olympia Exhibition Centre, Kensington, London

After cautioning the man, believed to be wearing a black suit, Security Officer Gorman proceeded to try to apprehend the figure as he lifted exhibit 301 from its showcase. Unfortunately, he had not accommodated for the presence of a second party to the crime, a man of rotund features in garish clothing, who rendered the officer unconscious.

Statement of Superintendent Walsh
New Scotland Yard

UNIT file
Investigation of Beacon Hill radar

Brigadier Lethbridge-Stewart, Captain Yates and the Doctor and Miss Grant of the Scientific Unit observed that both radar dishes had been drastically realigned. The upper operations cabin of tower one revealed evidence of sabotage to the programmed operations of the establishment. The Doctor theorized that the Nestene sphere taken from the exhibition had been connected to signalling mechanisms of the radar equipment, projecting the weak signal still within the meteorite into deep space and opening a homing beacon for further Nestene swarms.

The Doctor has identified the cause of the incident: a man who is believed to have encountered the Doctor at some previous time, known only as the Master. Any doubts were soon eradicated on the discovery of one of the missing scientists, Goodge, stored in his own lunch box. UNIT pathology has confirmed the Doctor's deduction that all the cells of the scientist's body had been systematically miniaturized.

UNIT Liaison has issued a description of the Master, as given by security staff from the Olympia exhibition, with a warning that according to the Doctor, the Master can change his appearance at any time.

Memo to all employees of Farrel Industries, Plastics Division

Owing to the imminent modernization of factory premises, all employees are given two days' notice for indefinite leave of absence. Half pay will be dispatched on a weekly basis to all your homes, and work will resume as soon as possible.

Colonel Masters will be joining us from tomorrow as director of Farrel Industries, running operations as usual with Mr Rex Farrel. Colonel Masters will be injecting considerable capital into the company with his introduction of new clients, people who never have enough plastic to fulfil their needs.

UNIT report

Sabotage attack on UNIT HQ

The zinc-lined ammunition box that housed the missing Nestene sphere was recovered from the abandoned car of the second missing scientist from Beacon Hill. A high-density explosive device with a hair-pin trigger timer had been set to detonate as the lid to the box opened; the rusty lid jammed, allowing time to eject the bomb into the river. Miss Grant is now recovering from hypnosis, believed to have been used by the Master to influence her to detonate the device.

Farrel Industries Ltd

Products

The Easy Slumber Chair. A flat black pad of plastic polythene, sensitive to human body temperature, it will inflate into the shape of a reclining chair that will form its base and back to fit around the spinal posture of the occupant.

The Troll Doll. Designed from authentic wood-cuts of early seventeenth-century Norwegian mythology, the troll doll becomes pliable in warm room temperatures, giving the hardened rubber framework within flexibility. In the right temperatures, the creature can be stood on its hind legs and seen to walk through the heat friction of its wire skeleton.

Colonel Masters — alias the Master.

The Troll Doll.

UNIT scientific advisor, codenamed the Doctor, with his assistant Miss Grant.

Note to Colonel Masters from Rex Farrel

It is truly devastating to think that one of our products killed McDermott; he has been with the company as long as I can recall. I am relieved that the product was not tested on the public first.

I wholeheartedly agree with your suggestion of giving the first Troll Doll off the production line to my father. He has always objected to innovation, and is positively distraught about your arrival in the company. Perhaps he will come round to our way of thinking.

UNIT file

The incident at Rossini's Circus

Enquiries in the local district led to the fact that the field where Phillips car had been left (scientist, reported missing from Beacon Hill), had been the site for a travelling circus a week or so previously. Electing to carry out the mission solo, the Doctor used his own transport to travel to Tarminster, the next venue for the circus.

Miss Grant accompanied the Doctor on his trip unofficially; it is also noted that the Doctor was not aware of this fact. She called for back-up assistance immediately the Doctor was apparently being held by officials at the circus for questioning. Brigadier Lethbridge-Stewart is noted as having seconded three F-Class UNIT transportation vehicles to ferry men to the scene. Reports indicate that the Doctor sabotaged the Master's means of transport, and that Phillips died under the influence of the Master's hypnosis.

The intervention of police officers saved the Doctor and Miss Grant from any serious injury, when the workers on the circus site were summoned to deal with him.

Urgent message to mobile UNIT vehicle, for the attention of Brigadier Lethbridge-Stewart. Tarminster police authorities deny all knowledge of sending police escort for the Doctor and Miss Grant. Repeat, it was not a police vehicle that took the Doctor and Miss Grant.

UNIT report
Tarminster Quarry

Strategic retreat after confrontation with Autons in abandoned quarry, one UNIT soldier killed.

Brigadier Lethbridge-Stewert.

The Doctor and Miss Grant were seen in a black Jaguar police vehicle heading towards quarry. F-Class UNIT transportation vehicle carrying Brigadier Lethbridge-Stewart, Captain Yates and one foot soldier apprehended vehicle shortly after its arrival in the quarry.

The police officers were found to be Autons. Fire was exchanged by either side. Captain Yates managed to knock one of the two Autons down a slope estimated at a height of fifty feet; the Auton rose unharmed. UNIT personnel escaped with the loss of one foot soldier.

The Autons were defeated — but the Master avoided capture by UNIT forces and escaped.

The daffodils of peace. Accept one from Farrel Plastic Products as a token of our appreciation to you, the public that has made us one of the most successful plastic suppliers in the United Kingdom. Display it in your home, and as you walk past, breathe in its delicate perfume and think of us, the master of plastic.

Promotional leaflet
Farrel Industries Ltd

MYSTERIOUS DEATHS PLAGUE THE HOME COUNTIES

Alarming reports are beginning to materialize of a series of deaths, as though a mysterious disease were spreading through the land.

Bodies both young and old, healthy and ill are being found in homes, with the cause of death being diagnosed as heart failure, shock or suffocation with no apparent cause.

Top Government scientists are believed to be working non-stop, to determine whether there is a link between the deaths.

In a gesture of respect, Farrel Industries Ltd is donating all money raised from its latest promotional campaign to set up a research facility to investigate the deaths.

Here, at *The Daily Chronicle*, we all carry Farrel's plastic daffodils as a mark of respect. Be sure to buy tomorrow's paper, when you can learn how to get your own daffodil, free with this paper.

Message to Brigadier Lethbridge-Stewart

The Doctor and Miss Grant have discovered a link between the first two deaths. Both deceased worked for Farrel Industries Ltd. John Farrel reported dead. A plastic doll has been retrieved from the scene. Widow reported doll to be jammed in window as though trying to get out. Doll being brought back to UNIT science laboratories for analysis.

UNIT file
Farrel Industries Ltd

Accounts statements indicate massive increase in cash-flow stability over the past three months, and massive expenditure on moulds and materials. Premises abandoned – all staff noted as being on permanent leave of absence. Records on file of Rex Farrel (son of John Farrel, proprietor) indicate the presence of new director, Colonel Masters, and the fact that a fifteen-seat coach has been hired for a promotional tour. Sample of Farrel product: a plastic daffodil, recovered from main office.

The presence of an Auton within the main safe of the office indicates that the working base for the Master has been discovered.

UNIT report
Sabotage attack, Miss Grant

Plastic doll recovered from the Farrel estate became active when subjected to an increase in heat. Its pre-programmed objectives were to kill all humanoid matter, in this case Miss Grant. The attack was stopped by Captain Yates, whose sharp shooting disintegrated the doll.

Unit report
Sabotage attack, the Doctor

A telephone flex under Nestene influence is believed to have wrapped around the throat of scientific adviser the Doctor, attempting strangulation. Brigadier Lethbridge-Stewart stopped assault by disconnecting the phone line. UNIT officials will contact phone company over installation earlier today; contracting company believed to be called Masterson Ltd.

UNIT scientific report
Analysis of Nestene Autojet

Exterior signs indicate the subject as being no more than a refined plastic daffodil. Spectrographic analysis shows pre-programmed instructions imbued into every molecule of its structure. The flower has been set to home in one the facial features of a human.

Triggered by high-frequency signal, the daffodil turns and searches for human tissue. On detection, the bulb of the flower sprays a jet of fine plastic film that adheres instantly to the skin. The victim is suffocated, losing consciousness within minutes and dying within ten. The film evaporates as traces of carbon dioxide come into contact with it.

Owing to the fatal nature of these flowers, a national warning has been issued. Early victims are believed to have set the daffodils off by using short-wave radios.

UNIT report
Tarminster Quarry

UNIT patrols tracked the tour coach used as a distribution point for the daffodils, following it to the site of the earlier Auton confrontation. With no apparent activity visible, Brigadier Lethbridge-Stewart instigated plans for an air strike by the RAF to eradicate the immediate Auton threat. The air strike was aborted owing to the unexpected presence of the Doctor and Miss Grant, who arrived in the company of the Master. The Master was presumably holding them hostage to prevent the air attack.

Boarding the coach, several minutes passed before it moved on, with its destination confirmed as the Beacon Hill radar station. UNIT forces followed by road.

UNIT report
Beacon Hill radar station

Successful confrontation with main Auton forces in field lying adjacent to main Beacon Hill complex: 14 wounded UNIT soldiers, 24 dead.

The Plastic Promotions coach veered off the main road and came to a stop in a field, where Autons, still wearing promotional uniforms, opened fire. Heavy UNIT casualties resulted.

The Master is believed to have retreated to the radio telescope radar facility; the Doctor pursued him to the main control room. Some soldiers report being distracted during the conflict by the moving radar dishes, which both turned into each other forming a large catchment area. The creature that partly materialized within the radar dishes was described at debriefing as the real manifestation of a Nestene. Sightings confirm a globe of bright light, with various tentacles of some description materializing from within. The manifestation vanished at the same moment as the sudden collapse of the Autons, which simply fell to the ground.

Close examination of the bodies revealed featureless Auton heads underneath the grotesque masks that they wore. It is apparent that they were the same type of creature UNIT encountered twelve months ago.

Urgent message to all mobile UNIT groups

Search for a man known simply as the Master, believed to have escaped from the Beacon Hill radar station during conflict with Autons. Descriptions will follow. This man is dangerous. Extreme caution is advised.

LEGEND

THE TIME OF THE NEW WORLD DAWNED. CENTURIES OF EVOLUTION HAD PASSED, AND NOW IT WOULD BE DESTROYED. THE NEW WORLD MOVED THROUGH THE STARS TOWARDS THE EARTH. SILURIAN SCIENTISTS LOOKED TO THE STARS AND KNEW WHAT WOULD BEFALL THEIR RACE.

AS THE NEW WORLD PASSED BY THE EARTH, OCEANS, FORESTS AND THE LAND ON WHICH THEY STOOD WOULD BE TORN FROM THEIR ROOTS. ALL OTHER LIFE WOULD DIE AS THEIR AIR WAS TAKEN.

CAVERNS AND CHAMBERS WERE PREPARED. THE SILURIANS AND THEIR BLOOD COUSINS OF THE SEA WOULD RETREAT TO HIBERNATION. SCIENTIST SILURIANS DEVISED WAYS OF BEING REVIVED AS THE AIR RETURNED.

ALL THE WHILE THE ANCIENT MASTERS OF THE WORLD SLEPT, WAITING FOR THE DAY WHEN THEY WOULD ARISE TO RECLAIM THEIR LANDS AND OCEANS.

BUT AS ALL OF THEIR KIND SLEPT, THE AIR DID NOT LEAVE THE WORLD. THE LIFE FORMS THEY REGARDED AS PETS FLOURISHED, AND WHOLE NEW SPECIES EMERGED, CULMINATING IN THE APPEARANCE OF HOMO SAPIENS.

MAN LOOKED UPON THE NEW WORLD IN THE SKIES AND CALLED IT THE MOON. HE REGARDED THE EARTH AS HIS WORLD.

THE SILURIANS AND THE SEA DEVILS

Is it not the ultimate arrogance of mankind to suppose that we have always been the dominant species of the planet? Could there not have been other species of intelligence and dignity, creatures who knew the grace, the beauty and wisdom of their kind? And could their ancestors now be subject to captivity in our zoological establishments? We cannot say for sure.

Extract taken from the transcript of Mr Darwin's lecture

The Natural History Museum Society Archives

The brand-new underground research complex, buried in the heart of Wenley Moor, for the study of advanced methods of producing sub-atomic energy, was declared open today with a ceremony performed by its director. Dr Lawrence later commented: 'Decades of work lie ahead for all my staff.'

The Derbyshire Echo

The journal of Doctor John Quinn
No date entered
The lower regions of excavation left open by the building operation to construct the research centre has left vast passageways and caverns wide open, ideal pickings for a pot-holer such as myself. I shall endeavour to unearth their infinite mysteries.

Journal entry
One week later, no date entered
The final evening of my casual sojourns to the lower depths has inspired me to continue exploring the area. There is a vast clawed footprint ingrained in the ancient soil of the cave floor – I had no idea creatures of prehistoric times dared venture underground. The possibility of alighting upon further evidence of their presence down here is tantalizing.

I have located new chambers leading even further down. I anticipate their complexity is such that I will have to chart every step of the way for a safe and secure route.

Journal entry
End of month one, no date entered
The unusual warmth of several rock faces on a lower cavern level gave rise to the idea of bringing a thermal-activity probe on my next descent. The water content of pools at that depth has a slightly acidic quality that is quite alarming. A high level of radium activity within the structure of the rock indicates my worst fears are a reality.

The initial firing sequence for the cyclotron atomic generator necessitated a small, but certainly dangerous, degree of nuclear energy being ejected into the rock craters below the building's base. News of a leak of this size must not get out to the national press.

The damp lower atmosphere must be effecting my equipment, because I have readings that indicate the presence of a generator within the rock, one that has absorbed the power that passed through it and become active, but this is hardly possible at these depths.

Journal entry
Seven weeks later, no date entered
I've made contact with them. They're very weak, but they are alive. They've been in there for centuries, perhaps since before the first Ice Age. They need more power, the leakage triggered the machinery that revived one or two of their kind, but they need more. If I can just divert the flow of energy for mere fractions of a second, perhaps it will be enough for their supply. It can be built up in small doses. I dare not risk discovery, but the potential rewards are vast.

In return for bringing their people out of the state of deep sleep, knowledge of ancient times will be mine. Knowledge that man knows nothing of, times so distant that only they can speak of it. I long to see them, but they refuse until they have sufficient power to emerge from their chambers, buried deep in the rock. I will do all I can for them. Perhaps they will be able to provide the missing link.

Medical report
Patient: Spencer, Malcolm

History: Employee of the research facility, recovered from the caverns underneath the station where he was involved in a pot-holing accident. The patient's state on initial recovery was near catatonic, and he has since developed violent tendencies.

Dr Meredith's analysis: Spencer has been deeply traumatized. In rare cases such as Spencer's, the shock reverts the patient's mind to an almost primeval state. The only treatment is a course of sedation with mental stimulation wherever possible to try to bring the patient out of it.

Spencer can be subdued simply by offering him felt-tip pens, which he uses to decorate the walls of his room with intricate designs of creatures and monsters. Some are vaguely familiar, as if they were meant to be prehistoric animals. Whatever the case, Spencer saw something in the caves that has thrown his psyche back years, perhaps millennia. A race memory of man has been broken open in his mind.

Memo from Doctor Lawrence
To all cyclotron maintenance staff

The increased amount of power being drained from the main generator plant has given cause for grave concern by our government supervisors. Coupled with the number of staff breakdowns, mental and physical, that have been occurring over the past few months, I have to tell you that a special investigations team will be arriving shortly. All members of the United Nations Intelligence Taskforce will be given free run of the station; please co-operate with them. Hopefully, their work will not be prolonged, and the set programme of research and work will continue on schedule.

UNIT report
Exploration of cave systems below station

On the Doctor's instigation, a squad of UNIT soldiers, Brigadier Lethbridge-Stewart, and Major Baker of the research centre security accompanied him on a reconnaissance of the caverns.

Major Baker was injured after encountering an unknown figure in the caves. Overcome by fear from a sighting similar to that of Spencer in the medical unit, Major Baker was carried to the sur-face by stretcher and admitted to the centre's hospital. The figure Major Baker opened fire on is believed to have sustained a wound from a bullet. Traces of blood were detected on the cave floor, samples of which were taken for analysis.

UNIT laboratory analysis

Chromosome indications suggest that the sample from the cave is of reptilian origin. Predict larger breed of reptile, adaptable to extreme heat. Approximate body density: equivalent to that of an average humanoid male. Species unknown. Corpuscle count suggests extremely low blood-flow rate. Low blood pressure. Slow heartbeat. Analysis complete.

The journal of Doctor John Quinn
No date entered

It's resting now. I've turned the thermostat up to the hottest temperature possible; it collapsed into a deep sleep once it saw that it was safe. The creature offered the open hand of peace, but that fool Major Baker had to let his military mind override common sense. Fortunately, the bullet wound seems to have healed quickly. The shock to its system of being shot must have sent it into a blind panic, and it fled to the surface, the first of its kind to see the sun for thousands of years. I have so many questions to ask, but I must let it rest.

I now have a sample of their technology to analyze: the calling device the other creatures gave me to help the wounded one find me is made of what appears to be raw metal, not crudely fashioned, but not as refined as the steel of today.

I am surprised the creature managed to avoid the UNIT troops that are swarming over the moors. It is not surprising that the owner of the barn it took refuge in died of fright when he saw it. My cottage had proved to be ideal sanctuary, miles from any other contact, only a select few at the research centre know of its existence. But how the Doctor from UNIT traced me to here, I just don't know.

The creature is stirring. The others instructed me to take it back to the caves as soon as possible, but I'm not prepared to let it go yet. Its appearance is basically what I suspected, a humanoid reptile covered in scales similar to that of a lizard, with mobile claw joints instead of fingers. The third eye on the forehead was not something that I would have predicted; I can-not see any particular purpose for its presence. I have endless questions to ask about their world, their culture and their languages. I must know, whatever the cost.

Memo to UNIT staff
Formal identification of enemy

The species inhabiting the cave systems below the research centre has been identified by the Doctor. Although the actual name of the race is unknown, they shall be referred to in all communications as Silurians, the chain of reptilian life forms that they are believed to have evolved from. Historically noted as having existed during the Palaeozoic Era, they predate the Stone Age and the Ice Age.

If sighted during surveillance of the cave systems, report the position first to headquarters and approach with extreme caution. It is not known whether the creatures possess any form of weapon, but it should be noted that several deaths have already been caused by them.

Emergency. All UNIT troops are to search the complex for Major Baker, head of the research centre security. Baker has been reported as missing from the sick bay. He is armed. Baker was spotted heading towards the caves armed with a rifle. Approach with extreme caution. Message ends.

UNIT file
Minutes of conference

Emergency meeting in mobile UNIT HQ, research centre conference hall, under supervision of Brigadier Lethbridge-Stewart.

Present at meeting: Permanent Under-Secretary Masters, Ministry of Energy/Defence; Dr Lawrence, head of research centre; the Doctor and Miss Shaw of UNIT; Brigadier Lethbridge-Stewart.

The Permanent Under-Secretary has been summoned from head office in London by Dr Lawrence, who wishes to register a formal complaint over UNIT's handling of what he regards as a situation of considerable delicacy. The operations of the centre are running behind schedule, Lawrence insists that the instant removal of UNIT will allow the schedule to be maintained.

Evidence has been presented to the Permanent Under-Secretary of UNIT's belief of a presence of creatures within the cave system under the complex. The evidence has been noted as being far from substantial proof of the claims.

Evidence presented by UNIT's scientific division clarifies the validity of the claims. Having just returned from a recent reconnaissance of the caves, both the Doctor and Miss Shaw are said to have gained access to the concealed chambers inhabited by the creatures, termed Silurians. Certain facts have now been established.

The power losses from the research station are being directed through the rocks to receiving beacons, which channel the energy into equipment used to revive Silurians from what appears to be cryogenic suspension.

Prehistoric carnivores, believed to have been preserved from the same period as the Silurians, are present in the base of the creatures, and are assumed to be responsible for the sightings that induced nervous shock in Major Baker and other hospitalized patients, such as technician Spencer.

A device retrieved from the late assistant director Quinn, of Silurian construction, is believed to have a multi-purpose function. Principally a homing signal, the fluting sound emitted from it is also used to gain entrance and exit from the Silurian chambers, as proved by the Doctor's expedition.

It has been confirmed that the missing Major Baker is held captive by the Silurians.

Permanent Under-Secretary Masters has confirmed that more evidence is needed of a conclusive nature before he can present the relevant facts to the Ministry at Whitehall.

A second expedition to achieve such objectives is currently under way, led by Brigadier Lethbridge-Stewart.

Alert to all UNIT staff. Communications with the search party in the cave system have been severed. The back-up squad has surveyed the area and concluded that a cave-in has blocked both entrance and exit to the tunnel. Derbyshire coal mining authorities are transporting drilling equipment to assist with the rescue mission. Please remain on standby. Message ends.

'Headquarters, this is Patrol Four. Confirm that expedition led by Brigadier Lethbridge-Stewart is now back at research centre. Another sighting has been made at the cave mouth. Major Baker has been seen returning towards Wenley Moor. Repeat, Major Baker is heading back. Over and out.'

Radio transmission received by research centre

Emergency, emergency. All research centre staff that have come into contact with Major Baker since his return are to report to the medical centre. Do not leave the complex. Seek immediate assistance. Repeat, this is an emergency.

UNIT file
Analysis of Silurian encounter

Based on information gathered by the Doctor on his second trip to the Silurian chamber under Wenley Moor, an unknown number of creatures are hibernating within the Silurians' system of storage facilities. Up to twenty of the species are currently revived and mobile.

A system of power ranking for authority exists, denoted by age and degree of scientific knowledge. The eldest of the creatures has expressed a willingness to communicate with humans to try to avoid conflict between the species. A postulation that the creatures could be offered outer desert regions of Earth as a domain has not been ruled out.

As a sign of co-operation, the creatures released the UNIT squad trapped in a cave shaft.

A rebellious faction inherent within the society of creatures is unwilling to integrate with mankind. As a demonstration of their power, Major Baker has been contaminated with a potentially lethal virus. A state of international emergency will be declared if a combative vaccine cannot be found within the next few hours. An error in transporting Major Baker to the Wenley Moor hospital has resulted in the disease claiming four lives. The entire area has been put in quarantine while the Doctor leads the fight to find a cure.

Message to UNIT HQ, Wenley Moor

Permanent Under-Secretary Masters has been found dead near Whitehall. Eighteen cases of the disease have been reported among passengers on Masters's train at Marylebone station, which has now been sealed off.

Incoming message to Wenley Moor Centre

All personnel: if symptoms of blistering facial skin become apparent, or you experience hot and cold flushes, please report to the medical centre. A vaccination should soon be available. The formula will be mass-produced as soon as the Doctor establishes the exact composition of the compound. Urgent! The Doctor has been reported as missing. If he is sighted, please inform Brigadier Lethbridge-Stewart.

UNIT report
Wenley Moor caves

Confrontation with mass Silurian forces attempting to exit from the cave system has been prevented. UNIT casualties total 26 dead, 12 injured.

Emerging from all corners of the cave system, the Silurians moved forward in groups of three. Sheer firepower repelled the attack.

Silurian weaponry consisted of a multi-purpose device within the third eye on the creature's forehead, capable of high-frequency audio vibratory attacks when directed at a human form. Autopsy reports have proved the theory that the sound waves effectively erased the brain, scrambling its structure within the skull and resulting in instantaneous death.

Dr Lawrence, director of the research centre, has fallen victim to the disease. Indications in the search for the Doctor show the possibility that the Silurians have infiltrated the centre and taken him. With ninety per cent of available UNIT troops guarding the cave entrances, the probability of repelling a second invasion of the centre is limited.

UNIT report
Silurian invasion attempt

The futile attempt to stop the Doctor countering the Silurian virus failed. Miss Shaw successfully retrieved a series of formula notations made by the Doctor, allowing MOD scientists the opportunity to find which one of the three worked.

Gaining access to the research centre by burning a hole through the wall, the Silurians returned en masse, holding the Doctor hostage. Certain UNIT casualties and staff fatalities

were sustained before the Doctor negotiated for them to stop killing, threatening to withdraw his reluctant assistance.

Using a device of Silurian construction attached to the cyclotron atomic generator, the power surge of activating the energy source would enable them to destroy the Van Allen Belt that protects the Earth from ultraviolet rays of the sun. Mankind would be wiped out instantly on its destruction and the Silurians would have an environment suited to their reptilian bodies.

Through energizing the cyclotron with too much power, the creatures were deceived into thinking that a thermo-nuclear detonation was about to eradicate the entire surrounding area. After retreating to their hibernation units to preserve their lives, the Doctor successfully realigned the power to a safe level. With the creatures dormant once more, Brigadier Lethbridge-Stewart ordered a high-explosive charge to be planted at key positions through the cave systems. The explosion has sealed the Silurians within their chambers permanently.

The Silurian threat is now regarded as negligible. No immediate operations will be carried out within the range of Wenley Moor until the power station is formally closed down within the next month.

The announcement today by the Ministry of Defence of the sale of the Portsmouth Sea Fort marks the end of a special piece of history. Built during the Second World War as an early warning station, the facility has remained empty for the past thirty years. A high-tech sonar testing facility will be developed after refurbishment and cleaning has finished. A certain degree of explosives will be used to clear the debris from the ocean floor; some small tremors may occur but there is no need for concern.

The **Portsmouth Echo**

Reports are being received of another disaster. The SS *Pevensey Castle* is believed to have vanished. Radar signals suggest that the ship sank at an alarming speed. Divers will be dispatched to search the area as soon as storm conditions clear. Transmissions received before all contact was lost suggest some form of attack behind the disaster. The nature of the attack and its accuracy of this have yet to be confirmed.

Communication sent to Ministry of Defence, London
From Captain Hart RN, HMS* Foxglove, *Portsmouth

The recorded history of Colonel Trenchard CBE
Date unknown

Of course, when I was told I was the only man for the job, I could not help but agree with them. Admiralty chaps recommended me for my years of honourable service to the Navy, and I should jolly well think so as well. Forty years of my life in endless wars, battling for all that Britannia represents, defending her name and country, and they retire me to a desk in Whitehall. I am a man of action, and maintain that age should not stop me from being in charge of operations once again.

I admit that the Hulke Canyon disaster could have been avoided, but my judgment at the time was to send the divers down to that depth. Nobody could have foreseen the implosion effect that the air pressure would cause on their lungs. I took the full responsibility, the press cover-up was maintained and my lips remained sealed. I feel my punishment was my silence, yet it is only now, fifteen years later, that I find myself restored to a position suitable for a man of my capabilities.

So this chap, what is his name, the Master, or something, was caught, and must now pay his dues. I find that the castle on the island is a bit grandiose for a mere prisoner, but it seems the security levels will be such that the isolation and guards are indeed needed to keep this man locked up. UNIT caught him, put him on trial so I understand, but the chap got off lightly. Life imprisonment, and a luxurious term of trial at that. Let's hear what this Master chap has to say for himself. He arrives tomorrow...

Trenchard's records
Date unknown
Well, having spent several weeks in the company of this so called 'epitome of evil incarnate', I feel I am in a position to pass judgement. Personally, he's a jolly nice chap, and tells an interesting story or two after dinner. He may have committed untold atrocities, but you can't judge a fellow for past sins when he repents.

He seems to be the victim of a mass cover-up, something I can relate to all too easily. It seems that there is an enemy contingent, some type of attack being planned against England. George Trenchard is one person who will honour the name of his family to the death, and perhaps assisting the Master to defeat this enemy would restore the name of Trenchard to the respect it deserves.

Trenchard's records
Date unknown
The chap that caught the Master paid a visit to the prisoner today – seems to be a high-ranking figure in UNIT. Had a sweet girl assistant with him . . . I think her name was Grant, Josephine Grant. He seems intrigued by the ship sinkings recently. As the Master has discovered, there is a distinct triangulation pattern that links all three wrecks, and right in the centre of the triangle is an old sea fort. I thought those things were obsolete, must be the last one left.

HMS *Foxglove* to UNIT HQ. Presence of two parties on government private property, claiming to be UNIT scientists. A Doctor and a Miss Grant. The Doctor was trespassing; he was examining a boat retrieved from one of the recent ship disasters. Claims the hole in the hull came from intense heat being fired at it from below the water, and that an aquatic reptile known as a Sea Devil was responsible for the death of one of the two-man sea fort crew and the catatonic state of the second. Please confirm status of personnel in UNIT.

Trenchard's records
Date unknown
When the Master first brought up the subject of getting him out of here for a few hours, I scoffed at the idea. Although I am all for his plans to rid England of the threat that this enemy poses, I shudder to think of the consequences of getting caught. But when he insisted that it was for vital supplies for his plans, I realized the trip was for the good of the safety of the country.

Infiltrating HMS *Foxglove*, with a simple admiral's disguise, our trip was a success. I admit to a certain degree of surprise on finding that infernal Doctor chap and Miss Grant in Captain Hart's office. Using my diplomatic skills of deception, I think I managed to divert their attention while the required stores were obtained. Our return to the castle was as easy as our exit.

Trenchard's records
Noted as same day
It's understandable, what with the Master being a natural man of honour, that he would want to rid himself of the Doctor, and what better way than a sword duel? I suspected that the Doctor realized something was wrong when he turned up here so unexpectedly.

The duel was inconclusive, and rightfully so, in retrospect. It would have been difficult to explain the death of the Master had the Doctor been triumphant. Well, he's the Master's prisoner now, and Miss Grant will soon be apprehended.

To cover up what's happened, I'll inform UNIT that they have left here to return to London. Better let Hart know as well, I suppose.

Alert to all coastguard facilities on the Portsmouth coast. Message from HMS *Foxglove*. A submarine on a mission to investigate for signs of wreckage left by the three recent ship sinkings has vanished from the radar monitors. At the first signs of debris or corpses, contact Captain Hart at the sea base. This is a priority message.

Trenchard's records
Third entry, same day

My sense of pride has led to my downfall yet again. I now realize that the intentions of the Master have been deceptive all along. The equipment from the naval base, a device, he said, that would repel the enemy – it's entirely the reverse, a homing beacon that is calling them to the island.

Those creatures are from beyond my nightmares. Damned giant lizards, covered in netting. Huge gill flaps and staring eyes, green and orange skin, and yet they walked like men. Carried their own weapons, some type of hand-held gun.

I don't know what the Master plans, and I doubt I shall find out. George Trenchard will not be said to have died a coward, the creatures are invading the castle as I write these final words. I wish the Doctor courage and speed in his fight against the Master... I have six cartridges left in my revolver; perhaps I can redeem myself with some of the lives of those creatures before I die.

Report to UNIT headquarters from Captain Hart of HMS *Foxglove* on board the HMS *Oakwood* under the command of Captain Briant

Evidence suggests that the Master has been taken from the prison by the Sea Devils. Colonel Trenchard was found dead, obviously having been involved in a battle to defend his prisoner.

The Doctor instigated a search of the sea bed alongside the sea fort. He descended in a standard class navy diving bell. No signal transmitted from the vessel showed indications of trouble. The bell was elevated from the water at the required speed, the Doctor was no longer in the diving bell. His presence at the current time is unknown. We shall instigate a search immediately.

'This is Robert Walker, Parliamentary Under-Secretary, security code triple K, private message to the Minister. Marcus, this is Bob, I've arrived at HMS *Foxglove*. I'll soon have this farce under control, no need to worry about that. Captain Hart claims to have lost one of his helpers, Doctor something or other . . . Shame, but sacrifices have to be made. If these things are holding him hostage under the sea, he'll get blown to bits with them I'm afraid. They'll be fish food before long. At least these naval types have managed to get a vague idea of where the creature's base is. We'll depth charge the whole area for safety's sake. Suggest a press release: say we found some old Nazi floating mines and detonated them harmlessly, don't want a load of panic over a few lizards, do we now? Pip pip for now, old chap.'

Message dictated and wired to Whitehall from HMS **Foxglove**

Message to HMS *Oakwood* from sea base

Acknowledge your first phase of depth charging is complete. Acknowledge that you have sighted bodies and debris from the creature's base. Stop phase two. Repeat, no more depth charges will be used as long as there is a chance that the missing submarine can be salvaged with its crew.

Those creatures, the Sea Devils. They broke through the hull of the submarine and started ploughing their way through the crew's quarters. Some didn't stand a chance, they just killed them instantly with those weird guns of theirs. The sub was brought into a dock hidden in an underwater cave system. All of the men were filed out and put in cells. Hours, perhaps a day passed, then this chap appears at the air vent, the Doctor or something. He freed us with one of those guns he'd managed to get. Before long the rest of the crew had been released – we all managed to get back to the sub which was surprisingly, still operative. A force of some kind held the sub in the dock and blocked the exit, but the Doctor managed to create a gap in it to allow us a chance to break free.

Statement of Lieutenant Ridgeway, acting commander of missing submarine

HMS *Foxglove* log entry
Entered by Captain Hart, no date given

The Doctor returned to the sea base maintaining that a solution on peaceful grounds was still viable. The Sea Devils are apparently creatures of peace by nature, and their king confided that his race is weak in number and would be unable to take on all the forces that mankind could throw at them. But with the Master on their side, their cause would be helped to such an extent that mankind could very be obliterated.

The creatures have invaded the sea base in force; my troops were taken by surprise and slaughtered. The Master is in need of more parts to repair the creatures' revivification machinery to bring the rest of the Sea Devils out of hibernation.

Before this crisis flared up, I checked with Lethbridge-Stewart at UNIT. It seems that the on-land creatures, the Silurians, posed the same kind of threat. He stipulated that should their colonies across the globe be successfully revived, mankind could be wiped out. It seems that the Silurians were here before man, and wanted their world back; the Sea Devils feel the same way about the situation.

Suffice to say, the Right Honourable Mr Walker MP lost some of his fighting prowess when confronted with the reality of the threat that the creatures represented. From a makeshift prison both he and Miss Grant were imprisoned with myself; I managed to open the air vent of the stationery cupboard so Miss Grant could get free. It seems that the Doctor turned the revivification apparatus against the Sea Devils, too high a frequency I think: the creatures were instantly stunned, allowing enough time for my men to regain hold of the sea base. The creatures have been repelled.

The Master managed to escape from his guard and get away on one of the troop's aqua-bikes; the Doctor was able to use a second one to pursue him.

Whatever happens now, the Sea Devil base will be bombarded by everything the Navy can throw at it. Mr Walker, I'm certain, will see to that.

Report to UNIT HQ from Captain Hart

Although believed dead, the Doctor has been recovered from the sea alive. The Sea Devil base was destroyed by him, triggering an explosive chain reaction in their revivification devices. The Master and the Doctor escaped to the surface in survival suits left in the base by the submarine crew. The Master managed to avoid capture, escaping from the base in a hovercraft. A search party found it abandoned several miles down the coast. His whereabouts are unknown. The Doctor and Miss Grant will be returning to UNIT HQ as soon as matters are tied up here.

United Nations Intelligence Taskforce
Aqua Division
Investigation of Sea Base Four
Date of Transmission 5–1–2084

Headquarters, this is investigation squad two. We have found no survivors on the base. Repeat, all personnel are dead. We are finding reptilian bodies amongst the dead. Two distinct species: one aquatic reptiles, the other dry-land reptiles. There has been an attempt to take over the nuclear capabilities of the base. Death of reptiles caused by hexachromite gas, lethal to all reptiles.

Nuclear missiles noted as being aimed at power blocs. Their launch has been aborted. Launch of missiles would have led to a world-wide nuclear confrontation, eradicating mankind and leaving Earth open for colonization by reptile species. Cause of defeat unknown.

UNIT officer Roberts reported sick, believed to have been affected by high density of gas. On entering storehold, he claims to have seen an ancient Earth police box, which disappeared in front of him.

The Earth Demons

From the time when man first learned the meaning of fear, there have always been demons: demons that wake you at the midnight hour; demons who haunt the thoughts and dreams of those in power; demons that live in the shadows of darkness, and the demons that lie within us all. For they are there: deep, primeval fears; jealousy that drives us to rage. The desire that covets all that is not ours. And the urge to conquer and rule whatever your domain may be. They are all demons of one sort or another. But can they be explained? Are demons all that they seem? Or is there meaning to their existence that man knows nothing of?

Extract from a speech by Professor de Richleau

The Mocata Memorial Lecture on Demonology, Queen's College, Cambridge

'When Beltane comes, tread softly,

For lo, the Prince himself is nigh,

All fear his might; the brave and lofty,

For then their blood will colour the sky.

Did the Dark One come and tread so gently,

Or was it merely a reflection in mine eye?'

Ancient English verse

Extracts from *The Demonologist's Casebook*

From the investigation and research by Miss Olive Hawthorne

Actual physical manifestation at Devil's End

I knew from the moment that Professor Horner announced he intended to excavate the Devil's Hump that there would be problems whose nature few people would understand, let alone be able to confront without dying of fright. The Devil's Hump had long been suspected as the ancient burial site of some long forgotten warrior king, somewhat akin to the discoveries made at Sutton Hoo, but an air of evil and superstition had been associated with the area long before any archaeologists started to express interest.

To the casual onlooker, the Devil's Hump appears to be no more than a small hill. Therefore protestations and petitions from the local villagers were ignored; the team working there even had the audacity to dismiss my knowledge of the area as nonsense. The supernatural heritage of the village church alone bears witness to the history of this particular community.

Every foundation stone bears the blood of sacrificial consecration from the Black Arts; satanic rituals have long been carried out in the cavern beneath what appears to be a normal church. The notoriety of the blood-letting reached Matthew Hopkins, the Witchfinder General, during the 17th century, who travelled from Huntingdon with his loyal followers to purge the area. But the disciples of evil were never found; their hideaway in the church proved most effective.

Word of the evil at Devil's End spread once more in the 18th century during the reign of terror of the Third Lord of Aldbourne. He knew little of the black arts, but relished the excuse they offered for brutality.

Actual sightings of 'something' began to occur towards the end of the 19th century, when Sir Marmaduke Percival opened a mining operation in the gully behind the Goat's Back, which led directly onto the Devil's Hump. Illness struck the miners before the mineral wealth, if any, of the land could be determined. Sir Percival lead a small band of workers barely able to walk, let alone dig, into the tunnel that had been created; only a few came out alive, and those able to talk claimed that the Devil himself had attacked them. So my apprehension concerning the excavation of the Devil's Hump itself is understandable.

Consultation with the talisman of Mercury, and casting the runes on 29 April confirmed that plans to broadcast the opening of the barrow live on BBC3 would bring mass devastation, and let evil into the world. My authority as a White Witch was dismissed as lunacy; nobody took heed of my warnings.

Yet the signs had already been seen. Only a few nights before, Old Josh Wilkins had been trampled by something in the church graveyard. The police later disclosed that every bone in his body had been crushed. I must say that the attitude of the Reverend Magister, on whose sacred grounds the tragedy had taken place, was less than sympathetic, but he had not found favour with the villagers since he suddenly replaced Canon Smallwood. Word spread through the village that Mr Magister was trying to revive the satanic cavern that operated many centuries before.

On the night of the tomb opening, the largest cavern gathering that the village had seen for three hundred years performed a Sabat that brought the presence within the Devil's Hump into the reality of this astral dimension. The death toll at the site was high but, of course, such power does tend to release atmospheric conditions that have adverse effects on the human body. Many of the bodies were found within the tunnels leading to the burial chamber, frozen solid and dead. One, however, survived: the scientist from UNIT made a remarkable recovery.

Some of his assistants found signs of hoof-marks across a field – the marks were of such a vast size that only a being some thirty feet high and weighing several tonnes would be able to make such indentations.

My suspicions of Mr Magister's behaviour had not been without validity; apparently he was using an alias, having been on the run from UNIT for quite some time: his real name is the Master. Using the power of the being he had summoned, a psycho-kinetic heat barrier was placed around the village, some ten miles wide and a mile high, with the church at the centre of the dome. Nothing could get in, and, most certainly, nothing could get out. The entire population was trapped.

The Doctor revealed the secret of the Devil's Hump: over one hundred thousand years ago, a race known as the Daemons arrived on Earth from their homeworld of Daemnos. Now I realize that such statements bear little credence with those of a logical and restricted mentality, but for those who are experienced the actual events that took place in Devil's End, the truth of the matter was all too believable. The Daemons practised a sophisticated science that bore similarities to the ancient satanic rituals of Earth. When they arrived on Earth, they eradicated the Neanderthal primitives to allow mankind to evolve; they gave the Egyptians technology that enabled them to construct pyramids of stone that defy the engineering techniques of today. All knowledge and development of our race through the ages had been assisted by them, and now the last of their kind was residing in the local church in the company of a man whose very nature was a evil as the myths that surround the Daemons. But what of the Devil's Hump itself, and the hollow chamber within?

The actual vessel that carried the Daemon had landed on the site, and over the course of the ensuing centuries gradually miniaturized until it was no bigger than a paving slab, but hundreds of times heavier, of course. It would seem that primitive man built the stone wall surrounding it to form some form of long-forgotten temple of worship, with the fear of the creatures becoming an inherent race memory of mankind. The legends of demons and mythological creatures may well have stemmed from the Daemons. Is it possible that the entire evolution of mythology can be traced back to these beings?

Bok, the stone gargoyle that had sat on the church spire for centuries, was given life through the power of the Daemon, Azal. It now guarded the church with lethal psionic fireballs that it projected from its claw. Within the cellar, a bargaining match that could have altered the face of the planet took place. The Daemon had the power to pass on his powers to the human that proved worthy of them; if a suitable specimen of *homo sapiens* could not be found, it was the law of the Daemons that the planet should be destroyed as a failure.

The Doctor managed to confront the Daemon, if only to rescue his pretty young assistant, a Miss Josephine Grant, from the human sacrifice that the Master was perfectly happy to turn her into. It seems that Azal realized the Doctor was equal in both intelligence and guile to the Master and offered him the power of his race, but this met with a blank refusal. Alas this only caused Azal to offer the power to the Master and decide to destroy the Doctor. Thankfully, the brave young girl, Jo, defended the Doctor and offered herself to take his place. Obviously a creature of the most pure forms of logic, Azal could not comprehend the willingness on her part to end her life to save that of another; it was the same raw emotional power that surged through the creature, the kind generated by the cavern that summoned him in the first place, only far more powerful. Azal imploded as a result of his confusion.

The fund-raising to rebuild the church is now well under way; I'm afraid a complete reconstruction is needed after the devastation that his death caused. The heat dome vanished, Bok became stone once more, and the May Day celebrations were allowed to continue in the time honoured tradition of relative peace.

The whole experience demonstrates two important factors. First, there is conclusive proof for those of an open mind and sufficient understanding that the life on the stars is not the proverbial little green man, and that there are far more complex powers in the physical and astral universe. Second, the Doctor from UNIT always seems to be on hand to solve the relevant dilemma that the creatures in question represent.

Actual physical manifestation through Fendahleen possession

I paid little attention to the announcement that a Professor Adam Colby was leading an archaeological expedition to the desert regions of Kilimanjaro, in Kenya, when *The Times* re-

ported news of his departure. What the press failed to ascertain was the level of success he had, and no one realized the implications at the time when what appeared to be a fairly common fossilized skull of the Jurassic era was excavated. The Nobel Prize-winning scientist joined the research programme at Fetch Priory, a small isolated scientific unit in the heart of rural England in a village called Fetchborough.

Run by the famous Dr Fendelman with financial resources provided by his multi-billion-pound electronic engineering conglomerate, the team at the priory aimed to establish the exact age of the skull and any possible evolution implications. This is where a most peculiar fact arises: the skull was estimated to be over twelve million years old, easily predating the first form of man to have walked on the Earth by some eight million years. And this in turn raised questions about the very nature of what is commonly regarded as the expected evolution of man.

Ten years previously, Doctor Fendelman worked on the reprogramming work to phase out any unstable elements in the power units of missiles. Certain equipment detected the presence of a sonic shadow, in effect an image of the weapon after it had taken off. The theory of such detection was developed until a device was constructed that could trace time backwards through sonic waves. This time scanner was capable of going back far enough to present images of the moment of death that took the life of the original owner of the skull. To avoid solar wave disruption, with heat from the sun distorting the sonic waves, all experiments had to be carried out at night.

There is a postulation, and it must be regarded as no more than that because no facts exist to validate it, that the skull may have influenced the cycle of human evolution itself. Traces of the time scanner indicated signs of a massive in-pouring of energy at the moment of death, centring on the cranium, which when X-rayed by Dr Fendelman, was found to have a pentagram ingrained in the dome of the head. It acted as a neuro-relay, a homing beacon for something, somewhere to find when the energy present within became reactivated.

It is theorized, and I am not one to question it, that the skull was not only from another culture, but from another world. My experiences with the Daemons taught me not to dismiss such things. The Fendahl, the nature of the species that projected the skull to earth, should they have lived, would surely have destroyed mankind. They are a gestalt life form – twelve mobile creatures with a central core, indestructible singly, and deadly when grouped together.

The Fendahl was an entity that fed on the essence of life itself, draining all the energy from any victim that crossed its track. When manifested, the creatures appeared somewhat akin to a mutated green caterpillar, with the upper torso giving way to a cavity of tendrils, through which life itself could be absorbed. But to enter this world, it needed a human core to house the central intelligence of the being, with the creatures acting like drones to feed it energy they gathered.

Doctor Thea Ransome had acted as assistant to Doctor Fendelman for a considerable time, and it was she whom the Fendahl possessed. They were brought into a state of complete physical manifestation through her by the energy of a black magic cavern. Another of Doctor Fendelman's scientists, a Doctor Maximillian Stael, realized the potential power of controlling the creatures. A cavern gathered in the cellar of Fetch Priory, the skull was electronically linked to the time scanner, creating a channel for the Fendahl to pass through, and Miss Ransome became a radiant angel of death. Had it not been for the intervention of the Doctor from UNIT and another assistant, Leela, Earth would surely have been doomed.

The Doctor encountered at first hand the methods of how the Fendahl creatures killed, using a form of telepathic paralysis that held a victim until their rather slow power of movement enabled them to reach and absorb their captive. Rock salt fired from a shotgun proved an admirable defence that allowed people to escape, and I must say that rock salt is a traditional weapon for the banishing of evil spirits, although not normally with a high velocity shotgun. To stop the Fendahl before they accumulated enough power from the time scanner's power banks to be able to leave the priory grounds, the Doctor created a controlled implosion with the equipment from the main lab, eradicating the threat permanently.

As for the skull, the Doctor apparently chose to dispose of it in his own way – something to do with a special furnace, a supernova. I'm told by sources close to the events that the creatures still do exist in the realms of unexplored space; according to the Doctor their home world of Planet 5 was trapped in something called a time-loop, and I just haven't got a clue as to what that is!

Manifestation reactivation in the village of Little Hodcombe

Instruments of war have always been part of any battle that has ever been fought through history, be they muskets to rifles, or spears to machine-guns, but I have always felt it is rather arrogant of mankind to assume that they can create the ultimate weapon, for surely that is something that will never be created: Death itself already exists. What, though, of a creature that projected psionic power to incite war? A being that feeds off the boiling hatred between opposing sides, growing in its own power to ensure death on both sides? Such a beast has been here for untold centuries: malice, malicious – words of hatred and anger – stem from an ancient, long forgotten name, the Malus.

A genetically engineered demon from an advanced, unknown race that lays lands to waste to make way for a greater invasion, the Malus was sent as part of an invasion that never happened. It came to rest in the village of Little Hodcombe in 1643, when the English Civil War reached its peak of ferocity. Fear lay in the hearts of the men that fought that battle, not fear of battle nor of death, but fear of the terrible vision they saw in the skies – the gargoyle face in the thunder clouds above. Gorged on the energy it had absorbed from death, the Malus slept, but the brave survivors of the village had no intention of ever letting it roam free to create war again.

The Malus was buried; a hill was built around it, and a church of the most consecrated stones was built round the head of the foul beast. Over two hundred and forty years passed. The First and Second World Wars came and went and the creature did not stir.

Professor Verney moved to Little Hodcombe to carry out research into the legends that surrounded the creature, finding the church overflowing with wood and stone carvings depicting the savagery that it caused. It was he who discovered what lay behind the walls of the church pulpit. The village magistrate, Sir George Hutchinson, a veteran war hero whose reputation for lack of mercy during his time at the Crown Courts of London ensured that he was posted to where he could cause least harm, was summoned by Verney. The disturbed nature of his mind reactivated the Malus's consciousness. Sightings of aged creatures and ghosts began to spring up throughout the community, as the Malus fed on their fears, projecting psychic images of their worst nightmares to draw energy.

Sir George studied the findings of Verney, and realized the potential power that would be released should the creature be freed. With the annual village pageant imminent, a war game celebrating the original battle that the Malus caused would create enough hatred and fear for it to break free from its prison. Verney found himself imprisoned so that nothing could stand in the way of the magistrate.

When anniversary day came, the walls of the church finally began to decay as the Malus's strength grew. The past began to merge with the present in the confused scenario, as villagers from 1643 were brought forward by the Malus, blending the world it knew with the one it intended to destroy.

It seems that my associate from UNIT arrived at the village – one of his companions was a relative of Verney's – and quickly discovered what was happening. The insanity began to burn through the mind of Sir George as the intensity of the creature's desire to break free grew; some way of blocking the mental link it had with all villagers had to be established before a repeat of the bloodshed from centuries before took place.

Technology has always been something that, as a subject matter for conversation and debate, eluded me completely, so I shall not pretend to explain the obvious level of sophistication involved in the equipment that the Doctor used to block the Malus's thought waves, jamming whatever kind of frequency it was that the accursed creature used to torment the minds of the villagers. It does seem to be rather the case that the Malus did not take to this concept very well; it turned its attentions on the Doctor and his companions, unsuccessfully trying to kill them as the Church began to crumble around them. One victim that was claimed was Sir George, who died as his tormented sanity broke under the influence of the Malus.

As to whether this creature was the only one of its kind, that is a question that nobody can answer. Certainly it is worth considering what happened in Little Hodcombe if ever another war breaks out.

Complete demonic manifestation at Carbury Castle

The legends of King Arthur and the myths that surround his name have been told incalculable times throughout the course of history, twisted and distorted until they are beyond recognition, with the facts of the truth lost in the realms of story-telling. The noble King fought his last and bloody battle on the shores of the heralded Lake Vortigern, where the son of his mortal enemy, Morgaine, slew him. Words tell of how the day will come when good King Arthur will rise once again, to lead his people to triumph in battle.

The battle between Morgaine, a witch priestess of the most malevolent power and cruelty, and the King's sorcerer, Merlin, never came to what could be termed a satisfactory conclusion. The tales of the past come to a halt when she banished Merlin to be frozen in the ice caves. I have proof that this was far from their last battlefield; their war stretched beyond the laws of time and death, drawing them to return to Lake Vortigern centuries later, in our modern age of technology.

During the late summer of 1999, the world was on the brink of catastrophe as the peace talks between world powers broke down yet again, but few realized that powers far greater than theirs combined had returned.

Beyond the terror of mere demons lies another form of being, creatures that evil itself cannot control, dark forces that absorb worlds and feed on them: they are the Destroyers. Through ancient powers, Morgaine held one as her slave, and it was the Destroyer that she summoned to eradicate Merlin. The silver chains that bound its limbs were the only thing that prevented the Destroyer unleashing its wrath on her – that and the fact that it had dwelt in her heart for centuries.

The power that Morgaine sought lay within Excalibur, the ancient sword of Arthur, which he used until he returned it to the Lady of the Lake. It has lain undiscovered for centuries, until, that is, the Doctor retrieved it.

When Morgaine's and Arthur's knights returned for the final battle by the shores of the lake, it was the Doctor's companion, a girl known only as Ace, who first beheld the Destroyer as Morgaine brought him into this world. It appeared as a towering presence of reptilian blue, with curled black horns. Its power grew as it fed on the death and slaughter of knights and UNIT soldiers, until Morgaine finally freed it to destroy Merlin. Why she thought the Doctor was he is something that quite eludes me.

The Destroyer's silver armour shattered as easily the creature's chains, the enchantment broke and the creature's mind soared free. It prepared to unleash its power on a world that had not seen its like for untold centuries. It was Brigadier Lethbridge-Stewart who confronted it, armed with weapons that legends said killed werewolves and creatures of the night: silver bullets. The critical moment was right, the bullets pierced the Destroyer's heart before the energy could be channelled, allowing the Brigadier to escape before energy exploded from every pore of the creature's body and wrecked the remains of Carbury Castle. With her main force destroyed and her forces wiped out, it seems that Morgaine was captured by UNIT, unable to be victorious after centuries of waiting and torment. My sources tell me something about these knights and Morgaine actually being from another dimension, where the Doctor was actually Merlin in his own future, which is our past that never happened except in another dimension. Or something like that, I'm not exactly sure myself.

Actual revivification of dead matter into vampiric manifestation

The term 'vampire' has been damaged beyond repair by the works of Bram Stoker, whose many imitators have, if anything, only accentuated the problem. The undead, those drinkers of blood that spend our waking hours in coffins, are very popular yet false mythology. The general public has an inbred ability to dismiss the unknown, and that which cannot be understood. It is harsh indeed to dismiss something as nonsense when it so nearly succeeded in taking over England when the country was at its most vulnerable, at the height of the Second World War.

To fully understand what the bleak months of 1943 uncovered off the coast of North Yorkshire, my research stretched back to the earliest records kept by the parish of the village

off Maiden's Point. Most coastal regions of the country were affected during the time of the Viking invasions, and many settlers' ancestors can still be traced through to the modern society of today, although of course, they have little knowledge of the relevance of their roots.

Not all Vikings came to invade; some sought refuge. The ones who came to Maiden's Point, then named Bay of Maidens, had lost numerous men to the curse that followed them. It was a curse that would lay in wait for centuries.

As with many cases that I have investigated, the ancestors who stayed in the area where any given phenomena may have manifested showed definite evidence of race memory. Even today, over fifty years after the events during the war, the name of Maiden's Point still brings warnings from the villagers to stay clear, with threats of disturbing the inherent evil that may still be in the waters. I am certainly not the person to dispel such superstition, it is a rare commodity in these times and I embrace it with all my heart.

The power of Fenric, an ancient and twisted force of pure evil, was loosed after centuries of imprisonment. Like a ghastly parody of the djinn of the Arabian Tales, a simple bottle had held Fenric.

Through methods that are hard to comprehend, even on a metaphysical level, Fenric reached into the future of Earth, to the moment that mankind no longer existed. Only one being remained. Hundreds of thousands of years of unrelenting industrial pollution had finally taken their toll, reducing the lands and oceans to no more than a sea of boiling, acidic waste. Yet one creature survived, one that would become known as the Ancient One, a Haemovore, a creature that relied on blood to live, and yet despaired at the fate of his kind. There was nothing he could do but watch the final death throes of the planet, until Fenric drew him away.

Carried back through the history of the Earth in a storm of time, the Ancient One found a world he could neither comprehend nor understand. All it knew was that it had to wait for Fenric. Humans were abundant, and his need for the natural plasma the body produces could readily be satisfied, so it was there in Transylvania during the ninth century that the legends of the vampire were born. The creature followed the bottle as it travelled through various countries in the hands of various races; each one was affected by the curse that the creature brought with it. If it fed, the victims became one of its kind, following the Ancient One wherever the bottle led it, and eventually to the Bay of Maidens.

A naval base developing chemical weapons in the area housed the latest equipment that technology could offer: the ULTIMA machine, a code-breaker to decipher German radio transmissions. Its crippled inventor, Doctor Judson, had spent time studying the legends that surrounded the area; when the bottle containing Fenric was found in the church crypts, he made a final, fatal mistake of connecting it to the machine. Fenric broke free and entered his body – at long last it had a new mobility and could continue its plan. The call came and the Haemovores rose from the depths, laying waste to the population of the area and slaughtering the troops at the base.

Although decay had set in to the flesh and limbs of the Ancient One, he rose to answer Fenric. A confrontation between the Ancient One and Fenric saved the future of the Earth: the Ancient One took its own life and destroyed Fenric. The Haemovores, who had followed it through untold centuries, were destroyed.

In a sense, a temporal paradox had been formed with the Ancient One existing both in 1943 and at the end of the world: if it died in the past, how could it exist in the future? Perhaps the realization that its sacrifice would break the temporal trap and possibly avert the future made the Ancient One take its life, but the question as to whether the Earth will die in the manner that this creature saw it is something that nobody in this lifetime will discover.

One puzzle remains, perhaps more perplexing than the entire mystery of the Haemovores put together. How is it that the Doctor chap from UNIT could be present in 1943, and, if legends are correct, have imprisoned Fenric in the flask centuries before? I can accept that the chap I knew at Devil's End was old enough to have worked for Naval Intelligence during the war, but not that he had lived centuries before. That would make him hundreds of years old, and we know that such a thing is just not possible. Don't we?

APPENDIX:

The Monster Makers

As long as the need for dreams stays within us, there will always be monsters. For surely the imagination would die if there were not things to scare us, things that we did not understand or believe in. The mind is a desolate place as sleep overcomes it, and it is up to creatures, the beasts that stalk the land of dreams, to bring us back to reality. If there is one man who can truthfully say that he has never been frightened, made to jump or get alarmed by monstrous and creepy thoughts, he's probably lying!'

James Thurber

The shadows that loom upon us up the wall,

The creatures that stand towering, dwarfing all,

Are they real? Are they just imagination?

Is it just some form of mental prestidigitation?

Surely not, for I hear your answer as you call,

The power to make monsters lies within us all!'

John Hawksworth

From 'The Dreams of Distant Monsters'

Introduction

Before this section of the book was put together, I came to two conclusions. First, to cover the production history of each one of the stories covered in the first part of this book would take a volume. Second, there is a vast amount of material already available on this subject, so each chapter of *The Monster Makers* is divided into the following sub-sections:

Production data

A brief analysis of the behind-the-scenes work on each relevant story that went into creating the monsters, varying from details of how the costumes were made to problems that were experienced on set during filming. Much of this material has been drawn from the memories and anecdotes of people who worked on the programme at the time.

Technical data

Each story has detailed listings of the studio work for each episode, with 'film inserts' denoting that either model work or location material was later edited into footage shot during that recording session. Take note of the varying amounts of time the production teams had between filming the episode and getting it ready to broadcast: the early stories have little under a few weeks and the later ones have months. In some instances, there were only a matter of days before transmission was scheduled.

During the reigns of the first, second, third and fourth Doctors, stories were usually recorded with one episode per filming day. This changed in later years as stories were shot in blocks: all the scenes on any set used in a story were filmed in one go, thereby shooting the story out of sequence. Dates for the recording blocks are noted for later stories rather than trying to divide up what was shot for any one episode on the day in question.

Broadcast dates

The transmission date and time are listed for the first screenings of each episode. Stories marked with an asterisk indicate that the story was repeated at a later date; this information has not been listed owing to the amount of space the information would take up.

Cast details and production credits

Basic cast lists give all the names of actors with speaking parts denoted in the original scripts. Listings of all the extras and walk-on performers would be too vast to list here, but emphasis has been made on listing all actors who played the monsters in each story. The production credits give a basic indication of who worked on the main elements of a production.

Additional data

Notes of the novelizations and video releases are given after each story, along with any other details of interest.

THE ICE WARRIORS

Production data

The prospect was now a reality that there would be no more Dalek stories beyond *Evil of the Daleks* at the climax of the fourth season of the programme. Terry Nation was taking his creations to America to try to instigate production on their own series, so *Doctor Who*'s producer, Innes Lloyd, set about bringing a veritable army of new monsters to the screen for the good Doctor to fight. It was 1967; *Doctor Who* was entering its fifth year of production.

Writer Brian Hayles had already worked on two scripts during Innes Lloyd's time with the series – *The Celestial Toymaker*, which was filmed for the third season, and *The Smugglers*, which was broadcast at the start of the fourth season – so he was quickly commissioned to create a new monster.

The basic idea of the Ice Warriors was triggered by an article based on science fact. Lloyd always tried to ensure that his writers brought realistic elements into their work, no matter how fantastic, so that there was an element of reality that the audience could relate to. In Hayles's case, it came from the story of some Soviet scientists discovering the body of a baby mammoth perfectly preserved in ice.

Above: **An Ice Warrior.**

Left: **Ice Warrior Zondal (Roger Jones) stands beside the sonic cannon in *The Ice Warriors*.**

Above: **Bernard Bresslaw in his Ice Warrior costume, holds his young son.**

Hayles's original concept of the Ice Warriors, however, made them partly cybernetic beings, but the idea of wiring round the throat that lit up when the Martians spoke bore too close a similarity to the Cybermen, who were also appearing in season five. The final appearance of the noble warlords, as seen on screen, was developed by costume designer Martin Baugh, who was intent on giving them a more reptilian look.

Derek Martinus, the director chosen for the first story, had also overseen the Cybermen's debut in *The Tenth Planet*. He ensured that all the actors hired to play the human characters were far shorter than those playing the Ice Warriors, to emphasize the aliens' size and power. These were creatures of nobility and heraldry, an intelligent species that was radically different from some of the earlier monsters in the series. They were a success, and proved popular enough to warrant a return during the next season.

With the advent of *The Seeds of Death*, a stock company of Ice Warrior actors began to form. Alan Bennion played the scheming Slaar in his first appearance as an Ice Lord, while Sonny Caldinez returned as an Ice Warrior after playing one in the previous story.

The costumes for this story were the same heavy fibreglass shells that Baugh had developed. The heavy rubber leggings were supported across the shoulders by strong braces, which the sleeves could be clipped on to when pulled up to neck level. The bulky body armour could then be fitted over this, with the helmet being fitted last, after suitably reptilian skin had been added to the only visible part of the actor, his lips. In fact, the materials used to make the suits was so difficult to control that their construction was handled by an industrial engineering firm, which was well experienced with such things for making boats and so on, but seldom, if ever, for making monsters!

The Ice Lord's sleek appearance was achieved through less arduous means, with a simple body suit, somewhat similar to a diving suit, with the chin and neck of the actor covered in the reptilian flesh, owing to the exposure of that area from the design of the character's high-domed helmet. Both types of creature retained the claw-like pincers. Like Martinus before him, director Michael Ferguson hired actors who were easily dwarfed by the Martian invaders.

The effects of the sonic weapons clamped to the Ice Warriors' wrists were perhaps the simplest effect to achieve in both of these complex stories. The actor subjected to internal sonic distortion was simply filmed in the reflection of laminated foil; when this was tapped from behind it created the effect of the body twisting and distorting.

Only a single warrior and Ice Lord appeared in *The Curse of Peladon*, with Caldinez and Bennion now firmly established in their roles. With this story marking the first colour appearance of the creatures, the Ice Lord's body suit showed a unified colour scheme that was far brighter than that of the normal warrior, which had been a basic bottle green colour from the first story onwards. The colour scheme was deliberately changed to darker shades between this and Bennion's final appearance to date in the next story. The addition of a flowing cape added more bulk to the Ice Lord, who had seemed considerably weaker than his warriors in their first appearance together.

Several of the older costumes were repaired and brought out of retirement for *The Monster of Peladon*, including the distinctive one worn by *Carry On* film star Bernard Bresslaw as Varga in The *Ice Warriors*, but the suit that represented the leader of Ice Warrior forces was now no more than a trooper's. It is sad to note that when preparations were underway for the aborted story *Mission to Magnus*, which would have teamed the Ice Warriors with Sil, a check with the costume storage facilities at the BBC revealed that only one original suit had survived.

Technical Data

The Ice Warriors
Production code 00, season five, six episodes

Episode one
Studio recording on 21 October 1967
Rehearsal 10.30 a.m.–1 p.m., 2 p.m.–7 p.m.
Studio filming 8.30 p.m.–9.45 p.m.
Studio D at Lime Grove on 2in tape, filmed inserts
Broadcast Saturday 11th November 1967, BBC1 5.25 p.m.–5.50 p.m.

Episode two
Studio recording on 28 October 1967
Rehearsal and studio filming as episode one
Broadcast Saturday 18 November 1967, BBC1 5.25 p.m.–5.50 p.m.

Episode three
Studio recording on 4 November 1967
Rehearsal and studio filming as episode one
Broadcast Saturday 25 November 1967, BBC1 5.25 p.m.–5.50 p.m.

Episode four
Studio recording on 11 November 1967
Rehearsal and studio filming as episode one
Broadcast Saturday 2 December 1967, BBC1 5.25 p.m.–5.50 p.m.

Episode five
Studio recording on 18 November 1967
Rehearsal and studio filming as episode one
Broadcast Saturday 9 December 1967, BBC1 5.25 p.m.–5.50 p.m.

Episode six
Studio recording on 25 November 1967
Rehearsal and studio filming as episode one
Broadcast Saturday 16th December 1967, BBC1 5.25 p.m.–5.50 p.m.

Cast: Patrick Troughton (the Doctor); Frazer Hines (Jamie); Deborah Watling (Victoria); Peter Barkworth (Leader Clent); Wendy Gifford (Miss Garrett); George Waring (Arden); Malcolm Taylor (Walters); Peter Diamond (Davis); Angus Lennie (Storr); Peter Sallis (Penley); Roy Skelton (computer voice); Bernard Bresslaw (Varga); Roger Jones (Zondal); Sonny Caldinez (Turoc); Tony Harwood (Rintan); Michael Attwell (Isbur).

Production credits: Brian Hayles (writer); Derek Martinus (director); Peter Bryant (script editor); Jeremy Davis (designer); Sylvia James (make-up); Martin Baugh (costumes); Dudley Simpson (incidental music); Bernard Wilkie and Ron Oates (visual effects); Innes Lloyd (producer).

The Seeds of Death
Production code XX, season six, six episodes

Episode one
Studio recording on 3 January 1969
Rehearsal 10.30 a.m.–1 p.m., 2 p.m.–7 p.m.
Studio filming 8.30 p.m.-10 p.m.
Studio D at Lime Grove on 2in tape, filmed inserts
Broadcast Saturday 25 January 1969, BBC1 5.15 p.m.–5.40 p.m.

Episode two
Studio recording on 10 January 1969
Rehearsal and studio filming as episode one
Broadcast Saturday 1 February 1969, BBC1 5.15 p.m.–5.40 p.m.

Episode three
Studio recording on 17 January 1969
Rehearsal and studio filming as episode one
Broadcast Saturday 8 February 1969, BBC1 5.15 p.m.–5.40 p.m.

Episode four
Studio recording on 24 January 1969
Rehearsal and studio filming as episode one
Broadcast Saturday 15 February 1969, BBC1 5.15 p.m.–5.40 p.m.

Episode five
Studio recording on 31 January 1969
Rehearsal and studio filming as episode one
Broadcast Saturday 22 February 1969, BBC1 5.15 p.m.–5.40 p.m.

Episode six
Studio filming on 7 February 1969
Rehearsal as episode one
Studio filming 8.30 p.m.–10.15 p.m.
Broadcast Saturday 1 March, BBC1 5.15 p.m.-5.40 p.m.

Cast: Patrick Troughton (the Doctor); Frazer Hines (Jamie); Wendy Padbury (Zoe); Philip Ray (Eldred); Louise Pajo (Gia Kelly); John Witty (computer voice); Ric Felgate (Brent); Harry Towb (Osgood); Ronald Leigh-Hunt (Commander Radnor); Terry Scully (Fewsham); Christopher Coll (Phipps); Martin Cort (Locke); Derek Slater (Guard); Graham Leaman (Marshal); Hugh Morton (Sir James Gregson); Peter Whittaker (weather station operator); Alan Bennion (Slaar); Sonny Caldinez, Tony Harwood, Steve Peters (Ice Warriors).

Production credits: Brian Hayles (writer); Michael Ferguson (director); Terrance Dicks (script editor); Paul Allen (designer); Sylvia James (make-up); Bobi Bartlett (costumes); Dudley Simpson (incidental music); Bill King and 'Trading Post' (visual effects); Peter Bryant (producer).

The Curse of Peladon*
Production code MMM, season nine, four episodes

Episode one
Studio recording on 17 January 1972
Rehearsal 11.30 a.m.–1 p.m., 2 p.m.–6.30 p.m.
Studio filming 8 p.m.–10.30 p.m.
Studio TC4, TV Centre on 2in tape, filmed inserts
Broadcast Saturday 29 January 1972, BBC1 5.50 p.m.–6.15 p.m.

Episode two
Studio recording on 18 January 1972
Rehearsal 10.30 a.m.–1 p.m., 2 p.m.–6 p.m.

Above: **Alpha Centuari (Stuart Fell) was another federation delegate on Peladon along with the Ice Warriors.**

Studio filming 7.30 p.m.-10.30 p.m.
Studio TC4, TV Centre on 2in tape, filmed inserts
Broadcast Saturday 5 February 1972, BBC1 5.50 p.m.–6.15 p.m.

Episode three
Studio recording on 31 January 1972
Rehearsal as episode one
Studio filming 8 p.m.-10 p.m.
Studio TC3, TV Centre on 2in tape, filmed inserts
Broadcast Saturday 12 February 1972, BBC1 5.50 p.m.–6.15 p.m.

Episode four
Studio recording on 1 February 1972
Rehearsal as episode one
Studio filming 7.30 p.m.–10 p.m.
Broadcast Saturday 19 February 1972, BBC1 5.50 p.m.–6.15 p.m.

Cast: Jon Pertwee (the Doctor); Katy Manning (Jo Grant); Henry Gilbert (Torbis); David Troughton (Peladon); Geoffrey Toone (Hepesh); Gordon StClair (Grun); Nick Hobbs (Aggedor); Stuart Fell (Alpha Centauri); Ysanne Churchman (voice of Alpha Centauri); Murphy Grumbar (Arcturus); Terry Bale (voice of Arcturus); George Giles (Captain); Wendy Danvers (Amazonia); Alan Bennion (Izlyr); Sonny Caldinez (Ssorg).

Production credits: Brian Hayles (writer); Lennie Mayne (director); Terrance Dicks (script editor); Gloria Clayton (designer); Sylvia James (make-up); Barbara Lane (costumes); Dudley Simpson (incidental music); Ian Scoones (visual effects); Barry Letts (producer).

The Monster of Peladon
Production code YYY, season eleven, six episodes

Episode one
Studio recording on 28 January 1974
Rehearsal 11 a.m.–1 p.m., 2 p.m.–6.30 p.m.
Studio filming 8 p.m.-10 p.m.
Studio TC8, TV Centre on 2in tape, filmed inserts
Broadcast Saturday 23 March 1974, BBC1 5.30 p.m.–5.55 p.m.

Episode two
Studio recording on 29 January 1974
Rehearsal 10.30 a.m.–1 p.m., 2 p.m.–6 p.m.
Studio filming 7.30 p.m.-10 p.m.
Studio details as episode one
Broadcast Saturday 30 March 1974, BBC1 5.30 p.m.–5.55 p.m.

Episode three
Studio recording on 11 February 1974
Rehearsal 11 a.m.–1 p.m., 2 p.m.–6 p.m.
Studio filming 7.30 p.m.–10 p.m.
Studio TC6, TV Centre on 2in tape, filmed inserts
Broadcast Saturday 6 April 1974, BBC1 5.30 p.m.–5.55 p.m.

Episode four
Studio recording on 12 February 1974
Details as episode two
Broadcast Saturday 13 April 1974, BBC1 5.30 p.m.–5.55 p.m.

Episode five
Studio recording on 26 February 1974
Details as episode three
Broadcast Saturday 20 April 1974, BBC1 5.30 p.m.–5.55 p.m.

Episode six
Studio recording on 27 February 1974
Details as episode two
Broadcast Saturday 27 April 1974, BBC1 5.30 p.m.–5.55 p.m.

Cast: Jon Pertwee (the Doctor); Elisabeth Sladen (Sarah Jane Smith); Ralph Watson (Ettis); Donald Gee (Eckersley); Gerald Taylor (Vega Nexos); Nina Thomas (Queen Thalira); Frank Gatcliffe (Ortron); Michael Crane (Blor); Stuart Fell (Alpha Centauri); Ysanne Churchman (voice of Alpha Centauri); Terry Walsh (Captain); Rex Robinson (Gebek); Graeme Eton (Preba); Nick Hobbs (Aggedor); Roy Evans (Rima); Max Faulkner (Miner); Alan Bennion (Azaxyr); Sonny Caldinez (Sskel); David Cleeve, Terence Denville, Alan Lenoir, Kevin Moran, Graham Leaman (Ice Warriors).

Production credits: Brian Hayles (writer); Lennie Mayne (director); Terrance Dicks (script editor); Gloria Clayton (designer); Elizabeth Mon (make-up); Barbara Kidd (costumes); Dudley Simpson (incidental music); Peter Day (visual effects); Barry Letts (producer).

Additional data

An Ice Warrior was seen in episode ten of *The War Games* (story ZZ) broadcast 21 July 1969. Tony Harwood wore the costume for this fleeting appearance.

The following episodes are preserved in the BBC film archives: *The Ice Warriors* – 1, 4, 5 and 6; *The Seeds of Death* – all episodes remain; *The Curse of Peladon* – all episodes remain; *The Monster of Peladon* – all episodes remain.

Episode ten of *The War Games* exists, along with the rest of the story.

Novelizations
Doctor Who and the Ice Warriors
Brian Hayles
Number 33 in the Target novelization series.

Doctor Who – The Seeds of Death
Terrance Dicks
Adapted from the original scripts by Brian Hayles. Number 112 in the Target novelization series.

Doctor Who and the Curse of Peladon
Brian Hayles
Number 13 in the Target novelization series.

Doctor Who and the Monster of Peladon
Terrance Dicks
Adapted from the original scripts by Brian Hayles
Number 43 in the Target novelization series.

Doctor Who and the War Games
Malcolm Hulke
Adapted from the original scripts by Malcolm Hulke and Terrance Dicks. Number 70 in the Target novelization series.

Doctor Who – Mission to Magnus
Philip Martin
The Ice Warriors feature in this adaptation of the proposed story from the aborted 23rd season of the programme.

Commercial video releases
Doctor Who – The Seeds of Death
BBC Video
Episodes edited together to form one 136-minute film. End titles missing from episodes 1, 2, 3, 4 and 5; beginning titles missing from episodes 2, 3, 4, 5 and 6.

Doctor Who – The War Games
BBC Video
All episodes uncut.

THE ZARBI AND MENOPTRA

Butterflies, ants and venomous grubs

Production data

Two species of gigantic insectoid life forms at war with each other – not any mere battle over land or food, this involves the conquest of a world and the fight to get it back. This was the premise of what was to become one of the most ambitious and costly stories to have been produced during the black and white era of *Doctor Who*. Up until that point, there had always been a token human contingent present in the stories, but Bill Strutton's scripts called for no recognizable human shapes. Apart from the regular TARDIS crew, the rest of the cast would be required to wear costumes varying from intricate to bulky extremes.

The Menoptra were, perhaps, the simplest of the four native species of Vortis to realize. The actors playing the creatures donned a black vinyl body suit with rings of yellow fur attached in circles round the main body, the arms and the legs. The wings of the creatures were made out of light plastic sheeting with black veins painted on the surface, and a simple mechanism that could be triggered on cue to spread the wings open to a span of some five feet across.

Black and white face paints were used to achieve the skin coloration on the head, with a hood fitted on with gauze pads that covered the eyes and wire antennae fixed to the dome of the head. The renowned choreographer Roslyn de Winter was hired by director Richard Martin to help create an alien feel to the movements of the actors, and devise a style of precise and clipped speech intonation. In fact, de Winter was so successful that she was asked to take on the part of Vrestin.

The Optera were achieved by using the same kind of principle as the Menoptra, with the costumes being built up in sections round a basic black body suit. A more albino-like appearance was given to them, to emphasize the fact that they had been living underground for generations. With the Menoptra, continual hand and arm movements made them very expressive creatures; the Optera costumes were deliberately designed so that the actors could barely move their arms above elbow level, and had to hop to move anywhere because of their restricted leg mobility. All this was done to show the natural regression of the once proud creatures that had fled the Zarbi centuries before.

The Zarbi themselves were made of heavy glass fibre; the weight was such that the natural stoop of the creatures may have been more unintentional than would appear on screen. The actors were fitted into the costumes in three stages, with black leggings being supported by braces over which the main body section could be set, with the head secured last. The field of vision was limited, with only a small hole covered in black gauze to provide visibility.

This might go some way to explaining why, at one point in the story, a Zarbi quite clearly charges into a camera and makes the picture shake. The heat inside the costumes generated from the studio lighting made it near unbearable for the actors to stay inside for long periods.

The Venom Grubs were a simple glass fibre shell that could be supported by an actor concealed underneath it, on all fours, shielded by the numerous tendrils hanging down from the main part of the body. When movement was needed for chase scenes, it was mounted on a simple wheeled platform that could be operated off camera with wires. The gun mechanism was triggered by an operator and consisted of a small powder charge fired by a low-voltage electrical current, with suitable sound effects added in post production.

Some of the more effective sequences called for the Menoptra to be seen in flight as their main invasion force attacked Vortis. Although this was achieved by the then relatively common use of Kirby wires, a simple overhead harness support on invisible wires, the fully open wings of the creatures concealed this fact quite well.

The Zarbi were planned to be the next major monster for the series, following the phenomenal success of the two Daleks' stories that had been made up to that point, and a sufficiently vast publicity drive before and during broadcast ensured that they were indeed popular with the viewers. The problem was that the sheer technicalities that the script called for were such that the story went way over budget, which had an undesired effect that costs had to be cut on the stories that followed it.

The production team found the whole operation tiring when compared with their normal run of operations. Nevertheless, negotiations were entered into with Bill Strutton about writing a follow-up for the third season of the programme in the following year.

Verity Lambert, the producer, and her script editor, Dennis Spooner, left the programme shortly after the second season had been completed. Strutton's ideas never reached the screen, with the new production team veering towards a different style of story. The appearances of the Zarbi and Menoptra may have been brief, in terms of the overall history of the series, but they certainly made an impact that has not been forgotten.

Technical data

Below: **A Menoptra and a Zarbi from** *The Web Planet.*

The Web Planet
Production code N, season two, six episodes

Episode one: The Web Planet
Studio recording on 22 January 1965
Rehearsal 10.30 a.m.–1 p.m., 2 p.m.–7 p.m.
Studio filming 8.45 p.m.–10 p.m.
Riverside 1 Studio, on 2in tape with film inserts
Broadcast Saturday 13 February 1965, BBC1 5.40 p.m.–6.05 p.m.

Episode two: The Zarbi
Studio recording on 29 January 1965
Rehearsal and studio details as episode one
Studio filming 8.30 p.m.–9.45 p.m.
Broadcast Saturday 20 February 1965, BBC1 5.40 p.m.–6.05 p.m.

Episode three: Escape to Danger
Studio recording on 5 February 1965
Rehearsal 10.30 a.m.–1 p.m., 2 p.m.–7 p.m.
Studio filming 9 p.m.–10.15 p.m.
Studio details as episode one
Broadcast Saturday 27 February 1965

Episode four: Crater of Needles
Studio recording on 12 February 1965
Rehearsal and filming details as episode three
Broadcast Saturday 6 March 1965, BBC1 5.40 p.m.–6.05 p.m.

Episode five: Invasion
Studio recording on 19 February 1965
Rehearsal and filming details as episode three
Broadcast Saturday 13 March 1965, BBC1 5.40 p.m.–6.05 p.m.

Episode six: The Centre
Studio recording on 26 February 1965
Rehearsal 11.30 a.m.–1 p.m., 2 p.m.–7 p.m.
Studio filming 9.30 p.m.- 10.45 p.m.
Studio details as episode one
Broadcast Saturday 20 March 1965, BBC1 5.40 p.m.–6.05 p.m.

Cast: William Hartnell (the Doctor); William Russell (Ian Chesterton); Jacqueline Hill (Barbara Wright); Maureen O'Brien (Vicki); Roslyn de Winter (Vrestin); Arne Gordon (Hrostar); Arthur Blake (Hrhoonda); Jolyon Booth (Prapilius); Jocelyn Birdsall (Hlynia); Martin Jarvis (Captain Hilio); Ian Thompson (Hetra); Barbara Joss (Nemini); Catherine Fleming (Voice of the Animus); Robert Jewell, Gerald Taylor, Kevin Manser, Hugh Lund, Jack Pitt, John Scott Martin (Zarbi).

Production credits: Bill Strutton (writer); Richard Martin (director); Dennis Spooner (script editor); John Wood (designer); Sonia Markham (make-up); Daphne Dare (costumes); BBC Radiophonic Workshop (incidental music); John Wood (visual effects); Verity Lambert (producer).

Additional data

All six episodes of *The Web Planet* are preserved in the BBC film archives.

Novelization
Doctor Who and the Zarbi
Bill Strutton
Number 73 in the Target novelization series.

Commercial video releases
Doctor Who – The Web Planet
BBC Video
Episodes released in their complete form. Caption crediting the next episode, 'The Lion' (episode one of *The Crusade*), has been cut from the end of episode six. The incidental music at the end of episode six has been altered.

THE YETI

The abominable creatures of the snow

Production data

During the early 1930s, the first expedition to Mount Everest since the tragedy of Mallory and Irvine's in 1925 reached Tibet. Local legends that the Sherpas spoke of told of a hermit of the snows, a lost creature that lived in the higher reaches of the mountains, feeding on fruits, berries and wild roots.

Reports of this were sent back to England, but the message got confused with a description of the weather the explorers were experiencing at high altitude, so the phrases 'Man of the Mountains' and 'this abominable snow' got twisted to form 'the Abominable Snowman', and thus the phrase was coined that has stuck with the creatures ever since.

With Innes Lloyd's production team looking for elements of realism to introduce to the programme, it was

Below: **A Yeti attacks a visitor to the *Daily Mail* Boys and Girls exhibition.**

only natural that the idea of an Abominable Snowman should be suggested. Only a few years previously, the *Daily Mail* had mounted an expedition to try to track down the elusive beings. The evidence it found certainly proved that something was up there, so the topic was still relatively fresh in the mind of the public.

The writing team of Mervyn Haisman and Henry Lincoln structured a plot that worked so well, and the resulting costumes created to bring the creatures to the screen were so successful, that the pair were commissioned to write a sequel to *The Abominable Snowman* while the first story was still in production.

The finished scripts for the first story called for the main bulk of the action to take part in the heart of the Himalayas, in one of the fabled monasteries that lie around the foothills of the mountains. The monastery could easily be realized within the confines of the studio, but the normal locations that the production team used for the programme could in no way double for mountains. The logistics were such that a location trip moving further afield than normal was possible. For the first time the production team, headed by director Gerald Blake, went beyond the normal 'forty miles outside London' rule for TV filming and went to Snowdonia for a week of exterior shooting.

A total of four Yeti costumes were constructed, with heavy leg and arm coverings built into their main framework, giving the creature its vast bulk. Looped wooden and bamboo canes for the lower half of the body were layered with specially treated fur, with darker patches covering the face area and chest unit.

A small cavity was built into the chest area, enclosed behind a fur-flap, to conceal the control spheres carried inside the Yeti. Heavy rubber was used for the feet and claws, cast in dark black shades; the nails were painted on afterwards in white enamel.

The control spheres were made through a simple process of vac-forming some glass fibre, but many smashed casualties resulted from the heavy rain during the filming in north Wales. No matter how hard they tried, the actors just could not keep their balance inside their costumes. The sight of a Yeti somersaulting and landing on its back, covered in mud, was not as unique as it sounds.

One of the make-up assistants later recalled that dozens of hairdriers were wired up to extension cables so that the Yeti's fur could be dried and fluffed up for each scene. There was, however, one compensation for the Yeti actors. They were nowhere near as cold as the rest of the cast, who didn't have the luxury of heavy fur costumes to protect them from the bitterly cold winds on the mountain.

During the studio recording, the sets had to be carefully constructed to allow plenty of room for the Yeti to move around, with specially fragile props being constructed for the finale of episode six, when the creatures storm the monastery and destroy anything that stands in their way.

One of the final scenes of the story involved Professor Travers, downhearted that he might never find a Yeti, spotting a real Yeti on a rocky ridge overhead. One of the Yeti costumes simply had the bamboo leg structures removed, creating the effect of a slimmer creature than its robotic replicants, and allowing the actor to run more easily as Travers set off in pursuit.

Nearly three months to the day passed, and the Yetis were back in the studio once more, this time in *The Web*

Above: **A Mk I Yeti costume.**

Above: **The production crew rehearse a scene on the side of a Welsh mountain during *The Abominable Snowmen*.**

Right: **A Yeti meets the local children whilst on location for *The Abominable Snowmen*.**

Above: **Professor Travers (Jack Watling) as he appeared in his second story** *The Web of Fear.*

Left: **A Yeti minus head, during location filming for** *The Abominable Snowmen* **in Wales.**

Below: **The scenes of the Yeti on the slopes of the Himalayas in** *The Abominable Snowmen* **were actually filmed in North Wales.**

of Fear. The appearance of the creatures had been altered under the orders of the new producer, Peter Bryant, who was somewhat concerned that they looked far too 'cuddly'. The production office had received many letters that indicated younger viewers thought the creatures were like teddy bears.

The dark patch of fur around the face was taken away, and powerful eye lights being implanted in the head of the costume, to eerie effect. As many of the scenes would be set in the tunnels of the London Underground system, an altogether slimmer, more mobile creature was created, with movement for the actors inside now slightly easier because the costumes were lighter.

When permission was denied by London Transport to film on some disused underground stations, director Douglas Camfield resorted to using several large sets, filming them from dif-ferent angles and viewpoints to create the effect of unending tunnels. The results were so convincing that the Underground authorities were at one point threatening to sue the BBC for filming on their property without consent.

Professor Travers returned for this story and was again played by Jack Watling, who had to endure long make-up sessions to show the ageing effect necessary to account for the years that had passed between stories. A third appearance by the character was proposed for the sixth season Cyberman story, *The Invasion*, but owing to prior commitments, Watling was unable to appear.

The only surviving Yeti costume was used fifteen years later for a brief appearance by the creature in the programme's twentieth-anniversary story *The Five Doctors*. Suffice to say, that after such a long period of time, it looked slightly moth-eaten.

Mervyn Haisman and Henry Lincoln did start work on a third Yeti story that would have acted as the debut adventure for the third Doctor and been the final story for Jamie. The six-part adventure told of how the Doctor was trying to return Jamie to his own time, only to find his native village trapped in an energy barrier, stopping anyone getting in or out. The local laird's castle had been taken over by the Great Intelligence, intent on invading the Earth at a time where no technology existed that could threaten or harm it, and a small army of Yeti were present to protect it.

Owing to a disagreement with the production team over their other tale, *The Dominators*, and the fact that an episode was cut, shortening its six episodes to five without their permission, the writers never saw the third Yeti saga on screen. Nevertheless the Yeti still remain one of the most popular monsters to have emerged from the era of the second Doctor.

Technical data

The Abominable Snowman
Production code NN, season five, six episodes

Episode one
Studio recording on 15 September 1967
Rehearsal 10.30 a.m.–1 p.m., 2 p.m.-7 p.m.
Studio filming 8.45 p.m.–10 p.m.
Studio D at Lime Grove on 2in tape, film inserts
Broadcast Saturday 30 September 1967, BBC1 5.25 p.m.–5.50 p.m.

Episode two
Studio recording on 16 September 1967
Rehearsal as episode one
Studio filming 8.30 p.m.–9.45 p.m.
Studio details as episode one
Broadcast Saturday 7 October 1967, BBC1 5.25 p.m.–5.50 p.m.

Episode three
Studio recording on 23 September 1967
Rehearsal and filming as episode two
Broadcast: Saturday 14 October 1967, BBC1 5.25 p.m.–5.50 p.m.

Episode four
Studio recording 30 September 1967
Rehearsal and filming as episode two
Broadcast Saturday 21 October 1967, BBC1 5.25 p.m.–5.50 p.m.

Episode five
Studio recording on 7 October 1967
Rehearsal and filming as episode two
Broadcast Saturday 28 October 1967, BBC1 5.25 p.m.–5.50 p.m.

Episode six
Studio recording on 4 October 1967
Rehearsal 10.30 a.m.–1 p.m., 2 p.m.–6.45 p.m.
Studio filming 8.15 a.m.–9.45 p.m.
Studio details as episode one
Broadcast Saturday 4 November 1967, BBC1 5.25 p.m.–5.55 p.m.

Cast: Patrick Troughton (the Doctor); Frazer Hines (Jamie); Deborah Watling (Victoria); Jack Watling (Professor Travers); Norman Jones (Khrisong); David Spencer (Thomni); David Grey (Rinchen); Raymond Llewellyn (Sapan); Charles Morgan (Songsten); Wolfe Morris (Padmasambhava); David Barron (Ralpachan); Tony Harwood, Reg Whitehead, Richard Kerley, John Hogan (Yeti).

Production credits: Mervyn Haisman and Henry Lincoln (writers); Gerald Blake (director); Peter Bryant (script editor); Malcolm Middleton (designer); Sylvia James (make-up); Martin Baugh (costumes); Ron Oates and Ulrich Grosser (visual effects); Innes Lloyd (producer).

The Web of Fear
Production code QQ, season five, six episodes

Episode one
Studio recording on 13 January 1968
Rehearsal 10.30 a.m.–1pm, 2 p.m.–3.30 p.m., 4 p.m.-7 p.m.
Studio filming 8.30 p.m.- 9.45 p.m.
Studio D at Lime Grove on 2in tape, film inserts
Broadcast Saturday 3 February 1968, BBC1 5.25 p.m.–5.50 p.m.

Episode two
Studio recording on 20 January 1968
Rehearsal 10.30 a.m.–1 p.m., 2 p.m.–3.45 p.m., 4.15 p.m.–7 p.m.
Studio filming 8.30 p.m.–9.45 p.m.
Studio details as episode one
Broadcast Saturday 10 February 1968, BBC1 5.25 p.m.–5.50 p.m.

Episode three
Studio recording on 27 January 1968
Rehearsal and filming as episode one
Broadcast Saturday 17 February 1968, BBC1 5.25 p.m.–5.50 p.m.

Episode four
Studio recording on 3 February 1968
Rehearsal and filming as episode one
Broadcast Saturday 24 February 1968, BBC1 5.25 p.m.–5.50 p.m.

Episode five
Studio recording on 10 February 1968
Rehearsal and filming as episode one
Broadcast Saturday 2 March 1968, BBC1 5.25 p.m.–5.50 p.m.

Episode six
Studio recording on 17 February 1968
Rehearsal 10.30 a.m.–1 p.m., 2 p.m.–3.45 p.m., 4.15 p.m.–6.45 p.m.
Studio filming 8.15 p.m.–9.45 p.m.
Studio details as episode one
Broadcast Saturday 9 March 1968, BBC1 5.25 p.m.–5.50 p.m.

Cast: Patrick Troughton (the Doctor); Frazer Hines (Jamie); Deborah Watling (Victoria); Jack Watling (Professor Travers); Tina Packer (Anne Travers); Nicholas Courtney (Colonel Lethbridge-Stewart); Frederick Schrecker (Julius Silverstein); Rod Beacham (Lane); Ralph Watson (Knight); Richardson Morgan (Blake); John Rollason (Harold Chorley); Jack Woolgar (Sergeant Arnold); Stephen Whittaker (Weams); Derek Pollitt (Evans); Bernard G. High (Soldier); Joseph O'Connell (Soldier); Bert Sims (Newspaper Seller); John Levene, John Lord, Colin Warman, Gordon Stothard, Jeremy King, Roger Jacombs (Yeti).

Production credits: Mervyn Haisman and Henry Lincoln (writers); Douglas Camfield (director); Derrick Sherwin (script editor) David Myerscough-Jones (designer); Sylvia James (make-up); Martin Baugh (costumes); incidental music from stock material; Ron Oates (visual effects); Peter Bryant (producer).

Additional data

A Yeti was seen in episode ten of *The War Games* (ZZ); see additional data for the Ice Warriors. John Levene wore the suit for this fleeting appearance.
A Yeti was seen in *The Five Doctors* (6K) broadcast on 25 November 1983. The costume was an original from the first Yeti story, on this occasion worn by Lee Woods.
The following episodes are preserved in the BBC film archives: *The Abominable Snowmen* – 2; *The Web of Fear* – 1.
Episode ten of *The War Games* exists with the rest of the story. *The Five Doctors* exists as a 90-minute film and a four- episode story. Colour 16mm home movie footage on location in Wales is known to exists among specialist collectors. The film was shot by the director of *The Abominable Snowmen*, Gerald Blake.
One of *The Abominable Snowmen* Yeti costumes was used in one of the episodes of *Whicker's World* from 1968. The presenter Alan Whicker is seen wandering through a cemetery, commenting on the mythical creature, when it appears and kidnaps him.

A Yeti costume was used at the press photocall when the identity of the actor playing the third Doctor was revealed during summer 1969. The creature was seen carrying the actor in its arms.

Novelizations
Doctor Who and The Abominable Snowmen
Terrance Dicks
Adapted from the original scripts by Mervyn Haisman and Henry Lincoln. Number 1 in the Target novelization series.

Doctor Who and the Web of Fear
Terrance Dicks
Adapted from the original scripts by Mervyn Haisman and Henry Lincoln. Number 72 in the Target novelization series.

Doctor Who and the War Games
Malcolm Hulke
Adapted from the original scripts by Malcolm Hulke and Terrance Dicks. Number 70 in the Target novelization series.

Doctor Who – The Five Doctors
Terrance Dicks
Number 81 in the Target novelization series.

Commercial video releases
Doctor Who – The Troughton Years
BBC Video
Compilation tape of episodes existing from incomplete stories in the BBC film archives. All of *The Abominable Snowman* episode 2 is included, with an extract from the beginning of *The Web of Fear*. Presented by Jon Pertwee, he is seen at one point standing with the one remaining Yeti costume to have survived, now over 24 years old.

Doctor Who – The War Games
BBC Video
All episodes uncut.

Doctor Who – The Five Doctors
The 90-minute version, uncut, as broadcast 25 November 1983.

THE WIRRN

Giant insects and infectious blister-pack

Production data

The basic concept of an insectoid life form that lays eggs in the human body, which then gestate, take over the body and transform it into an altogether different being may sound a bit familiar. In more ways than one, the acclaimed series of *Alien* films bear a striking similarity to the ideas behind *The Ark in Space*, and this story preceded it by at least four years.

The third story to be recorded for the newly arrived fourth Doctor, as personified by Tom Baker, had sets designed by Roger Murray-Leach that were used in an ingenious way to save money on the already tight budgets that the production team worked under. The sets were reused on the next story, *Revenge of the Cybermen*, having been slightly redressed so that in the context of the story, the Doctor and his companions were visiting the space wheel before it became the Nerva Beacon seen in this story, in a totally different time zone.

The life cycle of the Wirrn took a clearly structured pattern: the queen Wirrn was the first creature to be seen, dead and mummified. An inanimate full-body prop was built for sequences involving her, and with no actor inside required to operate it, the lower end of it could be sealed; the other costumes were left open to allow the actor to move. This is the only instance that the tail of a Wirrn is clearly seen on screen, with a gigantic pair of pincers made out of glass fibre.

The Wirrn larva that is seen on several occasions was achieved by encasing the actor, Stuart Fell, in a cocoon of heavy polythene blister-pack, which had been given a suitably insectoid green tint, and a layer of large pink suckers on its underbelly. Fell had to move the costume by crawling, arching his back and moving forward with his hands, dragging his feet at the rear. With help, Fell could stand, allowing the scenes where the creature tries to break through a doorway to be filmed showing its suckers. Blister-pack was a then relatively new industrial packing material, and was used to great effect for the transformation of Noah.

To show the gradually spreading infestation of Wirrn spores throughout the character's body, several stages of make-up were required. Noah's hand is first seen with the flesh putrefying into no more than a hooked green claw. This was a glove-like appliance that allowed the actor to move his hand around inside to create the effect of mutating flesh.

The next stage involved the entire arm, the upper parts of the torso and the side of the head, which were covered with the same material. The final stages show Noah with only half his face left free, while only one arm remains human on the upper body. The left eye has taken on the shape of the Wirrn's optical nerves, suggesting the shape of things to come.

The adult Wirrn costumes were supported over the actors by a bamboo cane structure, with the moulded glass fibre head held over the actor's; the latex abdomen and antennae could be moved from within. Difficulties with the weight of the costume made the desired effect difficult to achieve on screen, and only the Wirrn mandibles can be seen moving significantly.

The only full shots of living Wirrn are seen as the invasion swarm of the creatures crawls over the surface of the space station. Simple puppets were used to achieve this effect, with wires nearly, but not quite, invisible against the space backdrop.

Several animatroic armatures were constructed specifically for use in the scenes where the Wirrn's tendrils are seen as they try to break through the air ducts, but also for use in the sequen-ces showing the point of view from the queen Wirrn when she arrived on Nerva Beacon The sounds heard when the Wirrn communicate were created by the Radiophonic Workshop based on the shrill sound of crickets and other such insects.

When fully fitted on the actor, the Wirrn stood over six feet tall, which required careful co-ordination as the material used on the creature's main body could rip easily, and limited studio recording time would in no way allow for emergency repair work.

The script by Robert Holmes was based on a submission by John Lucarotti, author of several Hartnell stories, such as *Marco Polo* and *The Massacre*. The cost of the alien Delc that his scripts called for – headless, multilimbed creatures – made it near impossible to realize, so Robert Holmes reworked the script in just over two weeks, retaining the basic elements such as the space ark and the cryogenically frozen humans.

Although the Wirrn were popular, if not one hundred per cent successful, *The Ark in Space* remains their only appearance to date, apart from a fleeting appearance of one of the costumes in the hundredth *Doctor Who* story, *The Stones of Blood*. The body of one of the creatures is seen lying, severely decayed, in a prison cell on a space station. The story featured no location work, with the director, Rodney Bennett, having shot *The Sontaran Experiment* back to back with this adventure.

Technical data

The Ark in Space*
Production code 4C, season twelve, four episodes

Left: **A Wirrn** from *The Ark in Space.*

Below: **A Wirrn costume.**

Episode one
Studio recording on 28 October 1974
Rehearsal 11 a.m.–1 p.m., 2 p.m.–6 p.m.
Studio filming 7.30 p.m.–10 p.m.
Studio TC3, TV Centre on 2in tape, film inserts
Broadcast Saturday 25 January 1975, BBC1 5.30 p.m.–5.55 p.m.

Episode two
Studio recording on 29 October 1974
Rehearsal 10.30 a.m.–1 p.m., 2 p.m.–2.30 p.m.
Studio filming 2.30 p.m.–3.30 p.m.
Rehearsal 3.30 p.m.–6 p.m.
Studio filming 7.30 p.m.–10 p.m.
Studio details as episode one
Broadcast Saturday 1 February 1975, BBC1 5.30 p.m.–5.55 p.m.

Episode three
Studio recording 11 November 1974
Rehearsal and filming as episode one
Studio TC1, TV Centre on 2in tape, film inserts
Broadcast Saturday 8 February 1975, BBC1 5.30 p.m.–5.55 p.m.

Episode four
Studio recording 12 February 1974
Rehearsal and filming as episode two

Above: **Tom Baker relaxes on a Wirrn during a break in recording for *The Ark in Space*.**

Studio TC1, TV Centre on 2in tape, film inserts
Broadcast Saturday 15 February 1975, BBC1 5.30 p.m.–5.55 p.m.

Cast: Tom Baker (the Doctor); Elisabeth Sladen (Sarah Jane Smith); Ian Marter (Surgeon Lieutenant Harry Sullivan); Wendy Williams (Vira); Kenton Moore (Noah); Christopher Masters (Libri); John Gregg (Lycett); Richardson Morgan (Rogan); Peter Tuddenham (voices); Gladys Spencer (High Minister's voice); Stuart Fell (Wirrn Larva); Stuart Fell, Nick Hobbs (Wirrn); Brian Jacobs (Dune).

Production credits: Robert Holmes (writer); Rodney Bennett (director); Robert Holmes (script editor); Roger Murray-Leach (designer); Sylvia James (make-up); Barbara Kidd (costumes); Dudley Simpson (incidental music); John Friedlander and Tony Oxley (visual effects); Philip Hinchcliffe (producer).

Additional data

A Wirrn, in actual fact the body of the queen Wirrn, was seen in episode four of *The Stones of Blood* (5C), broadcast on Saturday 18 November 1978.

An edited omnibus version of *The Ark in Space* was broadcast on 20 August 1975, running for seventy minutes.
Both *The Ark in Space* and *The Stones of Blood* are held in their entirety in the BBC film archives.

Novelization
Doctor Who and the Ark in Space
Ian Marter
Adapted from the original scripts by Robert Holmes. Number 4 in the Target novelization series.

Commercial video release
Doctor Who – The Ark in Space
BBC Video
Episodes edited together to form one 94-minute film. Beginning titles missing from episodes 2, 3 and 4. End titles missing from 1, 2 and 3.

SIL AND THE MENTORS

Production data

The financially erudite slugs

When Philip Martin first submitted the idea for a possible story to the production office, they were somewhat surprised. Martin had a reputation for creating tough, realistic thrillers such as the highly acclaimed classic series *Gangsters*. His concept of a society where the populace had their natural aggression pacified by an unrelenting system of broadcasts, showing violent combat, war and executions went through various drafts under various titles – *Domain, Planet of Fear* and so on — until it finally went before the cameras under the name of *Vengeance on Varos*, the second story of season 22.

The one true alien life form featured in the story was a Mentor, a native of the planet Thoros Beta called Sil. In many ways this one character represented the most difficult challenge for the production team on the entire story.

Science fiction writer Isaac Asimov once wrote about the nature of aliens in literature, and pointed out that in all of the science-fiction books that had been written and the films that had been made, with only a few exceptions, you never saw an alien life form that was water-based. Martin's original descriptions called for Sil to be seen totally immersed in a tank of water, communicating through speakers attached to the sides, but this would have proved a technical nightmare. The presence of water on any television set is liable to unnerve even the most experienced of directors, but had this been attempted, there was a continual threat of drowning involved for the actor playing the part. Even with the most stringent of safety precautions, accidents can and do happen.

A compromise was reached. Sil would sit on a small platform over a water tank, and be continually sprayed with the liquid by his assistants. But the character still had to be cast, and for director Ron Jones, the search was on.

It was obvious that Sil would have to be small, so endless auditions for dwarfs and midgets followed, with Ron Jones trying to find the right actor. Eventually, Nabil Shaban, an actor who suffers from brittle bones, was found and won the part.

Sil's was by far the most complex costume in the story, and consisted of a complete latex body costume and head appliances. With most of Sil's scenes shot from angles facing him directly, the seal at the back of the body suit remained unseen. The tail of the costume was operated by Shaban, moving his legs around inside, giving it a life all of its own.

The facial make-up was achieved by using a domed cowl, which was placed over his head, with a collar of loose skin surrounding it to cover the body's neck-line. The rim of the hole at the front of the cowl was glued to the actor's face, while face paints blended the colour to his skin.

The voice translator on Sil's chest was a simple electronic mechanism that responded to the vocal tracts of

Left: **Lord Kiv (Christopher Ryan)**
receives medical attention from Crozier
(Patrick Ryecart). *The Trial of a Time
Lord.*

Shaban's voice as he said his lines, flashing on and off to the rhythm of his words. A similar idea was used in one of the episodes of *Gangsters*, where one of the characters had a voice-box that was jammed, uttering nothing other than expletives.

One prop that Shaban relished and used at every opportunity were the marsh-minnows, a delicacy of live fish caught in the waters of Thoros Beta and which Sil couldn't get enough of. In reality they were mashed peaches and pears, turned a pale shade of green with some food colouring.

Sil was due to return in the next season of the programme, but the fate of the original season 23 lay with higher powers in the BBC. *Doctor Who* was put on hold for eighteen months and the story that Martin had written draft scripts for, *Mission to Magnus*, was replaced by a totally different script when the show returned. Sil was to have been seen working in allegiance with the Ice Warriors, who planned to turn the planet where their last colony lay in residence in the polar cap into an ice-world suitable for their habitation. Sil would have been on the sidelines ready to sell his supply of thermal vests and jumpers to the freezing natives of the world.

Mindwarp, which had the working title of *Planet of Sil*, was the second sequence in the epic adventure *The Trial of a Time Lord*, which became the revised season 23. As the working title suggests, more than one Mentor costume was going to be needed during filming.

The basic body suit for Sil was the same that Shaban had worn in *Vengeance on Varos*, although the colour scheme had now been changed to green rather than the previous brown. The head mask was totally different, with a far tighter-fitting latex appliance without the high cranial dome that the previous one had. Strips of ridged flesh were stuck round the edge of the face, blending into the main part of the latex, and allowing Shaban more flexible facial movements than before. Again, make-up blended the skin into the colour of the latex, the tongue was given a green tint and the teeth were painted with black to make them into points like fangs.

The same methods were used on Christopher Ryan, who played Lord Kiv, leader of the Mentors, except that several bulging lumps were moulded on to his head to indicate where his expanding brain was breaking through the lining of his skull. The body used for the brain transplant sequences was a life-size latex model of the costume later worn by Ryan for Kiv's new persona, with the face modelled from a cast of Ryan's face.

In the final battle at the end of the story, with Brian Blessed as King Yrcanos seemingly blowing everything to pieces, it seems more than likely that Sil may have died. But perhaps he will return one day to wheel and deal again.

Left: Sil (Nabil Shaban) as he appeared in his first story *Vengeance on Varos.*

Technical data

Vengeance on Varos
Production code 6V, season twenty-three, two episodes

Episode one and episode two
Story recorded in two separate recording blocks
Block one
Rehearsal 9–17 July 1984
Filming 18–20 July 1984
Block two
Rehearsal 21–31 July 1984
Filming 1–3 August 1984

Episode one broadcast Saturday 19 January 1985, BBC1 5.20 p.m.–6.10 p.m.
Episode two broadcast Saturday 26 January 1985, BBC1 5.20 p.m.–6.10 p.m.

Cast: Colin Baker (the Doctor); Nicola Bryant (Peri); Martin Jarvis (the Governor); Nabil Shaban (Sil); Jason Connery (Jondar); Forbes Collins (Chief Officer); Stephen Yardley (Arak); Sheila Reid (Etta); Geraldine Alexander (Areta); Owen Teale (Maldak); Graham Cull (Bax); Nicholas Chagrin (Quillam); Hugh Martin (Priest); Keith Skinner (Rondel); Bob Tarff (Executioner); Jack McGuire (Madman); Alan Troy (Madman).

Production credits: Philip Martin (writer); Ron Jones (director); Eric Saward (script editor); Tony Snoaden (designer); Dorka Nieradzik and Cecile Hay-Arthur (make-up); Ann Harding (costumes); Johnathan Gibbs (incidental music); David Barton (visual effects); John Nathan-Turner (producer).

The Trial of a Time Lord
Episodes five to eight
Mindwarp
Production code 7B, season twenty-three, four episodes

Episodes one to four
Story recorded in two separate recording blocks, with two days' location filming following completion of studio material.
Block one

Below: Lord Kiv (Christopher Ryan) in *The Trial of a Time Lord.*

Rehearsal 17 May–27 May 1986
Filming 28 May 1986
Block two
Rehearsal 31 May–9 June 1986
Filming 10 June 1986

Episode one (five of fourteen) broadcast Saturday 4 October 1986, BBC1 5.45 p.m.–6.10 p.m.
Episode two (six of fourteen) broadcast Saturday 11 October 1986, BBC1 5.45 p.m.–6.10 p.m.
Episode three (seven of fourteen) broadcast Saturday 18 October 1986, BBC1 5.45 p.m.–6.10 p.m.
Episode four (eight of fourteen) broadcast Saturday 25 October 1986, BBC1 5.45 p.m.–6.10 p.m.

Cast: Colin Baker (the Doctor); Nicola Bryant (Peri); Michael Jayston (the Valeyard); Lynda Bellingham (the Inquisitor); Brian Blessed (King Yrcanos); Nabil Shaban (Sil); Patrick Ryecart (Crozier); Christopher Ryan (Lord Kiv); Alibe Parsons (Matrona Kani); Trevor Laird (Frax); Gordon Warnecke (Tusa); Thomas Branch (the Lukoser); Richard Henry (Mentor).

Production credits: Philip Martin (writer); Ron Jones (director); Eric Saward (script editor); Andrew Howe-Davies (designer); Dorka Nieradzik (make-up); John Hearne (costumes); Richard Hartley (incidental music); Peter Wragg (visual effects); John Nathan-Turner (producer).

Additional data

In episode fourteen of *The Trial of a Time Lord*, the conclusion of *Mindwarp* is revealed to be a hoax; Peri was rescued by Yrcanos and taken to his home world to be his queen. A clip showing both Brian Blessed and Nicola Bryant was used to show this.

Novelizations

Doctor Who – Vengeance on Varos
Philip Martin
Number 106 in the Target novelization series.

Doctor Who – Mindwarp
Philip Martin
Number 139 in the Target novelization series.

Doctor Who – Mission to Magnus
Philip Martin
Sil featured with the Ice Warriors in this adaptation of one of the proposed stories for the aborted season 23.

THE SONTARANS

Irongron's toad and other warriors

Production data

A perfect fighting force, genetically produced warriors with a single, all-consuming thought in their minds of victory and glories of honour: the Sontarans. Robert Holmes came up with the concept of a race stuck in perpetual war with an enemy it had never seen, the Rutans, one of which featured in Terrance Dicks's story from season 15, *The Horror of Fang Rock*.

For the first story of the eleventh season, producer Barry Letts and his script editor, Dicks, decided to revive the historical format of stories for the programme, which had last been used in season four with *The Highlanders*, and this format was one that Holmes was certainly not enamoured with. To add an interesting twist to what he thought was restrictive story-telling, he devised the plot of a Sontaran ship crashing in Earth's past, the pilot of which would travel through time to take scientists and equipment he needed for repair work to his ship, and inevitably encounter the Doctor. The idea was sent to Dicks in the form of a battle report to Sontaran officer Terran Cedicks, from Officer Hol Mes, explaining the consequences of the dire fate that their colleague, Linx had met.

Alan Bromley was hired to direct the first of four Sontaran stories to date, with Kevin Lindsay cast as Linx. Lindsay wore a heavily padded suit of body armour to create the bulk that is characteristic of the muscular, squat race, with a glass fibre helmet resting on the ridge of a high collar, with the probic vent sticking out of the back of it. The make-up consisted of an extremely thick latex mask, with only the actor's lips and eyes left uncovered, and even these were blended in with make-up to match the latex. The mask's thin lips made breathing difficult and with the added weight of the helmet, it became near impossible to get enough air, which in turn created terrible problems for Lindsay during the studio filming when the Doctor and Linx's climactic fight was staged, with recording often stopping to allow him to get his breath back.

The Sontaran spaceship was built as a functioning prop, with several operating control panels inside, seen at the end of episode four. The general appearance can best be compared to the shape of a golf ball, it was made from a glass fibre shell supported by a wooden framework within. The prop was used again for the second story, *The Sontaran Experiment*, the following year. The script called for a barren wasteland after solar flares have laid waste to the surface of the earth, so the production team trekked into the wilds of Dartmoor to record the story entirely on location over a six-day shooting period.

As Field Major Styre, Lindsay wore a slightly redesigned mask, adapted to take into consideration the

Above: **The Doctor (Jon Pertwee) with Linx (Kevin Lindsay), in** *The Time Warrior*.

Below: **Kevin Lindsay has his mask adjusted during location filming for** *The Sontaran Experiment*.

problems experienced on *The Time Warrior*. This mask was made of a lighter latex material, so that the weight of the mask would not rest entirely on the head, making it far easier to speak and breathe. The lower lip was operated by a brace support in the actor's mouth to keep the lip in sync with his own. The same mask was used by Lindsay when he doubled as the Sontaran marshal, seen only on a monitor screen, with the only discernible difference being two raised bosses on the character's collar front. For the fight scene in episode two, Stuart Fell was brought in to take the place of Lindsay, who was suffering from a heart condition, while Terry Walsh doubled for Tom Baker, who had broken his collar bone earlier in the shoot.

When the proposed six-part finale for season 15 fell through, producer Graham Williams and script editor Anthony Read had to race to create a replacement while Williams had the additional problem of a BBC strike to contend with. *The Invasion of Time* can almost be divided into two separate stories; the first four episodes deal with the Vardans' attempted invasion of Gallifrey, with the climax of episode four revealing the true villains to be the Sontarans, whom the Doctor has to combat for the remaining instalments, thanks to Robert Holmes giving Williams permission to use them at the last minute.

Sadly, Kevin Lindsay had by now died, so Derek Deadman was brought in to play the lead Sontaran, Commander Stor. Four Sontaran costumes were put together for this story, including the ones used in past stories, with the three main warriors being used again and again to create an impression of a heavy invasion presence on the planet.

The mask was redesigned yet again, although only the face of Stor was seen unmasked. The mask was now even lighter to wear, but the large mouth had been phased out, with the edge of the mask simply being glued round the actor's mouth, making the creatures markedly different from those seen before.

During the making of *The Five Doctors*, the twentieth-anniversary story of the programme, former Doctor Patrick Troughton so much enjoyed the chance to return that he asked if it were possible for his Doctor and Frazer Hines as Jamie to return in another story. Robert Holmes set about drafting *The Two Doctors* to serve this purpose, with the added bonus of a return appearance by the Sontarans.

Two entirely new costumes were created for Clinton Greyn and Tim Raynham, with the head masks now reverting to the kind of design last seen in *The Time Warrior*. The eyes and lips were left free, while the rest of the actor's head was encased in the inevitable latex. Most of the location filming took place in Spain, which meant the heat inside the costumes was unbearable for much of the time.

Perhaps the most intriguing thing about the design of the Sontaran costumes are the hands. The creatures seen in all of the stories, except for *The Sontaran Experiment*, have had three digits, while Styre, for some mysterious reason, possessed five fingers. Although he didn't write this story, Robert Holmes was asked about this years later and answered that he felt that Sontarans probably found it easier to break human bones with five fingers!

Technical data

The Time Warrior
Production code UUU, season eleven, four episodes

Episode one
Studio recording on 28 May 1973
Rehearsal 11 a.m.–1 p.m., 2 p.m.–6.30 p.m.
Studio filming 8 p.m.-10 p.m.
Studio TC6, TV Centre on 2in tape, film inserts
Broadcast Saturday 15 December 1973, BBC1 5.30 p.m.–5.55 p.m.

Episode two
Studio recording on 29 May 1973
Rehearsal 10.30 a.m.–1 p.m., 2 p.m.–6 p.m.
Studio filming 8.30 p.m.–10 p.m.
Studio details as episode one
Broadcast Saturday 22 December 1973, BBC1 5.30 p.m.–5.55 p.m.

Episode three
Studio recording on 11 June 1973
Rehearsal and filming as episode one
Studio TC1, TV Centre on 2in tape, film inserts
Broadcast Saturday 29 December 1973, BBC1 5.30 p.m.–5.55 p.m.

Episode four
Studio recording on 12 June 1973
Rehearsal and filming as episode two
Studio details as episode three
Broadcast Saturday 5 January 1974, BBC1 5.30 p.m.–5.55 p.m.

Cast: Jon Pertwee (the Doctor); Elisabeth Sladen (Sarah Jane Smith); Nicholas Courtney (Brigadier Lethbridge- Stewart); Kevin Lindsay (Linx); David Daker (Irongron); John J Carney (Bloodaxe); Sheila Fay (Meg); Donald Pelmear (Professor Rubeish); June Brown (Lady Eleanor); Alan Rowe (Edward of Wessex); Gordon Pitt (Eric); Jeremy Bulloch (Hal); Steve Brunswick (Sentry); Jacqueline Stanbury (Mary).

Production credits: Robert Holmes (writer); Alan Bromly (director); Terrance Dicks (script editor); Keith Cheetham (designer);

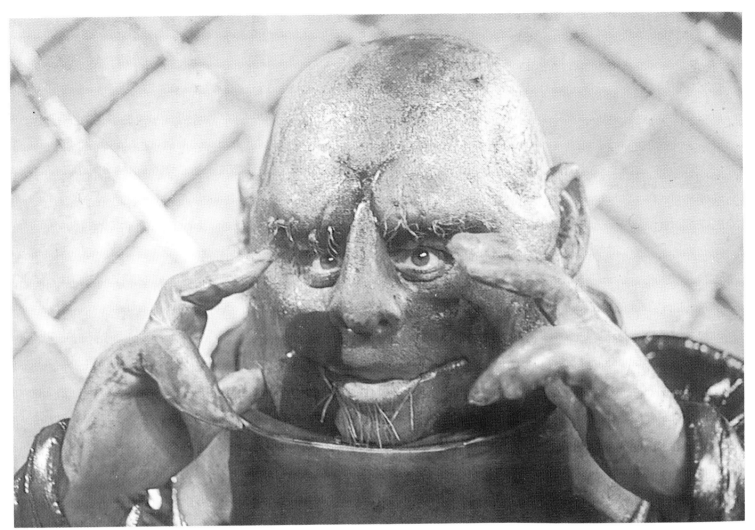

Sandra Exelby (make-up); James Acheson (costumes); Dudley Simpson (incidental music); Jim Ward (visual effects); Barry Letts (producer).

Above: **Linx (Kevin Lindsay) in** *The Time Warrior.*

The Sontaran Experiment*
Production code 4B, season twelve, two episodes
Episode one and two
Filmed entirely on location between 26 September and 1 October 1974, with several days' rehearsal beforehand on location.
Episode one broadcast Saturday 22 February 1975, BBC1 5.30 p.m.–5.55 p.m.
Episode two broadcast Saturday 1 March 1975, BBC1 5.30 p.m.–5.55 p.m.

Cast: Tom Baker (the Doctor); Elisabeth Sladen (Sarah Jane Smith); Ian Marter (Surgeon Lieutenant Harry Sullivan); Kevin Lindsay (Field Major Styre); Peter Walshe (Erak); Terry Walsh (Zake); Glyn Jones (Krans); Peter Rutherford (Roth); Donald Douglas (Vural); Brian Ellis (Prisoner); Kevin Lindsay (Sontaran Marshal).

Production credits: Bob Baker and Dave Martin (writers); Rodney Bennett (director); Robert Holmes (script editor); Roger Murray-Leach (designer); Sylvia James (make-up); Barbara Kidd (costumes); Dudley Simpson (incidental music); John Friedlander and Tony Oxley (visual effects); Philip Hinchcliffe (producer).

The Invasion of Time
Production code 4Z, season fifteen, six episodes
The filming of this story was heavily affected by a BBC strike, with much of the story shot out of sequence.
Rehearsal 26 October to 5 November 1977
One three-day recording block took place from 6 to 8 November 1977. All scenes in the Panopticon and the alien spaceships filmed.
All scenes outside the main Gallifrey city filmed from 13 to 15 November 1977.
With the absence of studio space, all remaining scenes for episodes two to six were filmed from 16th to 18th November and 5 to 16 December 1977.
Locations were used at St Anne's Hospital, Redstone Hill and the British Oxygen HQ in Hammersmith, London.

Episode one broadcast Saturday 4 February 1978, BBC1 6.25 p.m.–6.50 p.m.
Episode two broadcast Saturday 11 February 1978, BBC1 6.25 p.m.–6.50 p.m.
Episode three broadcast Saturday 18 February 1978, BBC1 6.25 p.m.–6.50 p.m.
Episode four broadcast Saturday 25 February 1978, BBC1 6.25 p.m.–6.50 p.m.
Episode five broadcast Saturday 4 March 1978, BBC1 6.25 p.m.–6.50 p.m.
Episode six broadcast Saturday 11 March 1978, BBC1 6.25 p.m.–6.50 p.m.

Cast: Tom Baker (the Doctor); Louise Jameson (Leela); John Leeson (Voice of K9); Milton Johns (Castellan Kelner); John Arnatt (Borusa); Stan McGowan (Vardan Leader); Chris Tranchell (Andred); Denis Edwards (Gomer); Tom Kelly (Vardan); Reginald Jessup (Savar); Charles Morgan (Gold Usher); Hilary Ryan (Rodan); Max Faulkner (Nesbin); Christopher Christou (Chancellery

Above: **Stike (Clinton Greyn) holds the second Doctor (Patrick Troughton) captive.** *The Two Doctors.*

Guard); Michael Harley (Bodyguard); Ray Callaghan (Ablif); Gai Smith (Presta); Michael Mundell (Jasko); Eric Danot (Guard); Derek Deadman (Stor); Stuart Fell, Norman Rochester, Martyn Richards (Sontarans).

Production credits: David Agnew (Graham Williams and Anthony Read) (writers); Gerald Blake (director); Anthony Read (script editor); Barbara Gosnold (designer); Maureen Winslade (make-up); Dee Kelly (costumes); Dudley Simpson (incidental music); Richard Conway and Colin Mapson (visual effects); Graham Williams (producer).

The Two Doctors
Production code 6W, season twenty-two, three episodes

Episodes one to three
Extensive location filming in Seville, Spain, 9–16 August 1984. Story completed with studio filming over three recording blocks.
Block one
Rehearsal 18–24 August 1984
Filming 30–31 August 1984
Block two
Rehearsal 1–12 September 1984
Filming 13–14 September 1984
Block three
Rehearsal 15–26 September 1984
Filming 27–28 September 1984

Episode one broadcast Saturday 16 February 1985, BBC1 5.20 p.m.–6.10 p.m.
Episode two broadcast Saturday 23 February 1985, BBC1 5.20 p.m.–6.10 p.m.
Episode three broadcast Saturday 2 March 1985, BBC1 5.20 p.m.–6.10 p.m.

Cast: Colin Baker (the Doctor); Nicola Bryant (Peri); Patrick Troughton (the Doctor); Frazer Hines (Jamie); John Stratton (Shockeye); Jacqueline Pearce (Chessene); Laurence Payne (Dastari); James Saxon (Oscar); Carmen Gomez (Anita); Aimee Delamain (Dona Arana); Nicholas Farcett (Technician); Laurence Payne (computer voice); Fernando Monast (Scientist); Jay McGrath (Dead Androgum); Clinton Greyn (Stike); Tim Raynham (Varl).

Production credits: Robert Holmes (writer); Peter Moffatt (director); Eric Saward (script editor); Tony Burrough (designer); Katherine Davies (make-up); Jan Wright (costumes); Peter Howell (incidental music); Steve Drewett (visual effects); John Nathan-Turner (producer).

Additional data

Kevin Lindsay also appeared in another story during season eleven. In *Planet of the Spiders*, he can be seen as Cho-Je, who induces the regeneration that saves the Doctor's life at the story's climax.

All stories are preserved in the BBC film archives. One other Sontaran appearance is also to be found in the BBC series *Jim'll Fix It*. The benevolent DJ fixed it for Gareth Jenkins to appear in *Doctor Who*. A specially filmed short adventure was made, with Colin Baker as the Doctor and Janet Fielding returning as Tegan in *A Fix with the Sontarans*. The two costumes from *The Two Doctors* were used.

Heavily criticized at the time for the level of violence portrayed in the story, it is interesting to note that in the original draft of *The Two Doctors* by Robert Holmes, the death scene of Oscar was rather different. In the televised story, he is stabbed by Shockeye; in the draft, Shockeye rips his arm off and starts to eat it!

Novelizations

Doctor Who and the Time Warrior
Terrance Dicks
Adapted from the original scripts by Robert Holmes. Prologue acknowledgement written by Robert Holmes. Number 65 in the Target novelization series.

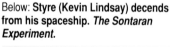

Below: **Styre (Kevin Lindsay) decends from his spaceship.** *The Sontaran Experiment.*

Doctor Who and The Sontaran Experiment
Ian Marter
Adapted from the original scripts by Bob Baker and Dave Martin. Number 56 in the Target novelization series.

Doctor Who and the Invasion of Time
Terrance Dicks
Adapted from the original scripts by David Agnew (Graham Williams and Anthony Read). Number 35 in the Target novelization series.

Doctor Who – The Two Doctors
Robert Holmes
Number 100 in the Target novelization series.

Commercial video releases

Doctor Who – The Time Warrior
BBC Video
Episodes edited together to form a 90-minute film. End titles missing from episodes 1, 2 and 3. Beginning titles missing from episodes 2, 3 and 4.

Doctor Who – The Sontaran Experiment/Genesis of the Daleks
BBC Video
Unedited episodes one and two. Story on a double-pack tape with the adventure that immediately followed it on the original broadcast run.

THE ZYGONS
The creatures of Loch Ness

Production data

It's somewhat surprising that the production team of the mid-1960s, particularly Innes Lloyd, in their quest for monsters with an element of reality behind them didn't turn their attentions towards the myths and legends surrounding Loch Ness. It wasn't until season 13 that Robert Banks Stewart's story, *The Terror of the Zygons*, brought the Doctor to the inland lake in Scotland, and indeed, the original working title for the story was *The Loch Ness Monster.*

This was changed on the grounds that to base a story solely round the one monster would be incredibly expensive and difficult to realize, so the more humanoid Zygons were introduced; these were not as important an element in the earlier drafts of the script as they later became. The legends of the monster of Loch Ness stretched back several hundred years. Unlike the Abominable Snowman, however, there is photographic evidence to support the belief that Nessie is real. The most remarkable is some black and white film shot towards the end of the 1930s that shows the creature swimming only ten feet or so from the shoreline.

The Zygons themselves were the creation of James Acheson, the stories costume designer, and his production team, including the in-house freelance monster specialist, John Friedlander. Acheson has since gone on to work on feature films, winning Oscars for his work on *The Last Emperor* and *Dangerous Liaisons*.

The look was intended to be quite unlike anything that had been seen on the series before; the shape of a human foetus was used as a starting point. The Zygons' vast domed heads and tiny faces can be recognized as originating from this idea, but the addition of suckers all over the body makes the creatures totally alien. The actual fitting of the three actors playing the creatures into their costumes took up endless, precious studio time, with painstaking care being taken to conceal the join of the two basic halves of the costume.

Above and Below: **Broton (John Woodnutt), leader of the Zygons.** *The Terror of the Zygons.*

The latex leggings were easily fitted, with heavy foot coverings blending into the trouser section. The entire head and chest section had to be carefully fitted, with the delicate glass fibre support frame that created the Zygon shape being all too easy to dent. The delicate paintwork on the body also had to be protected with great care; the make-up could then be applied to glue the mouth and eye holes round the rim of the actor's skin that was left bare. A very thin layer of latex was actually hooked into the mouth to form the lower lip. The main bulk of the body was made from expanded latex, which although quite heavy, was unusually comfortable for the actors within, with the arched back supporting the neck and spine.

Under the direction of Douglas Camfield, the actors developed a harsh, whispering sound for the Zygon voices, which caused problems for the studio's overhanging boom microphones. If the actor turned in any direction other than the one facing the microphone, the words simply faded away – the equipment was unable to pick them up. A small, mobile microphone was carefully concealed within the front of the Zygon costumes, hidden in one of the suckers just in front of the face, making it easy to record the appropriate dialogue.

The interior of the Zygon spaceship was designed to blend in with the creatures themselves, with the same colour scheme and organic feel that they had. No panels of switches and levers were in sight, just nodules and lumps that the Zygons manipulated, as though they were genetically linked to their ship. Actor John Woodnutt was the only one of the three Zygons to play both his human and alien counterparts.

The Loch Ness Monster itself was brought to life through several different methods, some of which were more successful than others. For the sequences involving the Doctor being chased across the moors by the creature, stop-motion animation was employed in one of the few instances in the programme's history when this technique has been used. For scenes where the creature is seen passing close by the screen, a camera was tracked alongside a full-length model of the monster. Unfortunately, when it came to filming the dramatic moment when the creature emerges from the waters of the River Thames, time had run out and a simple glove puppet was used, performing against a blue screen which had footage of the Thames embankment projected on to it with CSO in post-production. The matte shots of the Zygon ship, and the model shots of it stationed in the quarry and taking off are, by comparison, wonders to behold.

For a story that was based specifically round Loch Ness, the production team studied the logistical possibilities of going to the actual site. This proved far too costly, so they went to Bognor Regis instead.

Technical data

Terror of the Zygons
Production code 4F, season thirteen, four episodes

Episode one
Studio recording on 7 April 1975
Rehearsal 11 a.m.–1 p.m., 2 p.m.-6 p.m.
Filming 7.30 p.m.–10 p.m.
Studio TC3 TV centre on 2in tape, film inserts
Broadcast Saturday 30 August 1975, BBC1 5.30 p.m.–5.55 p.m.

Episode two
Studio recording on 8 April 1975
Rehearsal 10.30 a.m.–1 p.m., 2 p.m.–2.30 p.m.
Filming 2.30 p.m.–3.30 p.m.
Rehearsal 3.30 p.m.–6 p.m.
Filming 7.30 p.m.–10 p.m.
Studio details as episode one
Broadcast Saturday 6 September 1975, BBC1 5.30 p.m.–5.55 p.m.

Episode three
Studio recording on 22 April 1975
Rehearsal and filming as episode one
Studio TC4, TV Centre on 2in tape, film inserts
Broadcast Saturday 13 September 1975, BBC1 5.30 p.m.–5.55 p.m.

Episode four
Studio recording on 23 April 1975
Rehearsal and filming as episode two
Studio TC4, TV centre on 2in tape, film inserts
Broadcast Saturday 20 September 1975, BBC1 5.30 p.m.–5.55 p.m.

Cast: Tom Baker (the Doctor); Elisabeth Sladen (Sarah Jane Smith); Ian Marter (Surgeon Lieutenant Harry Sullivan); Nicholas Courtney (Brigadier Lethbridge-Stewart); John Levene (RSM Benton); John Woodnutt (Duke of Forgill); Hugh Martin (Munro); Tony Sibbald (Huckle); Angus Lennie (Angus McRanald); Robert Russell (the Caber); Bruce Wrightman (Radio Operator); Lillias Walker (Sister Lamont); Bernard G. High (Corporal); Peter Symonds (Soldier); John Woodnutt (Broton); Keith Ashley, Ronald Gough (Zygons)

Production credits: Robert Banks Stewart (writer); Douglas Camfield (director); Robert Holmes (script editor); Nigel Curzon (designer); Sylvia James (make-up); James Acheson (costumes); Geoffrey Burgon (incidental music); John Horton (visual effects); Philip Hinchcliffe (producer).

Additional data

During season seventeen a BBC strike curtailed production on *Doctor Who*, stopping work on the final story of the season, *Shada*.

One sequence was to have involved a space station and prison cells releasing their occupants. Apart from a Dalek and a Cyberman, a Zygon would have been seen as well. This was unfortunately never filmed.

Novelization
Doctor Who and The Loch Ness Monster
Terrance Dicks
Adapted from the original scripts by Robert Banks Stewart. Number 40 in the Target novelization series.

Commercial video release
BBC Video
Doctor Who – Terror of the Zygons
Episodes edited together to form a 94-minute film. End titles missing from episodes 1, 2 and 3. Beginning titles missing from episodes 2, 3 and 4.

THE AUTONS

Deadly dangerous dummies

Production data

Towards the end of the 1960s, plastic was a relatively new commodity that was economical, and at that time, easy to dispose of. The public thrived on it, but there were hidden implications that nobody thought about. Years passed and it became clear that once made, plastic could never be gotten rid of entirely; whereas glass could be melted down and reused, plastic couldn't. It was inevitable that the minds of TV writers would turn to this subject.

In the same year that *Spearhead From Space* was broadcast, the creators of the Cybermen, Kit Pedler and Gerry Davis, thought up a more brutal scenario based around the dangers of plastic. In the first episode of *Doomwatch*, 'The Plastic Eaters', a chemical virus was created to destroy the substance, but spread wildly out of control when it came into contact with it. Robert Holmes created the Autons to equal frightening effect for the younger viewer.

Two basic Auton designs were created for the first story. The Auton drone was the size of a normal man, with a smooth, almost clear, plastic featureless face, with blank dark eye sockets. This was simply achieved by using an overhead mask covering the actor's head entirely. The body of the Auton was covered by a blue boiler suit; a scarf round the neck concealed the edge of the mask.

The Auton gun was a simple hand-held prop: the actor held a false hand from within the sleeve of the boiler suit, and triggered a switch to drop the four main fingers of the hand down on a hinge. Another trigger could then be used to discharge an electrical powder flash down a thin nozzle. Although very effective on screen, the main problem with this was that the gun had to be reloaded after every shot, and quite often the charges would fail to go off, leading to endless retakes.

The basic Auton drones were used for the sequences in the invasion, where they are seen as shop-window dummies coming to life and slaughtering the general public. The costumes were slightly redressed, with several wearing dressing gowns and suits, and wigs covering their bald heads.

The second type of Autons, the replicants, were created by applying a simple plastic sheen to their faces of the actors playing them.

Owing to a strike at the BBC, this story was shot entirely on location, something that up until then the production teams could only dream of. Sets were erected inside buildings when studios would normally have been used. This resulted in the climax of the Nestene Consciousness materialization having to be done on set, when such effects would normally be staged in the controlled environment of a studio. Simple rubber octopus-like limbs are seen reaching out of the Nestene gestation tank, trying to strangle the Doctor and drag him into the tank.

Holmes's original script called for the creature to smash its way out of the tank and attack the Doctor, with a cat-and-mouse game of death ensuing as it stalked the Time Lord through the Auton laboratory. Unfortunately this was not to be, and the resulting effect was, to put it kindly, less than convincing. With the production team under such pressure, it's remarkable that director Derek Martinus achieved the overall results that he did with the story.

The success of *Spearhead From Space* immediately established the new Doctor, Jon Pertwee, as a successful replacement for Patrick Troughton. As production began to draw to a close on season seven, producer Barry Letts asked Holmes to write a sequel for the first story of season eight.

A basic formula had been devised to introduce a Moriarty-like figure for the Doctor to do battle with, and *Terror of the Autons* saw the debut of the Master, played by Roger Delgado. The story began with a Nestene sphere being stolen from a museum. The spheres were vac-formed glass fibre shells, roughly the size of a football, with flat patches running across areas of their surface. Several were fitted with simple lighting rods for scenes where the spheres are seen to become active.

The Autons were slightly redesigned for their second outing, with the faces of the creatures smoothed out even more, and the signs of noses and brows that had been there before now completely gone. The head was

Above: **Channing (Hugh Burden) was the most sophisticated of the Autons.** *Spearhead from Space.*

a shade of pale white and smooth, with the dark patches indicating where the eyes should be. For the large part of the story, the Autons are seen in disguise as policemen and so on, with simple latex masks worn over the Auton masks for scenes where the skin is pulled away to reveal their true identity. The hand-gun effects were the same as before, as were the costumes for the Auton drones when they made their brief appearances.

When the Master sends the Autons out to dispense the lethal plastic daffodils to the unsuspecting general public, vast hollow Happy Heads were worn by the actors, as well as a uniform consisting of a yellow blazer with red stripes, and white trousers. With the heads on for the rest of the story, the actors were not required to wear the tight Auton masks underneath on location. Director Barry Letts took the production unit to a real radar tracking station for the final battle at the end of episode four.

The effects of the Nestene chair was achieved by filming the sequences in reverse, with actor Harry Towb sitting on the chair as it deflated, and pulling its black plastic material across his face as if it were suffocating him. The Auton toy doll was played by an actor wearing a suit based on the foot-high doll that is planted in the car of Farrell's father in the story. The sequences involving the actors being attacked by the doll were achieved using CSO, matting the two images together. *Terror of the Autons* became somewhat notorious at the time of broadcast: the killer dolls and the kidnapping of the Doctor by policemen caused floods of complaints from parents who were worried about the effects this would have on their children.

The Autons were destined to return in one of the aborted stories from season twenty-three, with plans for Robert Holmes to write a story involving the Autons setting up a plastics factory in Singapore. Alas, such ideas as rubber bullets that bounce round corners after people, and Auton hands that when held over human heads melt until the head is encased in plastic, never got beyond basic discussion stages; not even a draft script was completed.

Technical data

Spearhead From Space
Production code AAA, season seven, four episodes

Episode one to four
Story recorded entirely on location, exact dates unavailable. Rehearsal over a period of five weeks in September 1969
Filming over a period of five weeks in October 1969

Episode one broadcast Saturday 3 January 1970, BBC1 5.15 p.m.-5.40 p.m.
Episode two broadcast Saturday 10 January 1970, BBC1 5.15 p.m.-5.40 p.m.
Episode three broadcast Saturday 17 January 1970, BBC1 5.15 p.m.-5.40 p.m.
Episode four broadcast Saturday 24 January 1970, BBC1 5.15 p.m.-5.40 p.m.

Cast: Jon Pertwee (the Doctor); Caroline John (Liz Shaw); Nicholas Courtney (Brigadier Lethbridge-Stewart); Hugh Burden (Channing); Neil Wilson (Seeley); John Breslin (Captain Munro); Anthony Webb (Doctor Henderson); Helen Dorward (Nurse); Talfryn Thomas (Mullins); George Lee (Corporal Forbes); Allan Mitchell (Wagstaffe); Prentis Hancock (Reporter); Derek Smee (Ransome); John Woodnutt (Hibbert); Betty Bowden (Meg Seeley); Hamilton Dyce (Scobie); Henry McCarthy (Doctor Beavis); Clifford Cox (Soldier); Edmund Bailey (Waxworks Attendant); Ellis Johns (Voice of Doctor Lomax); Iain Smith, Tessa Shaw, Ellis Johns (UNIT Staff); Pat Gorman (Auton).

Production credits: Robert Holmes (writer); Derek Martinus (director); Terrance Dicks (script editor); Paul Allen (designer); Cynthia Goodwin (make-up); Christine Rawlins (costumes); Dudley Simpson (incidental music); Derrick Sherwin (producer).

Terror of the Autons
Production code EEE, season eight, four episodes

Episode one
Studio recording on 9 October 1970
Rehearsal 11.30 a.m.-1 p.m., 2 p.m.-7 p.m.
Filming 8.30 p.m.-10 p.m.
Studio TC8, TV Centre on 2in tape, film inserts
Broadcast Saturday 2 January 1971, BBC1 5.15 p.m.-5.40 p.m.

Episode two
Studio recording on 10 October 1970
Rehearsal 10.30 a.m.-1 p.m., 2 p.m.-6 p.m.
Filming 7.30 p.m.-10 p.m.
Studio details as episode one
Broadcast Saturday 9 January 1971, BBC1 5.15 p.m.-5.40 p.m.

Episode three
Studio recording on 23 October 1970
Rehearsal and filming as episode one
Studio TC6, TV Centre on 2in tape, film inserts
Broadcast Saturday 16 January 1971, BBC1 5.15 p.m.-5.40 p.m.

Episode four
Studio recording on 24 October 1970
Rehearsal details as episode two
Filming 7.30 p.m.-10.30 p.m.
Studio details as episode three
Broadcast Saturday 23 January 1970, BBC1 5.15 p.m.-5.40 p.m.

Cast: Jon Pertwee (the Doctor); Katy Manning (Jo Grant); Roger Delgado (the Master); Nicholas Courtney (Brigadier Lethbridge Stewart); John Levene (Sergeant Benton); Richard Franklin (Captain Mike Yates); John Baskomb (Rossini); Dave Carter (Museum Attendant); Christopher Burgess (Professor Phillips); Andrew Staines (Goodge); Frank Mills (Radiotelescope Director); David Garth (Time Lord); Michael Wisher (Rex Farrel); Harry Towb (McDermott); Stephen Jack (Farrel Senior); Barbara Leake (Mrs Farrel); Roy Stewart (Strong Man); Dermot Tuohy (Brownrose); Norman Stanley (Telephone Repair Man); Les Conrad (Soldier); Pat Gorman (Auton/Auton Policeman); Terry Walsh (Auton/Auton Policeman); Tommy Reynolds (Auton Troll Doll); Les Clark, Bob Blaine, Ian Elliott, Charles Pickess, Mike Stevens, Nick Hobbs, Tom O'Leary (Autons).

Production credits: Robert Holmes (writer); Barry Letts (director); Terrance Dicks (script editor); Ian Watson (designer); Jan Harrison (make-up); Ken Trew (costumes); Dudley Simpson (incidental music); Michael-John Harris (visual effects); Barry Letts (producer).

Additional data

Robert Holmes's lost story from season twenty-three had the working title of Evil of the Autons. The character the Rani would also have been involved, as previously played by Kate O'Mara in *The Mark of the Rani* and *Time and The Rani*.
One of the earlier drafts of *The Five Doctors* by Terrance Dicks, before Tom Baker decided that he did not want to appear, had the third Doctor, Jon Pertwee, encountering an army of Autons in the Death Zone.

Novelizations

Doctor Who and the Auton Invasion
Terrance Dicks
Adapted from the original scripts by Robert Holmes. Number 6 in the Target novelization series.

Doctor Who and the Terror of the Autons
Terrance Dicks
Adapted from the original scripts by Robert Holmes. Number 63 in the Target novelization series.

Commercial video releases
Doctor Who – Spearhead From Space
BBC Video
Episodes edited together to form a 92-minute film. End titles missing from episodes 1, 2 and 3. Beginning titles missing from episodes 2, 3 and 4.

THE SILURIANS AND THE SEA DEVILS
Reptiles from the underworld and underwater

Production data

Perhaps the first interrelated monsters to have appeared in *Doctor Who*, the Silurians and Sea Devils both featured in individual stories with the Third Doctor before joining forces to fight the fifth Doctor several years later. Malcolm Hulke, their creator, had a fascination with the concept of what a race that had inhabited the Earth would have been like had it existed before man had even evolved from primitive apes. One thing was quite clear, the intense heat on the surface of the planet would have certainly meant they would have been a species of reptiles.

Timothy Combe was hired to direct the first, highly complex seven-part story, which introduced one of the most memorable intelligent monsters to have been seen on the programme. Textured body suits were worn by the actors playing the Silurians; they were covered in thick scales, with simple rubber gloves and shaped boots worn over the hands and feet, and claws stuck on the fingers and toes. The head masks were quite complex, with an electronic light fitted into a skull cap to illuminate the creature's third eye on the forehead. A rubber ridge resting against the chin of the actor enabled him to move the creature's mouth slightly to indicate that it was speaking. The older Silurians were given a slight change in skin colouration, to suggest their great age, and in some cases the sheer weight of the mask is quite clear, with some of the Silurian extras visibly stooping under the strain.

The dinosaur under Silurian control was achieved simply through using a rod puppet and projecting it against the cave wall with CSO. *The Silurians* was the first story shot in colour to be made in the studio (*Spearhead from Space*, which preceded it, was shot entirely on location); it was also the first one to take advantage of the relatively new process of colour separation overlay (CSO).

With extensive location footage being shot during the autumn of 1969, one of the sequences centred on filming point-of-view shots of a Silurian as it escaped across Wenley Moor. The actual monster costume was needed for only a few brief glimpses; other than that, a specially developed lens was used to show what the creature could see. Divided into three images, the top section was covered with a red filter, representing the third Silurian eye.

With *The Silurians* one of the successes of season seven, a form of sequel was requested by script editor, Terrance Dicks, from Malcolm Hulke the following year, but Hulke refused to take the obvious course of bringing the Silurians back. With the Silurians being cave-dwelling creatures, Hulke turned his attention to the sea. He developed the idea for the Silurians' aquatic cousins, the Sea Devils.

The Silurians had retreated into hibernation when the gravity of the Earth brought the moon into a natural orbit round the planet, fearing that a collision would take place. So was it too much to assume that a similar event

Above: **A Silurian from *Doctor Who and the Silurians*.**

Below: **A Sea Devil from *The Sea Devils*.**

Right: **A Sea Devil with its sonic gun.** *The Sea Devils.*

Right: **A Sea Devil with its sonic gun.** *The Sea Devils.*

had occurred with a water-based species, whose reactivation units had malfunctioned just as badly as the Silurians had done?

The Sea Devils were made of rather bulky rubber body suits, enabling the actor within to enter the sea without causing too much damage to the costume. With the Silurians' relatively simple head-mask, the actors had just the weight to contend with; the Sea Devils' heads were built round a head-piece so that they were, in effect, worn like a hat, with the actor being able to see out through a wire-mesh grille in the neck area. This, in turn, restricted the facial movements that could be used on the mask, with only the chief Sea Devil being able to move its mouth and blink its eyes.

The Silurians had not worn anything that could be compared to clothing, so they were in a sense naked, something that the director of *The Sea Devils*, Michael E. Briant, definitely didn't want in his story. So the creatures were duly decked out with vests made out of fishing-net, with Briant theorizing that they could have been made from trawler nets that had drifted to the bottom of the ocean.

The guns used by the Sea Devils can best be described as looking like squat hand-torches, with a glass lens mounted on a pronged cup that concealed the hand when holding one. A trigger within the cup could set off a powder flash charge, causing smoke to drift out of the front of the gun to great effect.

The voices for all the Silurians had been supplied by Peter Halliday, using a voice modulator similar to the ones used to create the voices for the early Cybermen. But for the Sea Devils, the actors inside the costume spoke their own dialogue in gently hissing voices, which were later treated for added effect in post-production.

One of the main problems experienced during filming was caused by the air that got caught between the top of the Sea Devil mask and the actor's head whenever they went under the surface of the water to prepare for scenes where the creatures had to rise from the depths. An air bubble was formed, resulting in the Sea Devils' heads frequently shooting into the air and breaking through the surface like a champagne cork before the actor had even begun to rise.

The opening story for the twenty-first season saw both breeds of creature return in *Warriors of the Deep*, with writer Johnny Byrne bringing them together to fight a common cause and invade an underwater nuclear base whose missiles could be used to wipe out the population of Earth, leaving the creatures free to take back the planet that was rightfully theirs.

To suit the futuristic nature of the story, the costumes for the monsters were suitably augmented, with the Silurians now fitted with an armoured shell like a tortoise, and the Sea Devils wearing a form of battle dress that can best be described as being similar to that of a Samurai warrior.

In a change from the original creatures, the Silurians' third eye now flashed in sync with their voicesto indicate which one was speaking. The eye had apparently lost its use as a weapon, as seen in their debut story.

With the dinosaur seen in *The Silurians* as a form of guard for the Silurian caves, the Sea Devils were revealed as having their own pet, the Myrka, used for fighting purposes in their battles. Unfortunately, the special-effects department at the BBC did not have enough time to finish building the creature properly, to the degree that they would normally be satisfied with. Suffice to say, there were considerable problems for the two men operating the creature during filming, with part of the trouble coming from the fact that the paint hadn't dried properly on its skin!

Technical data

Doctor Who and the Silurians
Production code BBB, season seven, seven episodes

Episode one
Studio recording on 8 December 1969
Rehearsal 10.30 a.m.–1 p.m., 2 p.m.–7 p.m.
Filming 8.30 p.m.–10 p.m.
Studio TC3, TV Centre on 2in tape, film inserts
Broadcast Saturday 31 January 1970, BBC1 5.15 p.m.–5.40 p.m.

Episode two
Studio recording on 22 December 1969
Rehearsal 11.30 a.m.–1.30 p.m., 2.30 p.m.–6.30 p.m.
Filming 8 p.m.–11 p.m.
Studio TC1, TV Centre on 2in tape, film inserts
Sequences for episodes three and four recorded on the same day, hence longer filming period
Broadcast Saturday 7 February 1970, BBC1 5.15 p.m.–5.40 p.m.

Episode three
Studio recording on 15 December 1969
Rehearsal and filming as episode one
Studio details as episode one
Episode three recorded before episode two
Broadcast Saturday 14 February 1970, BBC1 5.15 p.m.–5.40 p.m.

Episode four
Studio recording on 5 January 1970
Rehearsal and filming as episode one
Studio details as episode two
Broadcast Saturday 21 February 1970, BBC1 5.15 p.m.–5.40 p.m.

Episode five
Studio recording on 12 January 1970
Rehearsal and filming as episode one
Studio details as episode two
Broadcast Saturday 28 February 1970, BBC1 5.15 p.m.–5.40 p.m.

Episode six
Studio recording on 19 January 1970
Rehearsal 10.30 a.m.–1 p.m., 2 p.m.–6 p.m.
Filming 8.15 p.m.–10 p.m.
Studio TC8, TV Centre on 2in tape, film inserts
Broadcast Saturday 7 March 1970, BBC1 5.15 p.m.–5.40 p.m.

Episode seven
Studio recording on 26 January 1970
Rehearsal and filming as episode one

Above: **A Silurian costume.** *Doctor Who and the Silurians.*

Below: **The Silurians' pet dinosaur.** *Doctor Who and the Silurians.*

Studio details as episode six
Broadcast Saturday 14 March 1970, BBC1 5.15 p.m.–5.40 p.m.

Cast: Jon Pertwee (the Doctor); Caroline John (Liz Shaw); Nicholas Courtney (Brigadier Lethbridge-Stewart); John Newman (Spencer); Bill Matthews (Davis); Peter Miles (Doctor Lawrence); Norman Jones (Baker); Thomasine Heiner (Miss Dawson); Fulton MacKay (Doctor Quinn); Roy Branigan (Roberts); Ian Cunningham (Doctor Meredith); Paul Darrow (Hawkins); Nancie Jackson (Doris Squire); Gordon Richardson (Squire); Richard Steele (Hart); Ian Talbot (Travis); Geoffrey Palmer (Masters); Harry Swift (Robins); Brendon Barry (Doctor); Derek Pollitt (Wright); Alan Mason (Corporal Nutting); Pat Gorman (Silurian scientist); Dave Carter (Old Silurian); Nigel Johns (Young Silurian); Paul Barton, Simon Cain, John Churchill (Silurians).

Production credits: Malcolm Hulke (writer); Timothy Coombe (director); Terrance Dicks (script editor); Barry Newbery (designer); Marion Richards and Tessa Wright (make-up); Christine Rawlins (costumes); Carey Blyton (incidental music); Jim Ward (visual effects); Barry Letts (producer).

The Sea Devils★
Production code LLL, season nine, six episodes

Episode one
Studio recording on 15 November 1971
Rehearsal 11.30 a.m.–1 p.m., 2 p.m.–6.30 p.m.
Filming 8 p.m.–10 p.m.
Studio TC8, TV Centre on 2in tape, film inserts
Broadcast Saturday 26 February 1972, BBC1 5.50 p.m.–6.15 p.m.

Episode two
Studio recording on 16 November 1971
Rehearsal 10.30 a.m.–1 p.m., 2 p.m.-6 p.m.
Filming 7.30 p.m.-10 p.m.
Studio details as episode one
Broadcast Saturday 4 March 1972, BBC1 5.50 p.m.–6.15 p.m.

Episode three
Studio recording on 29 November 1971
Rehearsal and filming details as episode one
Studio details as episode one
Broadcast Saturday 11 March 1972, BBC1 5.50 p.m.–6.15 p.m.

Episode four
Studio recording on 30 November 1971
Rehearsal and filming as episode two
Studio details as episode one
Broadcast Saturday 18 March 1972, BBC1 5.50 p.m.–6.15 p.m.

Episode five
Studio recording on 13 December 1971
Rehearsal and filming as episode one
Studio details as episode one
Broadcast Saturday 25 March 1972, BBC1 5.50 p.m.–6.15 p.m.

Episode six
Studio recording on 14 December 1971
Rehearsal and filming as episode two
Studio details as episode one
Broadcast Saturday 1 April 1972, BBC1 5.50 p.m.–6.15 p.m.

Cast: Jon Pertwee (the Doctor); Katy Manning (Jo Grant); Roger Delgado (the Master); Clive Morton (Colonel Trenchard); Royston Tickner (Robbins); Edwin Richfield (Captain Hart); Alec Wallis (Bowman); Neil Seiler (Radio Operator); Terry Walsh (Barclay); Brian Justice (Wilson); June Murphy (Jane Blythe); Hugh Futcher (Hickman); Declan Mulholland (Clark); Eric Mason (Smedley); Donald Sumpter (Ridgeway); Stanley McGeagh (Drew); David Griffin (Mitchell); Christopher Wray (Lovell); Colin Bell (Summers); Brian Vaughn (Watts); Martin Boddey (Walker); Norman Atkyns (Rear Admiral); Rex Rowland (Griton); John Ceaser (Myers); Peter Forbes-Robertson (Chief Sea Devil); Pat Gorman, Brian Nolan, Steve Ismay, Frank Seton, Jeff Witherick, Jack Cooper, Mike Horsburgh, Mike Stevens, Marc Boyle (Sea Devils); Terry Walsh, Peter Brace, Stuart Fell, Bill Horrigan, Alan Chuntz (Sea Devil stunt doubles).

Production credits: Malcolm Hulke (writer); Michael E Briant (director); Terrance Dicks (script editor); Tony Snoaden (designer); Sylvia James (make-up); Maggie Fletcher (costumes); Malcolm Clarke (incidental music); Peter Day (visual effects); Barry Letts (producer).

Warriors of the Deep
Production code 6L, season twenty-one, four episodes

Episodes one to four
Story recorded in two separate recording blocks
Block one
Rehearsal June 1983
Filming June 1983
Block two
Rehearsal July 1983
Filming July 1983

Episode one broadcast Thursday 5 January 1984, BBC1 6.40 p.m.–7.05 p.m.
Episode two broadcast Friday 6 January 1984, BBC1 6.40 p.m.–7.05 p.m.

Episode three broadcast Thursday 12t January 1984, BBC1 6.40 p.m.–7.05 p.m.
Episode four broadcast Friday 13 January 1984, BBC1 6.40 p.m.–7.05 p.m.

Cast: Peter Davison (the Doctor); Janet Fielding (Tegan); Mark Strickson (Turlough); Tom Adams (Vorshak); Ingrid Pitt (Solow); Ian McCulloch (Nilson); Nigel Humphreys (Bulic); Martin Neil (Maddox); Tara Ward (Preston); Nitza Saul (Karina); James Coombes (Paroli); Norman Comer (Icthar); Stuart Blake (Scibus); Vincent Brimble (Tarpok); Christopher Farries (Sauvix); Steve Kelly, Chris Wolfe, Jules Walters, Mike Braben, Dave Ould (Sea Devils); William Perrie and John Asquith (the Myrka).

Production credits: Johnny Byrne (writer); Pennant Roberts (director); Eric Saward (script editor); Tony Burrough (designer); Jill Hagger (make-up); Colin Lavers (costumes); Peter Howell (incidental music); Mat Irvine (visual effects); John Nathan-Turner (producer).

Additional data

All episodes of all three stories are preserved in the BBC film archives. Colour copies suitable for transmission on British 625VT are sought for all episodes of *The Silurians*, and episodes 1, 2 and 3 of *The Sea Devils*.
One of the original costumes for the Sea Devils was found in the BBC costume warehouse in 1983, but enough time had elapsed for the latex mask to have decayed somewhat. The head can be seen at the occasional Who-related exhibition.

Novelizations

Doctor Who and The Cave Monsters
Malcolm Hulke
Number 9 in the Target novelization series.

Doctor Who and The Sea Devils
Malcolm Hulke
Number 54 in the Target novelization series.

Doctor Who – Warriors from The Deep
Terrance Dicks
Number 87 in the Target novelization series.

THE EARTH DEMONS

Devils and demons everywhere

Production data

The actual Daemon, Azal, did not make his appearance in *The Daemons* until the dramatic conclusion of episode four, although his presence had most certainly been felt up until that point, with his powers bringing the stone gargoyle, Bok, to life. Bok was simple enough for the costume department to make, with actor Stanley Mason wearing a white body stocking, clawed latex boots and gloves, and a head-mask that hid his features. A pair of wings and a tail were clipped on to his back as a finishing touch.

Left: **Bok (Stanley Mason) menaces the Doctor (Jon Pertwee).** *The Daemons.*

For the scenes when Bok returned to being his former stony self, a life-size polystyrene sculpture was made, and after filming had been completed, it spent many years residing in Jon Pertwee's garden, until the toil of the wind and rain eventually eroded it until nothing was left.

All the sequences featuring Azal were shot against a blue screen backdrop, so they could be matched with scenes shot of the church cellar by using CSO. Stephen Thorne wore a simple fur-lined body stocking over his lower half, with hoofed feet made out of thick latex. Thick black fur was stuck on to his chest and his back, with the horned wig carefully blended into it. While the lower half of his face remained free from being covered up, except for a set of suitably sharp fangs, a simple rubber mask finished the effect with a typically demonic face. Only Bok was required out of the two of them for both the studio filming, and the extensive location work in the village of Aldbourne, in Wiltshire, which up until a few years ago still had the pub sign created for the story hanging outside the local inn, The Cloven Hoof.

All the creature effects for *The Image of the Fendahl* were achieved in the studio, with the attack outside Fetch Priory being shot from their creatures' point of view, so that they aren't actually seen until the climax of episode three. The transformation of Thea Ransome into the embodiment of the Fendahl core was done with a combination of costume and make-up. Fabric of glittering gold and silver, mixed with facial colouring along the same lines created an eerie effect, with actress Wanda Ventham's eyes shut and painted over with white and black, creating a second, larger pair of eyes over her own. The Fendahl creatures themselves were a mixture of life-size props, stop-motion animation and simple puppetry, such as the sequence in which one of the Satanists was turned into one of the creatures.

The Awakening started life as a four-part script submitted to the then resident script editor, Eric Saward. It was consequently cut to two episodes when the decision was made that it would work better this way. Two aspects of the Malus creature are seen through the story, and both were made by Imagineering, a special effects company headed by Richard Gregory, who had been responsible for making the Cybermen for their return in *Earthshock*, two years previously.

The main Malus was quite literally the size of a wall, with only its head seen behind crumbling brickwork as it tried to break free. A certain degree of movement was needed for the prop, so it was given the ability to curl its lip back, move its head from side to side and roll its green eyes, illuminated with lights from behind. Smoke was duly pumped around it whenever it chose to move, and suitably angry roars were added in post-production.

The second aspect of the Malus showed its full body in miniature as a psychic projection inside the TARDIS, giving an idea of the sheer size of the creature which had been buried centuries before. This Malus was an elaborate rod-puppet, CSO'd on to a pre-filmed image of the TARDIS wall column. When the creature is seen to lose its control, and in a sense die, green slime was pumped through the neck and out of the mouth, giving it a suitably grisly death scene.

In 1983, the film *Legend* was released at the cinema, featuring stunning prosthetic effects by Rob Bottin, including the character of Darkness (otherwise known as the Devil), as played under the latex by Tim Curry. The script for *Battlefield* called for a similar creation, but without the technical resources of *Legend*'s budget.

The resulting effect, as played under the latex by Marek Anton, is a tribute to the ingenuity of the team who made it, with the Destroyer easily being one of the most impressive creations the series has seen in recent years. It was an animatronic head mask with multiple facial movements, such as curling back its lips to reveal fangs that slowly start to drool. The amount of cables needed to operate the head were such that they had to be carefully concealed under the flowing cape that the demon wore, and trailed out of the back of the head and down to the control units operated out of camera range. The actor's movements were carefully staged to avoid any damage or chance of wires being torn free accidentally.

For *The Curse of Fenric*, much the same principle was used to create the Ancient Haemovore, with an animatronic head mask being worn with a body costume of suitably mottled blue skin, and various pieces of equipment embedded in the flesh. The other Haemovores were achieved either through using simple clip-on masks for the most recent acquisitions to the race, or full face masks for the older creatures, whose features had been exposed to the water for longer.

With the level of sophistication in the special-effects industry of today, the job that was once relegated to the costume designer to achieve in between supervising all his other tasks has become a refined art form. Only imagination is needed to create any number of monsters or demons, and that's one thing that will certainly never run out.

Technical data

The Daemons★
Production code JJJ, season eight, five episodes

Episode one
Studio recording on 11 May 1971
Rehearsal 10.30 a.m.–1 p.m., 2 p.m.-3 p.m.
Filming 3.30 p.m.–4 p.m.
Rehearsal 4 p.m.–6 p.m.
Filming 7.30 p.m.–10 p.m.
Studio TC4, TV Centre on 2in tape, film inserts
Broadcast Saturday 22 May 1971, BBC1 5.15 p.m.–5.40 p.m.

Episode two
Studio recording on 19 May 1971
Rehearsal and filming as episode one
Studio details as episode one
Broadcast Saturday 29 May 1971, BBC1 5.15 p.m.–5.40 p.m.

Episode three
Studio recording – details not available
Rehearsal and filming as episode one
Studio details as episode one
Broadcast 5 June 1971, BBC1 5.15 p.m.–5.40 p.m.

Episode four
Studio recording on 26 May 1971
Rehearsal 10.30 a.m.–1 p.m., 2 p.m.–3.30 p.m.
Filming 3.30 p.m.–4 p.m.
Rehearsal 4 p.m.-6 p.m.
Filming 7.30 p.m.-10 p.m.
Studio TC3, TV Centre on 2in tape, film inserts
Broadcast Saturday 12 June 1971, BBC1 5.15 p.m.–5.40 p.m.

Episode five
Studio recording on 31 May 1971
Rehearsal and filming as episode four

Below: **Bok (Stanley Mason).** *The Daemons.*

Above: **The entire cast and crew of** *The Image of the Fendahl.*

Studio details as episode four
Broadcast Saturday 19 June 1971, BBC1 5.15 p.m.–5.40 p.m.

Cast: Jon Pertwee (the Doctor); Katy Manning (Jo Grant); Roger Delgado (the Master); Nicholas Courtney (Brigadier Lethbridge-Stewart); John Levene (Sergeant Benton); Richard Franklin (Captain Mike Yates); Damaris Hayman (Miss Hawthorne); Eric Hillyard (Doctor Reeves); David Simeon (Alistair Fergus); James Snell (Harry); Robin Wentworth (Professor Horner); Rollo Gamble (Winstanley); Don McKillop (Bert); John Croft (Tom Girton); Christopher Wray (Groom); Jon Joyce (Garvin); Gerald Taylor (Baker's man); Alec Linstead (Osgood); John Owens (Thorpe); Matthew Corbett (Jones); Robin Squire (TV Cameraman); Patrick Milner (Corporal); The Headington Quarry Men (morris dancers); Stephen Thorpe (Azal); Stanley Mason (Bok).

Production credits: Guy Leopold (Barry Letts and Roger Sloman) (writers); Christopher Barry (director); Terrance Dicks (script editor); Roger Ford (designer); Jan Harrison (make-up); Barbara Lane (costumes); Dudley Simpson (incidental music); Peter Day (visual effects); Barry Letts (producer).

Image of the Fendahl
Production code 4X, season fifteen, four episodes

Episode one
Studio recording on 20 August 1977
Rehearsal 2 p.m.–6 p.m.
Filming 7.30 p.m.–10 p.m.
Studio TC6, TV Centre on 2in tape, film inserts
Broadcast Saturday 29 October 1977, BBC1 6.10 p.m.–6.35 p.m.

Episode two
Studio recording on 21 August 1977
Rehearsal 10.30 a.m.–1 p.m., 2 p.m.–6 p.m.
Filming 7.30 p.m.–10 p.m.
Studio details as episode one
Broadcast Saturday 5 November 1977, BBC1 6.10 p.m.–6.35 p.m.

Episode three
Studio recording on 4 September 1977
Rehearsal 2 p.m.–6 p.m.
Filming 8 p.m.–10 p.m.
Studio details as episode one
Broadcast Saturday 12 November 1977, BBC1 6.10 p.m.–6.35 p.m.

Episode four
Studio recording on 5 September 1977

Rehearsal 10.30 a.m.–1 p.m., 2.30 p.m.–5.30p.m.
Press photocall 5.30 p.m.-6 p.m.
Filming 7.30 p.m.-10 p.m.
Broadcast Saturday 19 November 1977, BBC1 6.10 p.m.–6.35 p.m.

Above: **The Malus lets off steam in** *The Awakening.*

Cast: Tom Baker (the Doctor); Louise Jameson (Leela); Wanda Ventham (Thea Ransome); Denis Lill (Doctor Fendelman); Edward Arthur (Adam Colby); Scott Fredricks (Maximillian Stael); Edward Evans (Ted Moss); Derek Martin (Mitchell); Daphne Heard (Martha Tyler); Geoffrey Hinsliffe (Jack Tyler); Graham Simpson (Hiker); David Elliott and Roy Pearce (security guards)

Production credits: Chris Boucher (writer); George Spenton-Foster (director); Anthony Read and Robert Holmes (script editors); Anna Ridley (designer); Pauline Cox (make-up); Amy Roberts (costumes); Dudley Simpson (incidental music); Colin Mapson (visual effects); Graham Williams (producer).

The Awakening
Production code 6M, season twenty-one, two episodes
Episodes one and two
Story recorded in one studio block, four days of location work preceded it, 19-22 July 1983

Block one
Rehearsal 24 July-3 August 1983
Filming 4–6 August 1983

Episode one broadcast Thursday 19 January 1984, 6.40 p.m.–7.05 p.m.
Episode two broadcast Friday 20 January 1984, 6.40 p.m.–7.05 p.m.

Cast: Peter Davison (the Doctor); Janet Fielding (Tegan); Mark Strickson (Turlough); Polly James (Jane Hampden); Denis Lill (Sir George Hutchinson); Glyn Houston (Colonel Wolsey); Jack Galloway (Joseph Willow); Frederick Hall (Andrew Verney); Keith Jayne (Will Chandler); Christopher Saul (Trooper).

Production credits: Eric Pringle (writer); Michael-Owen Morris (director); Eric Saward (script editor); Barry Newbery (designer); Ann Ailes-Stevenson (make-up); Jackie Southern (costumes); Peter Howell (incidental music); Tony Harding (visual effects); John Nathan-Turner (producer).

Battlefield
Production code 7N, season twenty-six, four episodes

Episodes one to four
Story recorded in one studio block, twelve days of location work preceded it 6–17 May 1989
Block one

Rehearsal 18–29 May 1989
Filming 30 May to 1 June 1989
Episode one broadcast Wednesday 6 September 1989, BBC1 7.35 p.m.–8 p.m.
Episode two broadcast Wednesday 13 September 1989, BBC1 7.35 p.m.–8 p.m.
Episode three broadcast Wednesday 20 September 1989, BBC1 7.35 p.m.–8 p.m.
Episode four broadcast Wednesday 27 September 1989, BBC1 7.35 p.m.–8 p.m.

Cast: Sylvester McCoy (the Doctor); Sophie Aldred (Ace); Nicholas Courtney (Brigadier Lethbridge-Stewart); Jean Marsh (Morgaine); James Ellis (Peter Warmsley); Angela Bruce (Brigadier Winifred Bambera); Christopher Bowen (Mordred); Marcus Gilbert (Ancelyn); Angela Douglas (Doris); Noel Collins (Pat Rowlinson); June Bland (Elizabeth Rowlinson); Ling Tai (Shou Yuing); Dorota Rae (Flight Lieutenant Lavel); Robert Jezek (Sergeant Zbrigniev); Marek Anton (the Destroyer); Paul Tomany (Major Husak); Stefan Shwartz (Knight Commander).

Production credits: Ben Aaronovitch (writer); Michael Kerrigan (director); Andrew Cartmel (script editor); Martin Collins (designer); Juliet Mayer (make-up); Anushia Nieradzik (costumes); Keff McCulloch (incidental music); Dave Bezkorawajny (visual effects); John Nathan-Turner (producer).

The Curse of Fenric
Production code 7M, season twenty-six, four episodes

Episodes one to four
Story recorded entirely on location from 3–20 April 1989
Episode one broadcast Wednesday 25 October 1989, BBC1 7.35 p.m.–8 p.m.
Episode two broadcast Wednesday 1 November 1989, BBC1 7.35 p.m.–8 p.m.
Episode three broadcast Wednesday 8 November 1989, BBC1 7.35 p.m.–8 p.m.
Episode four broadcast Wednesday 15 November 1989, BBC1 7.35 p.m.–8 p.m.

Cast: Sylvester McCoy (the Doctor); Sophie Aldred (Ace); Dinsdale Landen (Doctor Judson); Alfred Lynch (Commander Millington); Tomek Bork (Captain Sorin); Nicholas Parsons (Revd Wainwright); Joann Kenny (Jean); Joanne Bell (Phyllis); Peter Czajkowzki (Sergeant Prozorov); Cory Pulman (Kathleen Dudman); Aaron Hanley (Baby); Marek Anton (Vershinin); Steve Rimkus (Captain Bates); Marcus Hutton (Sergeant Leigh); Janet Henfrey (Miss Hardaker); Anne Reid (Nurse Crane); Mark Conrad (Petrossian); Christien Anholt (Perkins); Raymond Trickett (Ancient Haemovore); Cy Town, Ian Elliott, Jennifer Crome, Ann Graham, Jacqui Nolan, Ian Collins, Graham Stagg, Perry Evans, Tony Ryan, Raymond Martin (Haemovores).

Production credits: Ian Briggs (writer); Nicholas Mallet (director); Andrew Cartmel (script editor); David Laskey (designer); Denise Baron (make-up); Ken Trew (costumes); Mark Ayres (incidental music); Graham Brown (visual effects); John Nathan-Turner (producer).

Additional data

All episodes of *The Daemons*, *The Image of Fendahl*, *The Awakening*, *Battlefield* and *The Curse of Fenric* are preserved in the BBC film archives. 625VT colour recordings are sought of *The Daemons* 1, 2, 3 and 5.

Novelizations
Doctor Who and The Daemons
Barry Letts
Adapted from the original scripts by Guy Leopold (Barry Letts and Robert Sloman). Number 15 in the Target novelization series.

Doctor Who and The Image of Fendahl
Terrance Dicks
Adapted from the original scripts by Chris Boucher. Number 34 in the Target novelization series.

Doctor Who – The Awakening
Eric Pringle
Number 95 in the Target novelization series.

Doctor Who – Battlefield
Marc Platt
Adapted from the original scripts by Ben Aaronovitch. Number 152 in the Target novelization series.

Doctor Who – The Curse of Fenric
By Ian Briggs
Number 151 in the Target novelization series.

Commercial video releases
Doctor Who – The Pertwee Years
BBC Video
Compilation of selected individual episodes from the era of the third Doctor, including *The Daemons* part 4. To be released during 1992.

Doctor Who – The Image of Fendahl
BBC Video
Unedited complete recordings of all four episodes. To be released during 1992.

Doctor Who – The Curse of Fenric
BBC Video
All four episodes re-edited to include additional material that was not broadcast on original transmission. Total running time 104 minutes.